australia's best
wine tours

About the author

Derek Barton is a book editor and writer with more than 20 years' experience in the publishing industry in Australia and the UK. He has worked on a range of travel books and wine guides, including *The Kiss Guide to Wine*, *The Great Australia Gazetteer* and *Top Tourist Destinations of Australia*.

australia's best
wine tours

the essential cellar-door touring companion

DEREK BARTON

Lothian
BOOKS

Thomas C. Lothian Pty Ltd
132 Albert Road, South Melbourne, 3205
www.lothian.com.au

Copyright © Derek Barton 2005
First published 2005

All rights reserved. No part of this publication may be reproduced,
stored in a retrieval system or transmitted in any form by any means
without the prior permission of the copyright owner. Enquiries
should be made to the publisher.

While every effort has been made to verify the information included in this publication, the author accepts no responsibility or liability for the accuracy of the content. It is in the very nature of the winemaking, tourism and hospitality industries to change—sometimes rapidly—in response to climate, popularity and fashion. In the course of researching this guide, a number of businesses have opened, merged, changed hands or closed. We are happy to hear from anyone who can correct inaccurate information, in the hope of improving future editions.

National Library of Australia
Cataloguing-in-Publication data:

Barton, Derek (Alan Derek).
    Australia's best wine tours.
    ISBN 0 7344 0682 7.
    1. Wine and wine making – Australia – Guidebooks. 2. Australia – Guidebooks. I. Title.

641.220994

The publisher gratefully acknowledges Tourism New South Wales for permission to reproduce photographs on pp. 1, 81, 149 and 233, as well as the details used for the 'Wineries' and 'Food and Dining' headings and the cover images of cheeses and grapes. The photograph of four chalets overlooking the Derwent River used for the 'Accommodation' heading was kindly supplied by Moorilla Estate in Tasmania. The photographs of Spray Farm (cover) and Scotchmans Hill (p. 175) were kindly supplied by Scotchmans Hill in Victoria. The photograph of vines on p. 93 at Chateau Leamon is by Mark Friswell.

Cover design by Mason Design
Text design by Mason Design
Main cover photograph by Jennette Snape
Typesetting by Cannon Typesetting
Maps by Laurie Whiddon, Map Illustrations
Printed in Australia by Griffin Press

Contents

Foreword	vi
Introduction	vii
How to use this book	ix
Wine regions of Australia map	xii
Acknowledgements	xiv

Australian Capital Territory and New South Wales — 1
- Canberra — 2
- Cowra–Canowindra — 14
- Hastings River — 23
- Hunter Valley: Lower Hunter — 30
- Hunter Valley: Upper Hunter — 49
- Mudgee — 58
- Orange — 70

Queensland — 81
- Granite Belt — 82

South Australia — 93
- Adelaide Hills — 94
- Barossa Valley — 104
- Clare Valley — 115
- Coonawarra — 127
- McLaren Vale — 137

Tasmania — 149
- Northern Tasmania — 150
- Southern Tasmania — 162

Victoria — 175
- Bendigo — 176
- Geelong — 185
- Grampians — 193
- Mornington Peninsula — 201
- Rutherglen — 212
- Yarra Valley — 222

Western Australia — 233
- Great Southern — 234
- Margaret River — 246
- Swan Valley — 258

Index — 269

Foreword

It is hard to imagine that no more than twenty years ago wine tasting was restricted to aficionados who drove to their favourite cellar doors (usually nothing more than a slab of wood propped up on a couple of empty casks in a corrugated-iron shed around the back of the vineyard), tasted a few drops of wines they had already fallen in love with, bought cases of their favourite vintage, and then headed back to their homes with smiles of success on their faces. How things have changed. Today literally millions of dollars can be spent just building the cellar door; restaurants and eateries abound in wine regions, and active Visitor Information Centres, knowing the value of having wine lovers stay an extra few nights in their regions, are eager to promote all the local attractions.

The best ideas are always the simplest, and most obvious, ideas. They are also the ideas that elicit the most jealousy and the most 'why didn't I think of that' envy. This book is one of those ideas. People now go to wine regions in vast numbers. Too commonly they go without a clear idea of which wines they want to taste or buy. And certainly they usually have little idea of what the region offers in the way of fine dining, interesting accommodation and must-see attractions. So these confused folk wander, quite randomly and without great purpose, from cellar door to cellar door until, if they are lucky, they stumble upon a wine they like or accidentally discover somewhere good to eat or to stay.

This book fills a huge gap and takes that stumbling and those accidents out of the equation. It is full of great advice, valuable suggestions and well-researched recommendations. Use it and you will find that your next visit to a wine region is much more than a wine lovers equivalent of 'pin the tail on the donkey'. The best part is that with this book you will not only purchase the right wines, you will stay in an interesting place, eat well and experience the beauties and attractions of the local area.

Bruce Elder
Travel Writer, Sydney Morning Herald

Introduction

Wine touring is a way of learning more about wines and wine-making, and also about the landscapes, culture and history of a region or country. In Europe, it has been a popular holiday pastime for many years, but only fairly recently has it become a viable option for Australians. Ten or twenty years ago, it would have required a great deal of effort to reach many of the country's wine regions, let alone find a comfortable place to stay, good food and locally made wine.

Today, the availability of discount airfares permits Australians to explore parts of the country that were previously beyond their financial or physical reach. Fine accommodation and top-quality food are available in all but the most remote wine areas, and it's no longer even necessary to go to the best or biggest hotel or the smartest restaurant in town to be sure of sampling wines from local vineyards—by the glass or bottle, they are available with lunch or dinner in most local restaurants.

Moreover, those who live and work in our wine regions increasingly display a great sense of pride, and work hard to please visitors. It has been a constant source of pleasure, during the research for this book, to meet people—young and old, in towns or the bush—who really do care, not only about the quality of the wines, but also the impression of the region that tourists will take away and pass on to others.

Major wine regions lie within easy reach of almost all state capitals. So, if you're visiting relatives or on business in Melbourne, why not set some time aside to explore the terrific providores and wineries of Geelong, the Mornington Peninsula or the Yarra Valley? Alternatively, mix wine-tasting with adventure or relaxation. Did you know, for example, that you can combine whale-watching in the Great Southern region of Western Australia with sampling some of the country's best wines? Or that a river cruise aboard the *Kalgan Queen*, departing from Emu Point in Albany, Western Australia will take you to a winery? Or that a short drive from the wineries of Hastings River in New South Wales, you can stroll along the pristine beaches of Port Macquarie?

Exploring the most beautiful regions of Australia and at the same time tasting examples of the fabulous wines being made around the country seems to me to be a fine way to take a break. And of course one of the greatest pleasures of wine touring is opening a bottle of wine weeks, months or years after a trip, and finding that simply taking a sip brings the whole experience back to you.

I hope you will enjoy discovering the wine regions of Australia as much as I have.

How to use this book

This book sets out to provide a detailed guide to wine touring in Australia. It includes information on all of Australia's major wine regions, providing details on which wineries to visit and when, where to stay and eat, and what else to do when you are there.

The guide is arranged by state (and territory, in the case of the ACT and New South Wales), and presents the wine regions in chapters, in alphabetical order. Each chapter features a detailed map and begins with a brief introduction to the wine region, its winemaking history and its wines, including tips on what to buy. This is followed by four subsections: *Wineries, Food and Dining, Accommodation* and *Travel Information*.

The wineries were selected on the basis that they provide, at the very least, an opportunity to taste and purchase wines in an agreeable environment. Some also offer a chance to learn more about wine. At others, great views, good food, music and atmosphere combine to create an especially rewarding destination.

The entries include the name and address of the winery, other contact details such as telephone number and email, opening hours, the name of the winemaker (whether the owner, a staff member or on contract and a description of the winery and its wines. Quick-reference abbreviations indicate other facilities you can expect to find there, such as picnic areas, barbecue facilities and eateries. Where relevant, information on wine tours and other activities is listed at the end of this section.

Note that the numbered lists of wineries below the maps are in alphabetical order by region or subregion and are *not* a recommended order in which to visit the wineries in the region—that's up to you to decide, depending on your interests and schedule.

Food and Dining covers local food producers and outlets, and offers recommendations for eating out. *Accommodation* lists the best of the area's hotels, motels, guesthouses and holiday houses. *Travel Information* not only explains how to get to the region and where to find more information, but also includes suggestions for other places to visit, activities for kids and lists of annual festivals and other events.

Making the most of your visit

The detailed information in this book will help you plan and enjoy your tour, but to get the most out of a trip keep in mind the following general pointers, too.

PLAN CAREFULLY

Contact local tourist offices to find out what's on and which are the busiest times. Visiting midweek or in the off-season can be especially rewarding as you are likely to receive more advice and attention at the cellar door, especially in the smaller family-run wineries, though you should check that the wineries you plan to visit are open (most are happy to make an appointment outside normal opening hours). Accommodation is likely to be less expensive at these times. It's worth remembering that almost all cellar doors are closed on Christmas Day and Good Friday.

Whenever you visit, it's advisable to book accommodation in advance, to avoid the highest rates as well as disappointment. Booking through websites can sometimes save money.

Generally, it's best to plan your accommodation and one or two special meals but incorporate some flexibility so that you can go where the mood, weather or wines take you. Mobile phones come into their own in wine regions, where it's well worth calling ahead to make sure a restaurant or winery is open, make a booking or find out about daily specials. Restaurants in particular always appreciate the advance warning.

TOURING, TASTING AND BUYING

Most of the access roads to wineries are now in good condition and only in extremes of bad weather are any out of service. In contrast, the signposting can be exasperating and even downright dangerous in places. *Always proceed with caution on unfamiliar roads.*

It's worth remembering that some wineries charge for tastings, particularly of older, premium or fortified wines, but this is usually refunded when you make a purchase. On the other hand, full-range tastings can attract a small charge, whether or not you decide to buy.

An increasing number of wineries provide food to accompany tastings, though many of the smaller ones do not. Offerings vary from cheese and biscuits, through tasting platters that are sufficient for a light lunch, to full à la carte meals. Matching local wines and foods is one of the great pleasures of wine touring, though this doesn't always need to be done in the context of a full meal.

It's not a good idea to transport wines in the boot of a car, especially during hot weather, unless you have some kind of thermal packaging. If that is not available, keep the wines inside the passenger compartment with you, and try to protect them from high temperatures and vibrations. Overall, the best option is to have the wines freighted back home. This can be achieved either by using a local courier or Australia Post, whose wine delivery services are now drawing compliments from many wine producers; they are quick, dependable and, for the most part, surprisingly cheap. Some wineries offer their own freight service, sometimes in conjunction with other wineries in the region, so that you can accumulate a dozen or two as you tour, then have them sent home from the last winery you visit.

Last but most definitely not least, do *not* drink and drive. Use the spittoon that is nearly always provided at cellar doors; if there isn't one, nobody will be offended if you ask. Professional wine tasters can assess a wine by tasting and spitting—and you can learn to do the same. Work out which wines you like and then buy a bottle or two to drink later, when you are at or can walk back to your accommodation. Alternatively, if you are travelling in a group, agree that someone will abstain from drinking in order to drive the others around safely. Or find out if transport between wineries is available. Some wineries now offer courtesy buses to ferry visitors from and back to their accommodation, and in many areas you can join an organised tour of local wineries.

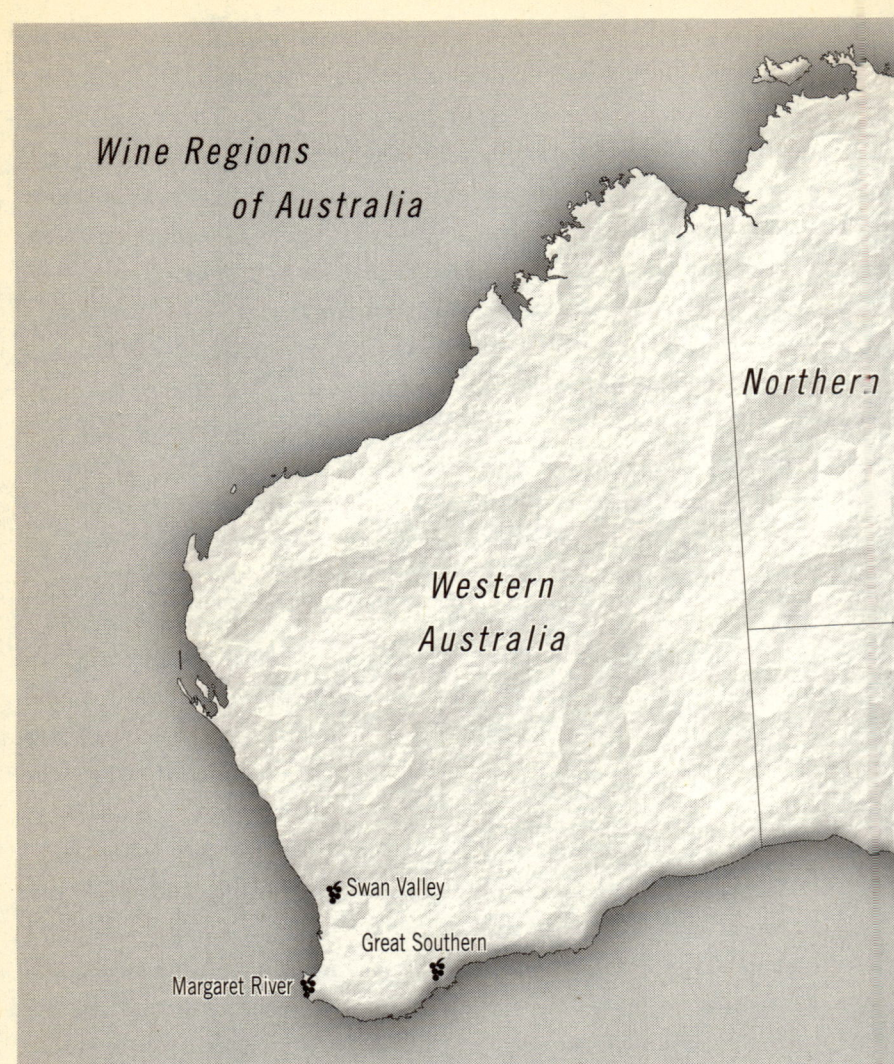

WINE REGIONS OF AUSTRALIA xiii

Acknowledgements

To thank everyone who provided information or encouragement for this book would be a tall order; however, for specific help and advice and photographs I would like to thank the following:

ACT/NSW Chris Barnes, Vigneron, President, NSW Wine Industry Association; staff at Orange Visitors Information Centre; Sue Lipscombe, Canberra Tourism and Events Corporation; Anne Scott, Hunter Valley Wine Society

Qld Christine Leslie, staff at Stanthorpe Visitors Information Centre

SA Steve Callery, Barossa Valley; Katie Cameron, Executive Officer, Adelaide Hills Wine Region Inc; Wendy Hollick, Hollick Wines, Coonawarra; Anne Weddle, Clare Valley

Tas Rod Cuthbert, Vignerons Association; Colin Corney; Judy Roberts, Bridestowe Lavender; K. & B. Jones, Geebin Vineyard, Birchs Bay; Joan and Tim Bradley

Vic Julie Stanley, Geelong Visitors Centre; Rachel Klitscher, Bendigo Tourism Information; Mark Friswell; Diana Howe; Richard Yallop

WA Vesna Borich, Carilley Estate; Julie Church; Pat Davidovic, Albany Visitor Centre; Sharon O'Reilly; Samantha Seymour-Eyles, Swan Valley Tourism; Fergus de Witt, Majestic Wines; Peter Rigby, Margaret River; Kaylene Walker, WA Tourism Commission, Sydney

My thanks are due to everyone who was kind enough to supply information for the book, but errors remain my responsibility. For future editions, please send any changes or updates to me at: dbarton@bigpond.net.au.

Thanks also to Scott Forbes and Cathy Smith for their thorough editorial work and determination to improve my efforts.

Finally, I'd like to thank my wife Margaret McPhee for her enthusiasm, patience, sound advice and constant willingness to explore unknown roads in pursuit of information—and the enjoyment of food and wine in this remarkable country.

Derek Barton
Sydney, January 2005

Australian Capital Territory and New South Wales

Canberra

Wine production in the Canberra region goes back to the 1850s when grapes were planted at nearby Yass, but the industry then languished for more than a century. A revival began in the 1970s, when several small wineries were established, notably by former civil servants including Ken Helm of Helm Wines, Edgar Riek of Lake George Winery, Ian Hendry of Affleck and Tim Kirk of Clonakilla. Today, the region is flourishing, with more than 33 wineries producing some of the nation's most diverse wines from an intriguing range of grape varieties.

The Canberra region is divided into three areas: Hall, Murrumbateman and Lake George–Bungendore (which includes Wamboin). The altitudes range from 500 to 860 m above sea level. Most of the wineries are still small, family-owned operations; many offer cellar-door sales and some conduct tours, though usually by appointment only. A number of new restaurants, cafes and bed and breakfasts have sprung up in the area, some attached to wineries. The varied terrain and surrounding hills ensure that many wineries also offer pleasant walks and views.

The picturesque hills and valleys around Canberra make for enjoyable touring. The distribution of the wineries means that you can take most of them in on a circuit tour, starting either from Canberra or from the Federal Highway from Sydney and travelling either clockwise or anti-clockwise. Generally the roads are in good condition, but signs to the wineries vary greatly and no standard signage has been adopted. Wine aside, the Canberra region of course has a great

Key

T	Telephone
F	Fax
E	Email
W	Website
WM	Winemaker
CD	Cellar door
P	Picnic facilities
PA	Play area for children
BBQ	Barbecue facilities
GT	Guided tours
C	Cafe
R	Restaurant
O	Opening hours
B&B	Bed and breakfast
H	Hotel/Inn
M	Motel
G	Guesthouse
SCA	Self-catering accommodation

deal to offer the tourist, from the cultural icons of the national capital, such as the War Memorial and the Australian National Gallery, to some of the best food in the country.

What to buy

The region specialises in crisp, cool-climate wines made from a range of grapes including Chardonnay, Riesling and Sauvignon Blanc, as well as Pinot Noir, Merlot, Shiraz and Cabernet Sauvignon (mainly in the warmer areas of Hall and Murrumbateman). Less well-known varieties also worth sampling include Gewurztraminer, Viognier and Touriga.

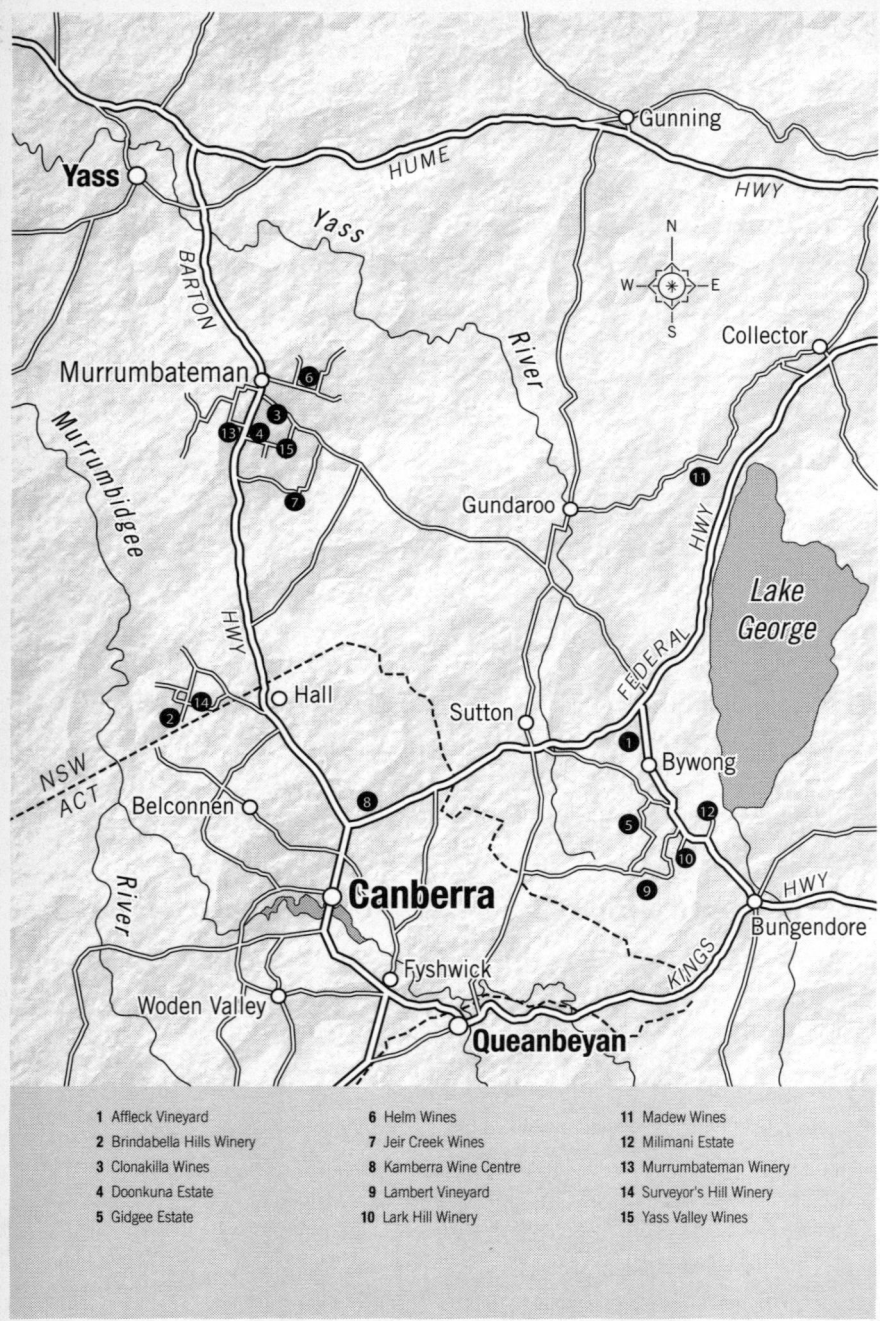

Wineries

Hall

Brindabella Hills Winery

*156 Woodgrove Cl, via Barton Hwy and Wallaroo Rd
(follow the signs from Hall)*
T 02 6230 2583 **F** 02 6230 2023

It's worth coming here for the views of the Brindabella Hills and Murrumbidgee River as well as for the top-rating cool-climate wines, which consistently win awards and critical acclaim. The Riesling and Shiraz are outstanding but you can also choose from Chardonnay, Semillon Sauvignon Blanc, Cabernet and Merlot. Twice a year the winery hosts a picnic lunch and jazz concert, as part of the April Harvest Festival and again during the Days of Wine and Roses in November.

Dr Roger Harris **WM**
10 am–5 pm **CD**
weekends and
public holidays,
or by appointment
P

Kamberra Wine Company

Cnr Northbourne Ave and Flemington Rd, Lyneham
T 02 6262 2333 **F** 02 6262 2300

A showcase for the BRL Hardy Company's Kamberra and Meeting Place ranges, this winery's slick, purpose-built visitor centre caters for large groups, including coach parties. Set in landscaped gardens with a pond—complete with ducks—it also houses the Meeting Place bistro. The wines range from reliable to very good indeed: try the Kamberra Riesling and Shiraz, and the Meeting Place Sauvignon Blanc.

Alex McKay **WM**
10 am–5 pm **CD**
daily or by
appointment
11 am daily **GT**
R

Surveyor's Hill Winery

215 Brooklands Rd, via Wallaroo Rd, Hall
T 02 6230 2046 **F** 02 6230 2048

Surveyor's Hill is best known for good-quality Sauvignon Blanc, Riesling and Cabernet Sauvignon, but don't forget to try the dry Rosado Touriga Rosé as well. The winery provides comfortable, fully equipped bed and breakfast facilities (two double rooms) in the old homestead on the property—ring ahead to book. The views over the Murrumbidgee Valley are lovely and guests can taste the wines at any time.

Dr Roger Harris **WM**
(contract)
10 am–5 pm **CD**
weekends and
public holidays,
or by appointment
B&B

Murrumbateman

Clonakilla

WM Tim Kirk
CD 11 am–5 pm daily

Crisps Lane, off Gundaroo Rd, Murrumbateman
T 02 6227 5877 **F** 02 6227 5871 **E** wine@clonakilla.com.au
W www.clonakilla.com.au

Highly skilled winemaking and a warm welcome make this small winery well worth a visit. Try the Semillon Sauvignon Blanc, Riesling or Chardonnay if you like whites, or the superb Shiraz Viognier blend or Cabernet Merlot if you prefer reds. The former sells out very quickly on release. Clonakilla's big Shiraz, made from fruit sourced in the Hilltops region, has good cellaring potential.

Doonkuna Estate

WM Malcolm Burdett
CD 11 am–4 pm daily
P
PA
BBQ

Barton Hwy, Murrumbateman
T 02 6227 5811 **F** 02 6227 5085

This is a good place to sample a local Chardonnay, and the Doonkuna is characteristic of the area—a light, elegant wine with peach and melon fruit. The Cabernet, Merlot, Shiraz and Cabernet Merlot blend are also skilfully made and reasonably priced. The winery has been rebuilt over the last couple of years and the land under vines extended in order to increase production considerably.

Helm Wines

WM Ken Helm
CD 10 am–5 pm
Thurs–Mon
P
PA
GT By appointment

Butts Lane Road, off Yass River Rd, Murrumbateman
T 02 6227 5811 or 5536 **F** 02 6227 0207 **E** khelm@enternet

The tasting room here is a delightful old wooden schoolhouse displaying photographs of the wines and the knowledgeable Ken, whose legendary status has earned him the title of 'honourary ambassador for the local wine industry'. The Rieslings are outstanding, but the Chardonnay, Merlot and Cabernet Merlot are also good.

Jeir Creek Wines

Gooda Creek Rd, Murrumbateman

T 02 6227 5999 **F** 02 6227 5900 **E** rob@jeircreekwines.com.au

This winery is set high on a vine-covered hill, commanding pleasant views over the surrounding countryside. Both reds and whites are made. The whites include excellent Riesling as well as Chardonnay and Sauvignon Blanc; prominent among the reds are Pinot Noir, Shiraz, Cabernet and Merlot. The winery participates in the Days of Wine and Roses Festival in November.

Rob Howell **WM**
10 am–5 pm **CD**
Fri–Sun and public holidays
P
By appointment **GT**

Murrumbateman Winery

Barton Hwy, Murrumbateman

T 02 6227 5584

Sparkling Chardonnay is a speciality here, but try the Cabernet Merlot blend, the rosé and port, too, and even the mead if it takes your fancy. This small winery also produces Riesling, Sauvignon Blanc and Verdelho as well as fortified wines. Surrounded by trees, the pretty cafe is often used for weddings and functions.

Duncan Leslie **WM**
10 am–5 pm **CD**
Thurs–Mon
C
P
BBQ

Yass Valley Wines

Crisps Lane, off Gundaroo Rd, Murrumbateman

T/F 02 6227 5592 **E** yasswine@cyberone.com.au

Grapes grown here range from Riesling, Semillon and Chardonnay to Shiraz and Merlot, and also include unusual varieties such as Traminer and Barbera, all well worth tasting. The on-site Crisps Lane Cafe offers light meals, salads and morning and afternoon teas.

Mick Withers **WM**
11 am–5 pm **CD**
weekends and public holidays
P
BBQ
C

Lake George–Bungendore

Affleck Vineyard

154 Millyn Rd, off Bungendore Rd, Bungendore

T 02 6236 9276 **F** 02 6236 9090

Local pioneers Ian and Susie Hendry established this tiny, family-owned vineyard in 1976 and now produce fine Pinot Noir and Chardonnay, as well as Shiraz, Merlot and Cabernet Shiraz. They also make a sweet white (Tokay style) as well as port, Muscat and a dry (Amontillado) sherry. Cheese platters can be purchased and light lunches arranged for groups (phone to book).

Ian Hendry **WM**
9 am–5 pm **CD**
most weekends
BBQ
P

Gidgee Estate

WM David Madew
(white wines),
Andrew McEwin
(red wines)
CD 12 noon–4 pm
most weekends

441 Weeroona Dr, Wamboin
T 02 6236 9506 **F** 02 6236 9070
This small winery offers the prize-winning Gidgee Estate Riesling, a fine Chardonnay and a pleasing blended red, Ensemble. The production volume is tiny, but the wines are of impressive quality.

Lambert Vineyard and Winery

WM Ruth Lambert,
Steve Lambert
CD 10 am–5 pm
weekends and
public holidays,
or by appointment
C Thurs–Sat for
dinner, Fri–Sun
for lunch

810 Norton Rd, Wamboin
T 02 6238 3414 **F** 02 6238 3855 **E** wine@lambertvineyards.com.au
This sparkling new winery, tasting room and cafe sits atop a breezy hill in the Wamboin Valley. The Riesling, Shiraz and Reserve Shiraz were the first wines to win awards but Lambert also produces Chardonnay, Pinot Gris, Cabernet Sauvignon and Pinot Noir of high quality. The stylish cafe has vineyard views and offers modern Australian dishes to match the wines.

Lark Hill Winery

WM Dr David Carpenter,
Sue Carpenter
CD 10 am–5 pm daily
except Tues, or by
appointment

521 Bungendore Rd, Bungendore
T 02 6238 1393 **W** www.larkhillwine.com.au
Located at an altitude of 860 m—level with the observation deck of the Black Mountain Tower—this is one of the highest wineries in the Canberra region. It's a bit hard to find but is definitely worth the effort: both the wines and the views are memorable. In particular, the Carpenters produce terrific, delicate Pinot Noirs, fine Chardonnays and award-winning Rieslings. They also make a rich Cabernet Merlot, a Méthode Champenoise sparkler and a big Cabernet called Exaltation.

Madew Wines

WM David Madew
CD 11 am–5 pm
Wed–Sun or by
appointment
R

'Westering', Federal Hwy, Lake George
T/F 02 4848 0026
One of Canberra's oldest vineyards, Madew is home to the acclaimed grapefoodwine restaurant (see Food and Dining) and music venue. Merlot is the best choice here, but the Riesling, Pinot Gris and Shiraz are also well worth trying. 'Opera by George', a weekend opera festival, is held at the vineyard each year in mid-March.

Milimani Estate Vineyard

92 Forest Rd, Bungendore
T 02 6238 1421 **F** 02 6238 1424

Andrew McEwin **WM**
(contract)
10 am–4 pm **CD**
most weekends
and public holidays,
or by appointment

P
BBQ

A small, family-run winery, Milimani Estate sells well-made Pinot Noir, Sauvignon Blanc and Chardonnay. The name is an Aboriginal term meaning 'in the hills' and the vineyards are some of Canberra's highest, offering great views over Lake George (when it's there) and the Brindabellas.

Wine tours and activities

The ACT Wine Industry Network does two especially useful things. It sells wine from several local wineries, including Tabart Heritage, Doonkuna, Clonakilla, Helm and Gidgee among others, at a stall at the Old Bus Depot Markets in the Canberra suburb of Kingston (10 am–4 pm every Sun). It also organises tours of several wine regions from Canberra, Young and Orange through to the South Coast and northern Victoria (**T** 02 6231 6997 or 0408 626 918 **W** www.actwine.com.au).

Food and Dining

Canberra has a fine range of restaurants and cafes, but when you are touring the vineyards it's not always easy to find a tasty meal, fresh produce or good takeaway food for a picnic. The Hall Markets at the Hall Showground (10 am–3 pm first Sun of every month except June) are well known in the district for the excellent local produce they offer. Entry is by gold-coin donation and the proceeds go to Hartley Lifecare Inc., formerly the ACT Society for the Physically Handicapped. Some of the best meat available locally is supplied by Dave Darmody at Sutton Country Meats, Camp St, Sutton (**T** 02 6230 3540 **O** 8 am–6.30 pm Mon–Fri, 8 am–2 pm Sat).

In addition to the following, there is a cluster of eateries at Gold Creek Village on the Barton Hwy in Hall.

Hall

Poacher's Pantry Smokehouse and Cafe, Nanima Rd, off the Barton Hwy, Hall **T** 02 6230 2487 **O** 10 am–5 pm Fri–Sun for lunch (bookings essential), 10 am–4 pm daily for coffee, cakes, product tasting and retail sales
Proprietors Susan and Robert Bruce make gourmet smoked goods such as kangaroo and emu prosciutto, smoked chicken breast, smoked tomatoes and garlic, and lamb with mountain pepper. You can taste samples of the meats matched with Wily Trout wines made from estate-grown grapes. The cafe terrace has a pleasant outlook over lawns and gardens.

Murrumbateman

Barrique Cafe Restaurant, Barton Hwy, Murrumbateman **T** 02 6227 5600 **F** 02 6772 5605 **E** barrique@barrique.com.au **O** 10 am–late Thurs–Mon for coffee and light meals, Thurs–Sat for dinner, weekends for brunch. Stylish food is served in a historic building that started out as the Traveller's Rest coaching inn. Outdoor dining under the trees is possible in summer. Barrique has a good local wine list and a cosy bar; it also serves England's Creek wines—including a delicious Riesling made by Ken Helm.

Lake George–Bungendore

Beetle Nutt Cafe, 12 Gibraltar St, Bungendore **T** 02 6238 0999 **O** 6 pm–9 pm Wed–Thurs, 6 pm–late Fri–Sat, from noon on Sun for lunch. An unusual range of pizzas, pastas and laksas as well as risottos and salads.

Cork St Cafe, Gundaroo **T** 02 6236 8217 **O** 4 pm–late Fri, 10 am–late Sat, 10 am–7.30 pm Sun. Good coffee, homemade cakes and focaccia, as well as salads and pizza. It's BYO too.

Gib Street Cafe, 2/15 Gibraltar St, Bungendore **T** 02 6238 1088 **O** 9 am–5 pm daily. This cafe offers pies, burgers and other hearty home-cooked fare, but also quiches and vegetarian dishes as well as cakes and cappuccinos. It is BYO and no corkage charge applies.

grapefoodwine, Madew Wines, 'Westering', Federal Hwy, Lake George **T** 02 4848 0165 **O** Fri–Sat for lunch and dinner, Sun for breakfast. Fast winning acclaim for its food and as a stylish events venue, grapefoodwine offers modern Australian food and a well-stocked cellar including a wide range of Australian and international wines.

Grazing, former Royal Hotel, cnr Cork and Harp Streets, Gundaroo
T 02 6236 8777   **F** 02 6236 8444   **E** mail@grazing.com   **O** Thurs–Sun for dinner, Fri–Sun for lunch, 9 am onwards on weekends for breakfast or brunch. Good food, wine and coffee are offered in a newly restored, National Trust listed property.

Gundaroo Wine Bar, Cork St, Gundaroo   **T** 02 6236 8155   **F** 02 6236 8655
W www.gundaroowinebar.com.au   **O** Roughly 3.00 pm–9.00 pm Mon–Wed, 1.00 pm–9.00 pm Thurs, 12.00 noon–late Fri–Sun, 'depending how busy we are'. The bar is in a splendid old building that was formerly a pub. There is a cafe serving pub-grub lunches on Fri–Sun, and dinners Thurs–Sun. Sunday roasts are very popular. The bar also sells local wines and holds tastings monthly—usually on Sun, when wines are available at discount. Plans are afoot to build a village square and old wares shops at the rear of the bar.

Further afield

The Lynwood Cafe, 1 Murray St, Collector   **T** 02 4848 0200   **O** 10 am–6 pm, Wed–Sun. Renowned for its high standard of seasonal food and for delicious jams and preserves, this cosy cafe has a strong following, so make sure you book in advance.

Accommodation

Murrumbateman

Country Guesthouse Schönegg, 381 Hillview Drive, Murrumbateman
T 02 6227 0344   **W** www.schonegg.com.au. Richard and Evelyn Everson's neat new bed and breakfast offers queen-sized beds, en-suite bathrooms and full country breakfasts included in the tariff. Meals are also available by arrangement and lunches are served on weekends in the restaurant/cafe. Fast becoming a 'must stay' for visitors to Murrumbateman.

Lake George–Bungendore

The Carrington Restaurant and Motel, 21 Malbon St, Bungendore **T** 02 6238 1044 **E** enquiries@thecarrington.com **W** www.thecarrington.com. If you're feeling flush, the Carrington is one of the best places to stay in the area. The historic building houses luxurious accommodation, with comfortable rooms and a lovely restaurant.

The Elmslea Homestead, 80 Tarago Rd, Bungendore **T** 02 6238 1651 **F** 02 6238 1988. This comfortable B&B provides beautifully furnished accommodation. Room tariffs vary depending on the number of beds and level of luxury—to spa or not to spa?—and dinner, bed and breakfast packages can be purchased at a slightly reduced cost.

The Old Stone House, 41 Molonglo St, Bungendore **T/F** 02 6238 1888 **E** stnhsebb@tpg.com.au **W** www.theoldstonehouse.com.au. Geoff and Carolyn Bunbury's comfortable B&B is elegantly furnished. Morning and afternoon teas as well as lunches and dinner are available by arrangement—and it is BYO.

Further afield

The Globe Inn, 70 Yossi St, Yass **T** 02 6226 3680 **E** stay@globeinn.com.au
Centrally located, this historic building has been meticulously restored. It has queen-sized bedrooms with good facilities.

Travel Information

How to get there
By road Canberra is a 3-hour drive from Sydney (305 km): take the M5 and Hume Hwy through the scenic Southern Highlands via Goulburn. From Melbourne, it's a 7-hour drive along the Hume Hwy (660 km).
By air Qantas flies direct from all state capitals except Darwin and Hobart, but no other major airline currently services the national capital.
By train Countrylink trains run from Sydney, taking about 3 hours (**T** 13 22 32).

Other attractions
The villages of Gundaroo, Collector and Bungendore all have cafes and a range of services, from artists' galleries to antique, pottery and bookshops. The Wood Works Gallery at Bungendore has some beautiful examples of Australian craftwork and a cafe that alone merits a visit.

For kids
The 'sheep's-back-to-garment' display at the Corriedale Clip farm spinning mill on Nanima Rd is fascinating. Ring beforehand (**T** 02 6227 5525). The Railway Museum at Yass has the shortest platform in Australia; refreshments and souvenirs are on sale (**T** 02 6226 2169). Gold Creek Village at Hall has a number of attractions for kids as well as food and drink. The National Dinosaur Museum offers great exhibits and fossil-making and plaster-painting for children (**T** 02 6230 2655). The dinosaurs' modern-day counterparts are the stars at the adjacent Reptile Centre (**T** 02 6253 8533). At Cockington Green, detailed miniature replicas of famous buildings (including Stonehenge) are complemented by landscaped floral displays; the centre also has a licensed cafe, BBQ and picnic grounds (**T** 02 6230 2273). In Canberra itself are the interactive science displays of Questacon, The National Science and Technology Centre (**T** 02 6270 2800), and the permanent exhibitions of the National Museum of Australia (**T** 02 6208 5000), both on the shores of Lake Burley Griffin.

Events
Mar: Annual Balloon Fiesta; Taste: Food, Wine and the Arts; Gundaroo bush races
Apr–May: International Chamber Music Festival
Apr: Harvest Festival
Sept–Oct: Floriade-Australia's Celebration of Spring
Nov: Days of Wine and Roses

Information
Canberra Visitors Centre,
330 Northbourne Ave, Dixon
T 02 6205 0044
W www.visitcanberra.com.au
W www.canberra.wines.com.au

Cowra–Canowindra

A very pleasant country town, Cowra has broad streets and some splendid old buildings. The pavements are wide and the shopping is good, and not far from the centre the banks of the Lachlan River are studded with trees and green parks. Cellar doors operate right in Cowra these days, there are vineyards on the edge of town, and you don't have to drive far to see rolling hillsides covered with carefully tended vines. Vineyards also surround the smaller agricultural centre of Canowindra to the north.

Following experiments in grape growing in the early 1970s, the focus of the local economy shifted from mixed farming and grazing to a combination of farming and winegrowing. The climate is warmer than other areas in the Central West and the range of wines reflects this. Chardonnay and Cabernet Sauvignon thrive, as well as Merlot, Tempranillo and Shiraz. The region first became known as a result of the success of wines (particularly Chardonnays) made with Cowra-grown grapes by the likes of Richmond Grove, Rothbury Estate and Arrowfield. More recently, local labels such as Cowra Estate and Wallington have blossomed, and the region is enjoying increasing local and international recognition for its wines.

As the wines and local services improve, Cowra is also becoming a popular wine-touring destination. The countryside varies between gently undulating grazing land, wooded hills and river flats along the Lachlan (Cowra) and Belubula (Canowindra) rivers. From Orange, you can approach the region either via Cudal or

Key

T	Telephone
F	Fax
E	Email
W	Website
WM	Winemaker
CD	Cellar door
P	Picnic facilities
PA	Play area for children
BBQ	Barbecue facilities
GT	Guided tours
C	Cafe
R	Restaurant
O	Opening hours
B&B	Bed and breakfast
H	Hotel/Inn
M	Motel
G	Guesthouse
SCA	Self-catering accommodation

Blayney on major roads, or via the village of Cargo on a good minor road that descends through a mixture of cleared and wooded scenic countryside—with a steadily increasing number of vines.

What to buy

The area produces excellent full-bodied Chardonnays and a wide range of other wines, most notably Cabernet Sauvignon, Shiraz, Pinot Noir, Sauvignon Blanc and Verdelho. Some growers are also experimenting with Merlot, Gewurztraminer, Sangiovese, Tempranillo, Grenache and even Petit Verdot.

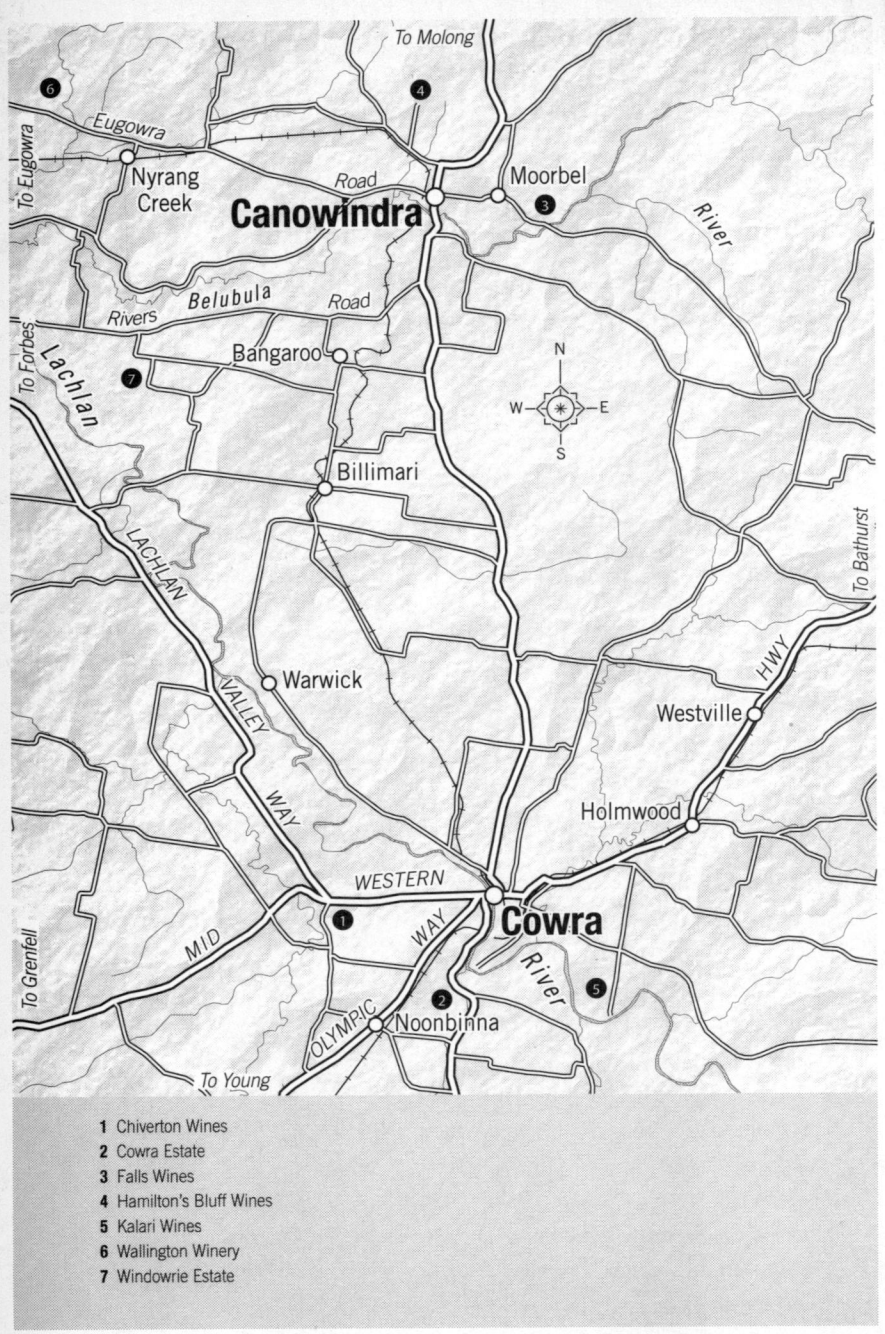

1 Chiverton Wines
2 Cowra Estate
3 Falls Wines
4 Hamilton's Bluff Wines
5 Kalari Wines
6 Wallington Winery
7 Windowrie Estate

Wineries

Chiverton Wines

605 Grenfell Rd, Cowra

T 02 6342 9308 or 02 6342 9270 after hours **F** 02 6342 9314
E chiverton@chivertonwines.com

The wines are sold under three labels—the premium Chiverton Estate, easy drinking Billygoat Hill and fruit-driven Nude Estate. Among the whites, Chardonnay predominates, though Semillon is also made. Of the reds, the pick are the soft Cabernet Sauvignon and the powerful Shiraz; Sangiovese and Merlot are also available. The cellar door is surrounded by spacious lawns that are ideal for picnics.

Simon Gilbert (contract) **WM**
10 am–5 pm daily, special twilight tastings Fri evening in summer **CD**

P

Cowra Estate

Boorowa Rd, Cowra

T 02 6342 3650 **F** 02 6341 4191

The oldest winery in Cowra (1973) is now in the same ownership as Chateau Tanunda in the Barossa. A range of grape varieties is grown—including Riesling, Gewurztraminer, Sauvignon Blanc and Pinot Noir—but the winery is best known for its Chardonnay and Cabernet Merlot blend. It also owns the Quarry Restaurant and Cellar Door in Cowra (see Food and Dining). The cellar door also sells Danbury Estate, Hungerford Hill, Mulyan and Richmond Grove wines.

Simon Gilbert (contract) **WM**
10 am–4 pm Tues–Sun **CD**

Falls Wines and Vineyard Retreat

Belubula Way, Canowindra

T 02 6344 1293 **F** 02 6344 1290 **E** thefalls@allstate.net.au
W www.fallswines.com

This grand old homestead and vineyard are set just 4 km from Cowra amid rolling vineyards and traditional sheep country. The wines range from full-flavoured Shiraz, Cabernet Sauvignon and Merlot to good local Chardonnay and Semillon. The facilities available to those who stay here include a tennis court and swimming pool with spa. The rooms are beautifully appointed and the dining room harks back to an era of stylish country living.

Jon Reynolds (contract) **WM**
10 am–4 pm weekends and public holidays, or by appointment **CD**

B&B
G

Hamiltons Bluff Wines

WM Andrew Margan (contract)
CD 10 am–4 pm weekends and public holidays, or by appointment

Longs Corner Rd (Tilga St), Canowindra
T 02 6344 2079 **F** 02 63442165 **E** info@hamiltonsbluff
W www.hamiltonsbluff.com.au

The winery is known for its prize-winning Chardonnays and for its splendid views across the countryside. The Canowindra Grossi Unwooded Chardonnay and Cowra Reserve Chardonnay are perhaps the best-known wines, but also available are Semillon, Méthode Champenoise, Cabernet Sauvignon, Shiraz and Sangiovese. Sales of the Canowindra Grossi range of wines now support the research work carried out by the Age of Fishes Museum in Canowindra—another good reason to drink the wines, if one were needed.

Kalari Wines

WM Jill Lindsay, Jon Reynolds (contract)
CD 9 am–5 pm Fri–Mon and public holidays, or by appointment

120 Carro Park Rd, Cowra
T/F 02 6342 1465 **E** kalari@westserve.net.au

This newly established boutique vineyard just outside Cowra has a pleasantly rustic tasting room overlooking gently sloping vineyards. Plantings of Chardonnay, Verdelho, and Shiraz have produced some award-winning wines. The word 'Kalari' is adapted from the local Aboriginal name for the Lachlan river. Food platters are available for groups of six or more by arrangement.

Wallington Straw Bale Winery

WM Murray Smith (contract)
CD First weekend of each month or by appointment
P

Nyrang Creek Vineyard, Nyrang Creek Rd, Canowindra
T 02 6344 7153 **F** 02 6344 7105

This is a boutique winery producing high-quality whites—Chardonnay and Semillon—as well as Cabernet Sauvignon and Shiraz. The picnic area has fine views of the vineyard, and on long weekends lunches and bush tucker are available.

Windowrie Estate

Windowrie Rd, Canowindra

T 02 6344 3264   **F** 02 6344 3227   **W** www.the-mill-winery.com.au

Established in 1988, the winery produces full-flavoured Chardonnay as well as Sauvignon Blanc, Shiraz, Cabernet Sauvignon, Merlot and Cabernet Franc. The wines are estate-made and of high quality. Tastings and sales can be arranged at the winery by appointment, but Windowrie's main tasting room and cellar door is 'The Mill' in the centre of Cowra. An immaculately restored three-storey building originally constructed in 1861, it overlooks verdant River Park on the banks of the Lachlan. Every year in October, the estate hosts a special musical event—either a picnic day or concert—that brings people from far and wide to enjoy the wines and the spectacular countryside.

Stephen Craig, **WM**
Rodney Hooper
(contract)
At 'The Mill', **CD**
6 Vaux St, Cowra
(**T** 02 6341 4141
F 02 6341 4411),
10 am–6 pm daily

Wine tours and activities

Australiana Tours at 1 Kendal St, Cowra, arrange tours of local wineries in their 14-seat minibus (**T/F** 02 6341 3350   **E** voriasa@tpg.com.au   **W** www.australianacorner.com). Operated by Des Bridekirk, Canowindra Motel Winery Tours runs half- and full-day tours to local wineries by arrangement (**T** 02 6344 1633).

Food and Dining

Cowra lies at the heart of an important food-producing region and much local produce finds its way to Sydney's markets and to some of its best restaurants. Fresh products can be sampled and purchased at the Farmers' Markets held at the Cowra Showground (8.30 am–12.30 pm, third Sat of each month). Cowra Smokehouse produces gourmet smoked trout and chicken, and a selection of other products ranging from home-style hams and bacon to marinated olives, sun-dried tomatoes, sauces, jams and pickles, and even to honey and fudge

(**T** 02 6341 1489). It also has a cafe (**O** 9.30 am–6 pm daily except Tues). Australiana Corner sells local jams, olives, pickles, honey and smoked trout as well as arranging wine tours (**T** 02 6341 3350). There are good restaurants in Cowra offering a range of cuisines and good value, and using fresh local produce.

Blue Gum Japanese Restaurant and Guesthouse, 22 Anderson's Lane, Cowra **T** 02 6342 3327 **F** 02 6341 3327 **E** bluegumfarm@ozemail.com.au **W** members@ozemail.com.au **O** 11.30 am–2 pm Fri–Sun for lunch, 6 pm–10 pm Wed–Sun for dinner. Set in a pleasant location surrounded by vineyards, this curiously named restaurant, orchard, farm and guesthouse offers both Japanese and Australian meals.

Neila, 5 Kendal St, Cowra **T/F** 02 6341 2188 **W** www.alldaydining.com **O** From 6 pm Thurs–Sat and public holidays. This modern Australian-Asian restaurant combines local produce and imaginative cooking; it also sell its own locally grown products including olives and olive oil.

The Quarry Cellar Door and Restaurant, Boorowa Rd, Cowra **T** 02 6342 3650 **W** www.cowraregionwines.com **O** Tue–Sun for lunch, Fri–Sat for dinner. Guests can dine inside or on a pleasant shaded terrace. They can also taste and purchase wines from a number of local vineyards, including Cowra Estate (owners), Coolinda, Mulyan, Nassau Estate, Fossil Creek, Danbury Estate and Kalari Vineyard.

Accommodation

Canowindra Riverview Motel, 3 Tilga St, Canowindra **T** 02 6344 1633 **E** riverview.motel@bigpond.co. The motel is centrally located and has thirteen comfortable queen-sized rooms, as a well as a couple of two-bedroom units. It also has a non-smoking level and a spa. Breakfasts and room service are available.

Civic Motor Inn, Young Rd, Cowra T 02 6341 1753 F 02 6342 3296 . An older-style motel, the civic is located close to the river. Its Oasis licensed restaurant has pleasant views over gardens and the Cowra golf course.

Cowra Breakout Motor Inn, 181–3 Kendal St, Cowra T 02 6342 6111. This modern, colonial-style motel, well located close to the centre of town, has standard rooms and two-bedroom suites. There is no restaurant, but room service and breakfast are available. A spa is open to guests.

The Falls Vineyard Retreat, Belubula Way, Canowindra T 02 6344 1293 F 02 6344 1290 E thefalls@allstate.net.au W www.thefallsvineyardretreat.com.au. The Falls provides comfortable accommodation in a renovated country property with immaculate grounds and is surrounded by vineyards. Meals are available if required, and the swimming pool is a great asset.

Vineyard Motel, Chardonnay Road, Cowra T 02 6342 3641 F 02 6342 6800 E vineyardhotel@dodo.com.au. This small family-run motel is set amidst vineyards 5 minutes from Cowra. It's a favourite with many winery visitors, so book ahead. There are barbecue facilities, and meals are available if pre-ordered. Guests also have the use of a small pool.

Travel Information

How to get there
By road Cowra is a pleasant 1-hour drive south of Orange (95 km away) and about 3.5 hours (325 km) direct from Sydney via Bathurst and Blayney.

Other attractions
Australia's World Peace Bell, a replica of the World Peace Bell that hangs opposite the United Nations building in New York, is to be found in Civic Square, Darling St, Cowra. It was awarded to Cowra in 1991 in recognition of the town's efforts towards reconciliation following the tragic events surrounding the Cowra Breakout of 1944. Those events and their aftermath are described by a nine-minute hologram display at the Cowra Visitor Information Centre at Olympic Park, Mid-Western Hwy; admission free (T 02 6342 4333). An avenue of cherry trees links the Japanese and Australian War Cemeteries, POW Campsite and Japanese Garden; when completed it will consist of over 2,000 trees. The Japanese cemetery at Binni Creek Rd, Cowra, contains the bodies of all those

Japanese POWs who lost their lives in the Breakout, as well as the remains of all Japanese nationals who died in Australia during World War II. The beautiful Japanese Garden represents the many landscapes of Japan and includes special features such as a Cultural Centre and Bonsai House (**T** 02 6341 2233 **O** 8.30 am–5 pm daily).

Darbys Falls Observatory, on Observatory Rd, Darbys Falls (30 km southeast of Cowra), offers one of the largest telescopes available to the public, a 500 mm Newton; if arriving after dark, you are requested to switch off headlights on approach (**T** 02 6345 1900 **O** 7 pm–10 pm, winter, 8.30–11 pm summer, weather permitting).

Australiana Corner in Kendall St, Cowra sells Australiana, Aboriginal artefacts, photography, wood and sheepskin products, and organises winery group tours (**T/F** 02 6341 3350). Don't miss the Age of Fishes Museum in Gaskill St, Canowindra, which has fossils that are over 360 million years old. Ask for a guided tour: it doesn't take long and the fossils—the real thing, not replicas—are astonishing (**T** 02 6344 1008 **W** www.ageoffishes.org.au). Canowindra is also one of the best places in Australia to go hot-air ballooning at dawn; you can even choose a package that includes a glass of sparkling wine (**W** www.aussieballoontrek.com).

For kids

The covered displays at the Fun Museum, Mid-western Hwy, Cowra, houses the War, Rail and Rural Museums (**T** 0500815 005 or **T/F** 02 6342 2801 **O** 9 am–5 pm daily). Wyangala Waters State Park, at the junction of the Lachlan and Abercrombie Rivers, 41 km from Cowra, has camping, fishing, mini-golf and water slides (**T** 02 6345 0877).

Events

Apr: Marti's Balloon Fiesta, Canowindra
May: Taste of Cowra
July: Cowra Picnic Races
Aug: Cowra Wine Show
Sept: Sakura Matsuri Cherry Blossom Festival at Japanese Garden
Oct–Nov: Cowra Spring Time Show
Nov: Cowra Food and Wine Weekend featuring Cowra Cork and Fork

Information

Cowra Visitor Information Centre, Olympic Park, Mid-Western Hwy, Cowra **T** 02 6342 4333
E tourism@cowra.nsw.gov.au
W www.cowratourism.com.au

Hastings River

The history of settlement in the Hastings River valley dates from 1821, when a military and penal outpost was established at Port Macquarie. It is thought that vines were first grown in the area in the 1830s, but the modern wine industry dates from the early 1980s when John Cassegrain, of French heritage, planted a vineyard with a view to reviving the viticultural fortunes of the region. His success, and that of those who followed him, was remarkable, for the region's warm, humid climate poses particular challenges. The introduction of hybrid vines—notably Chambourcin—was one of the solutions that has allowed the local industry to succeed when many were sceptical (some still are).

As in many other areas, there has been a marked increase in the number of vineyards in recent years. It will be interesting to see how the wines develop and whether the region's existing loyal following is sufficient to support the new wineries. But the great dedication of its winemakers, its tradition of bold and imaginative ventures, and an increasing local population should all ensure Hastings River continues to thrive.

What to buy

Not surprisingly Chambourcin is a favourite, though it is often blended with a range of other grapes now being grown successfully. The quality of local Cabernet Sauvignon and Shiraz has also improved recently. Of the whites, Verdelho and Chardonnay are good choices.

Key

T	Telephone
F	Fax
E	Email
W	Website
WM	Winemaker
CD	Cellar door
P	Picnic facilities
PA	Play area for children
BBQ	Barbecue facilities
GT	Guided tours
C	Cafe
R	Restaurant
O	Opening hours
B&B	Bed and breakfast
H	Hotel/Inn
M	Motel
G	Guesthouse
SCA	Self-catering accommodation

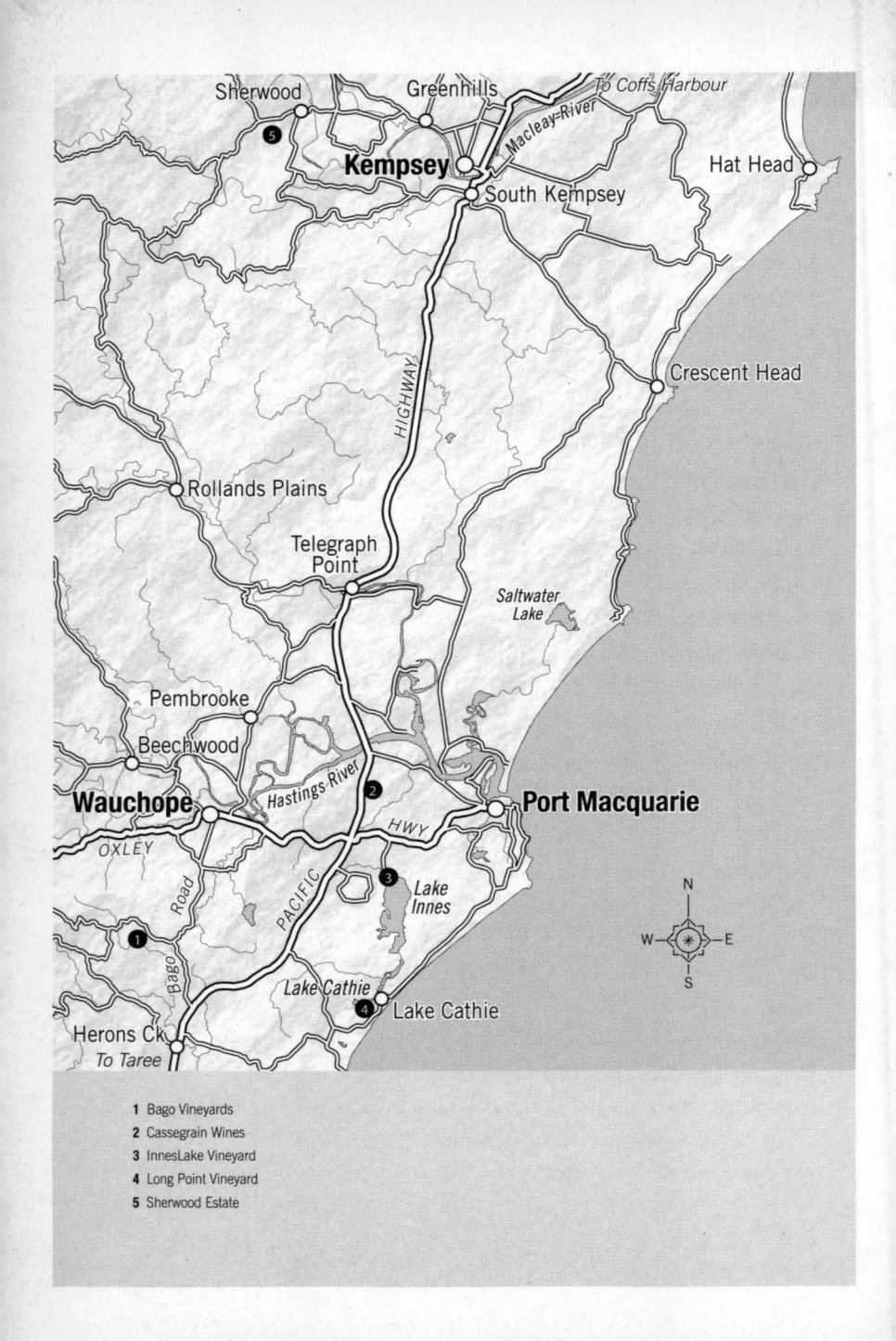

1 Bago Vineyards
2 Cassegrain Wines
3 InnesLake Vineyard
4 Long Point Vineyard
5 Sherwood Estate

Wineries

Bago Vineyards

Milligan's Rd, off Bago Rd
T/F 02 6585 7099 **E** info@bagovineyards.com.au
W bagovineyards.com.au

Chambourcin is the main attraction here, presented in an unusual array of styles ranging from rosé to medium-bodied reds and an award-winning Sparkling Chambourcin, which sells quickly. Other grapes grown include Chardonnay, Verdelho, Viognier, Merlot, Cabernet Sauvignon, Petit Verdot, Sauvignon Blanc and Pinot Noir (grown mainly as the basis for sparkling white and fortified wines). Platters of local cheeses can be purchased at the cellar door, and coffee and tea are available under the pergola overlooking the vineyards and adjacent state forest. As well as its main Bago label, Bago Vineyards has a second label branded 'Jazz'—Jazz Classic White, Jazz Chilled Red and Sparkling Jazz—which is appropriate as jazz (the music) is another big drawcard at the winery, with concerts being held on the second Sunday of each month.

WM Jim Mobbs
CD 9.30 am–5 pm daily
P
BBQ

Cassegrain Wines

281 Fernbank Road (cnr Pacific Hwy), Port Macquarie
T 02 6583 7777   **F** 02 6584 0354   **E** info@cassegrainwines.com.au
W www.cassegrainwines.com.au

This was the first of the new vineyards in the area, planted by Frenchman Gérard Cassegrain and his wife Françoise in 1980. The winery now produces four main ranges (Stone Circle, Premium, Discovery and Reserve) from a wide variety of grapes, including Chambourcin, Cabernet Sauvignon, Shiraz, Chardonnay, Merlot, Sangiovese, Durif and Verdelho. It has an attractive tasting area and an excellent restaurant, Ça Marche (see Food and Dining). Try the Chambourcin or Discovery Rosé for something out of the ordinary—the latter is especially good as a chilled summer wine—and the Reserve Fromenteau Chardonnay. The winery grounds, approached via a stand of eucalypts, have shaded picnic tables, and are an ideal place to pass a few restful moments away from the highway traffic.

WM John Cassegrain, Karen Leggett
CD 9 am–5 pm daily
P
R

InnesLake Vineyard

WM John Cassegrain (contract)
CD 10 am–5 pm daily
C From 10 am for morning tea and 11.30 am–2.30 pm for lunch

The Ruins Way, Port Macquarie

T 02 6581 1332 **F** 02 6581 0391

There is a newly refurbished cellar door here with a cafe serving light meals and specialising in local seafood. A small range of both reds and whites is on offer, including a Semillon, a Chardonnay and Summer White blend, as well as a Cabernet Merlot, a Cabernet Sauvignon, a Pinot Noir and a Shiraz. Also available are InnesLake Mist, a sweet white fortified dessert wine, and a tawny port. Charley Brothers gourmet produce can also be purchased at the cellar door.

Long Point Vineyard

WM Graeme Davies
CD 10 am–6 pm Wed–Sun and public holidays, or by appointment
P
BBQ

6 Cooinda Place, Lake Cathie

T 02 6585 4598 **E** longpointvineyard@tsn.cc

This is a family-owned operation producing a small range of wines including the area's speciality, Chambourcin, as well as Shiraz, Chardonnay, Cabernet Sauvignon and Traminer. There are two labels: the Long Point range, made only with grapes grown on the estate, and the Deckchair range, half of whose fruit is sourced elsewhere. In addition, Long Point makes a range of meads and liqueurs, including the popular, if curiously named, Agent Orange. The cellar door also sells gourmet products including Valla Beach Smokehouse goods (excellent smoked trout and smoked kangaroo), and condiments, olives, olive oil and macadamia oil made by Yarras (see Food and Dining).

Sherwood Estate

WM John Cassegrain (contract)
CD 11 am–4 pm Fri–Sun and public holidays
P
BBQ

1187 Gowings Hill Rd, Sherwood via Kempsey

T 02 6581 4900 **F** 02 6581 4728
E info@sherwoodestatewines.com.au
W www.sherwoodestatewines.com.au

Set in the lovely Macleay Valley, 40 minutes north of Port Macquarie, the Sherwood vineyards are planted with a range of grape varieties, from Chambourcin and Shiraz to Merlot, Cabernet Franc and Sangiovese in the reds, and Semillon, Sauvignon Blanc, Verdelho and Traminer Riesling in the whites. They have three labels: Gazebo, Middle Paddock and Sherwood Reserve. The

Semillon is a very pale green, lemony and zesty. They also make a dessert Semillon, Frost. Cheese platters are available at the cellar door and local produce is on sale. Musical performances take place here once a month on Sunday afternoons and you can take a picnic or use the barbecues.

Wine tours and activities

Macquarie Mountain Tours run half-day winery tours (1 pm every Thurs, Sat, Sun **T** 0419 557 166). The Sherwood Wine Embassy operates as a tasting and sales outlet for several vineyards, and sells regional food produce. It's located at the Highway Service Centre, at the intersection of the Oxley and Pacific Highways outside Port Macquarie (**T** 02 6581 4900 **O** 9 am–5.30 pm daily).

Food and Dining

Several wineries have a restaurant, cafe or snacks, and some sell local produce to complement their wines. Port Macquarie has a good selection of shops offering first-class food and the number and quality of restaurants has risen rapidly in the past few years. Local seafood is particularly good, ranging from oysters to the fresh fish available at the Fishermen's Co-op at the end of Clarence Street in Port Macquarie. Hastings River is also becoming known for its olive-growing, and an increasingly popular local speciality is olive oil infused with herbs and spices, particularly native varieties such as lemon myrtle and mountain pepper berries. One prominent producer, Yarras Olive Oil Products makes a variety of these oils as well as table olives (both natural and flavoured), salad dressings and dukkahs (nut-based mixes). The company sells its products through the wineries (Cassegrain, Bago and Long Point Vineyard) and retail outlets in Wauchope and Port Macquarie (**W** www.hastingsvalleyolives.com.au/retail). Another notable supplier of gourmet foods is Deli 66, Shop 1/114 William Street, Port Macquarie (**T** 02 6584 4600).

Ça Marche, Cassegrain Winery, cnr Pacific Hwy and Fernbank Creek Rd, Port Macquarie **T** 02 6582 8320 **E** camarche764@msn.com **O** 10.30 am–4.30 pm daily or by appointment. The restaurant occupies a lovely, airy space with a terrace overlooking lawns and vineyards. It serves a range of modern Australian food featuring regional and seasonal produce, including seafood. The proprietor, Phillip Down, also runs food and wine matching sessions ('wine education workshops') in the restaurant.

Crays Waterfront Restaurant, 74 Clarence St, Port Macquarie **T** 02 6583 7885 **O** From 6 pm daily, 12 noon–2 pm Sun–Fri. Fish and seafood are the focus here, but you can also tuck into steaks, chicken and vegetarian dishes.

Macquarie Seafoods, cnr Clarence and Short Sts, Port Macquarie **T** 02 6583 8476 **O** 11 am–8 pm daily. Classic takeaway fish and chips, as well as oysters, calamari and more.

Portabellos Cafe, Shop 6, 124 Horton St, Port Macquarie **T** 02 6584 1171 **O** Thurs–Sat for lunch, Thu–Sat for dinner. One of the most popular BYOs in the area (and there's no corkage charge!), Portabellos presents moderately priced, innovative food made with a host of fresh ingredients.

Accommodation

Country Comfort Inn, cnr Buller and Hollingworth Sts, Port Macquarie **T** 02 6583 2955 **F** 02 6583 7398 **W** www.constellationhotels.com. The hotel's Castaway Bar and Restaurant offers BYO with no corkage and 10 per cent discount on meals when you bring Cassegrain or Sherwood Estate wines.

Flynn's Beach Resort, cnr Pacific and Ocean Sts, Port Macquarie **T** 1800 833 338 **F** 02 6583 3111 **E** info@flynnsbeachresort.com.au **W** www.flynnsbeachresort.com.au. These refurbished beachside apartments have a pool, barbecues, a tennis court (fee applies) and a restaurant.

Tom's Creek Retreat, 223 Toms Creek Rd, Ellenborough **T** 02 6587 4313 **E** tomscreekretreat@bigpond.com **W** www.tomscreekretreat.com.au. This one is a bit off the beaten track, but if you want a peaceful rural setting and a comfortable place to savour your purchases it's well worth a look. The cabins have views through the valley woodlands and wildlife is abundant.

Travel Information

How to get there
By road From Sydney, it's approximately a 4.5-hour drive north to the Hastings Valley area along the Pacific Hwy.
By air QantasLink (**T** 13 13 13) flies to Port Macquarie (and return) from Sydney 4 times a day at 8.30 and 11.50 am, and 3.30 and 6.45 pm.
By train A service runs from Sydney to Wauchope three times a day, but only one (departing at 11.35 am) connects with the Countrylink bus service to Port Macquarie (arriving at 6.20 pm).

Other attractions
The Greater Port Macquarie area has many natural attractions. North Brother Mountain in Dooragan National Park offers spectacular views of the Camden Haven River. You can explore remnant rainforest at the Borganna Nature Reserve, located on the western edge of the Comboyne Plateau. Here a 1-km walking track leads to the top of Rawson Falls, where there are stunning views. But the Hastings River area is perhaps most famous for its beaches, and there are a number up and down the coast from Port Macquarie that offer opportunities for surfing, bathing or just pottering about on the sand. Two of the closest to the centre of Port Macquarie, both patrolled, are Town Beach and Flynn's Beach.

For kids
A classic Australian tourist experience, the Billabong Koala and Wildlife Park in Port Macquarie allows you to see (and cuddle) a range of Australian mammals in a suitably exotic park. Birds and fish are on show too, so there's plenty to keep kids interested (**T** 02 6585 1060).

The region's major tourist attraction is Timbertown pioneer village, a working replica of an 1880s sawmilling town, with a range of shops and galleries. The village has a blacksmith's forge, a station complete with steam train, a pub and barbecue facilities. Timbertown is on the Oxley Hwy 2 km west of Wauchope. Entry is by gold-coin donation; rides incur an additional charge (**T** 02 6585 2322; **O** 9.30 am–3.30 pm daily).

Events
Oct: Port Fest Food & Wine
Mar: Camden Haven Music Festival
Nov: Harvest, picnic and cultural festival (at Cassegrain)

Information
Port Macquarie Visitor Information Centre, cnr Clarence and Hay Sts, Port Macquarie **T** 02 6581 8000 or 1800 303 155 **F** 02 6584 0354
E tourism@hastings.nsw.gov.au
W www.portmacquarieinfo.com.au
North Coast Winegrowers Association
T 02 6585 7099

Hunter Valley: Lower Hunter

Key

T	Telephone
F	Fax
E	Email
W	Website
WM	Winemaker
CD	Cellar door
P	Picnic facilities
PA	Play area for children
BBQ	Barbecue facilities
GT	Guided tours
C	Cafe
R	Restaurant
O	Opening hours
B&B	Bed and breakfast
H	Hotel/Inn
M	Motel
G	Guesthouse
SCA	Self-catering accommodation

The Hunter Valley is divided between the Lower Hunter, centred on Pokolbin, and the Upper Hunter, which is centred on Denman, an hour or so to the north (see *Hunter Valley: Upper Hunter*). The Lower Hunter is one of Australia's premier winegrowing regions and was the first to be developed—vines were cultivated near the present site of Belford as early as the 1820s and the first Hunter Valley Vinegrowers Association was formed in 1847. In the 1850s and 1860s, vines were planted by James Busby, George Wyndham of Dalwood vineyard, Dr Henry Lindeman and Joseph Drayton. Notable figures of the 1880s included the forebears of another well-known Hunter family, the Tyrrells. Further expansion in the 1920s and 1930s saw several companies flourish, including McWilliams—founded in 1921 by the legendary Maurice O'Shea—and Lindemans.

In the early days, fortified wines were the main style of wine produced in the Hunter. But by the end of World War II, red wines had taken their place, with Shiraz matching Semillon as the most commonly grown grape. During the 1960s, a new generation of winegrowers, advocates and enthusiasts began to change the wine industry in Australia. In the Hunter Valley, they included Dr Max Lake, whose Lake's Folly is regarded as the first boutique winery and who was one of the first to achieve an international reputation, and Len Evans, who founded Rothbury Estate and has tirelessly promoted the region through the wine-show system and by developing overseas markets. Both helped put the Hunter Valley on the world wine map. Since then, winegrowers and winemakers have proliferated in the valley. Experimenting with different grapes, styles and winemaking techniques, they have transformed the area into one of Australia's most important wine regions and a hugely popular destination for wine lovers from all over the world.

Changing fashions in wine consumption have influenced the choice of grape varieties in the Hunter. The 1970s saw the reintroduction of Cabernet Sauvignon, while the popularity of Chardonnay in the early 1980s resulted in many hectares being converted to its production. More recently, the number of varieties grown in the Hunter has expanded as tastes have broadened, with Verdelho and Sauvignon Blanc becoming fashionable.

Despite a less than perfect climate—high humidity, with hail likely in spring and summer, and too much rainfall during the harvest—and poor soils in many areas, the Hunter continues to produce a huge variety of fine wines as well as large volumes of table wines whose popularity continues to grow apace.

The three main subregions of the Lower Hunter are Pokolbin, Broke–Fordwich and Lovedale. Pokolbin is the main commercial centre and has seen a good deal of recent development, both of wineries and of other establishments, including the Hunter Valley Gardens, housing estates, accommodation and golf courses, all of which has begun to change the character of the area.

The Broke–Fordwich subregion has experienced much less development, but has seen the planting of many new areas of vines, both by small operators and corporations. The soils are said to be more fertile here than in other parts of the lower Hunter and produce distinctive varietal wines. The Lovedale area is also part of the Lower Hunter but has sought, very effectively, to promote itself as a distinct destination through a host of special events such as the Lovedale Long Lunch.

There is simply too much in the Lower Hunter to experience in a short visit, although half-day and one-day tours are of course available. For the first-time visitor, it's probably best to start at the visitor centre in Pokolbin (see Travel Information), where you can pick up the latest guide and map (things change fast in the Hunter!) Then explore the best of the Pokolbin wineries, before branching out to Broke–Fordwich and Lovedale.

What to buy

The area produces both white and red wines, and is famous for Semillon and Shiraz. But although Semillon is seen as the classic Hunter white and has great cellaring potential in good years, Chardonnay and, more recently, Verdelho, Riesling and Pinot Gris are the pick of the whites. Shiraz is still the iconic red, but Cabernet Sauvignon, Merlot and other less well-known—and less popular—varieties such as Pinot Noir and Chambourcin are literally gaining ground. In addition, growers are experimenting with varieties such as Durif, Zinfandel and Mourvedre as well as Italian grapes such as Barbera and Sangiovese, though these are strictly in the minority.

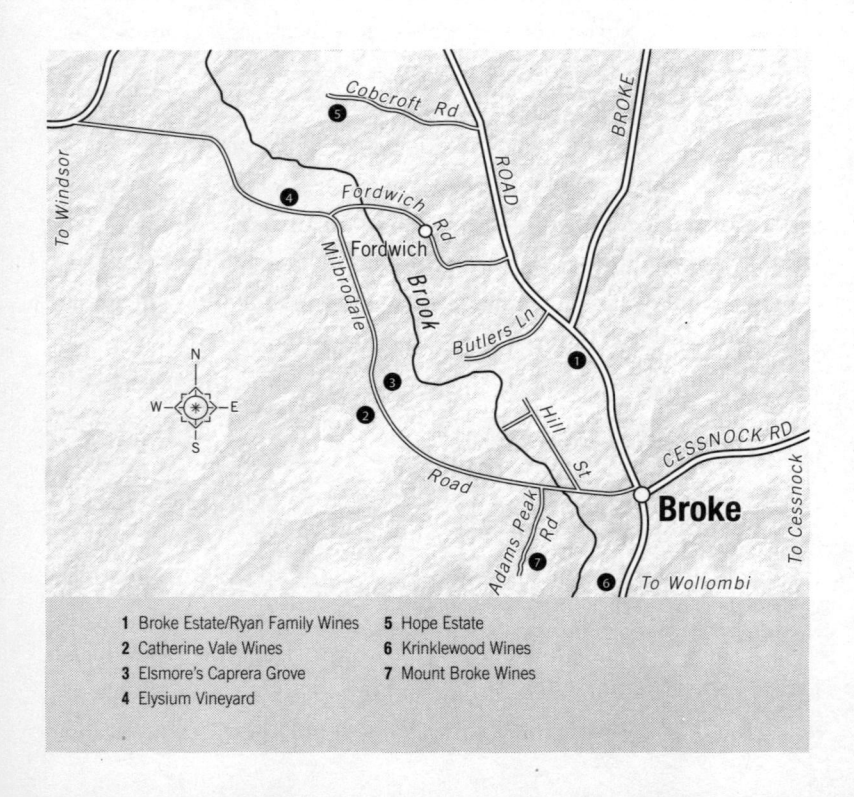

1 Broke Estate/Ryan Family Wines
2 Catherine Vale Wines
3 Elsmore's Caprera Grove
4 Elysium Vineyard
5 Hope Estate
6 Krinklewood Wines
7 Mount Broke Wines

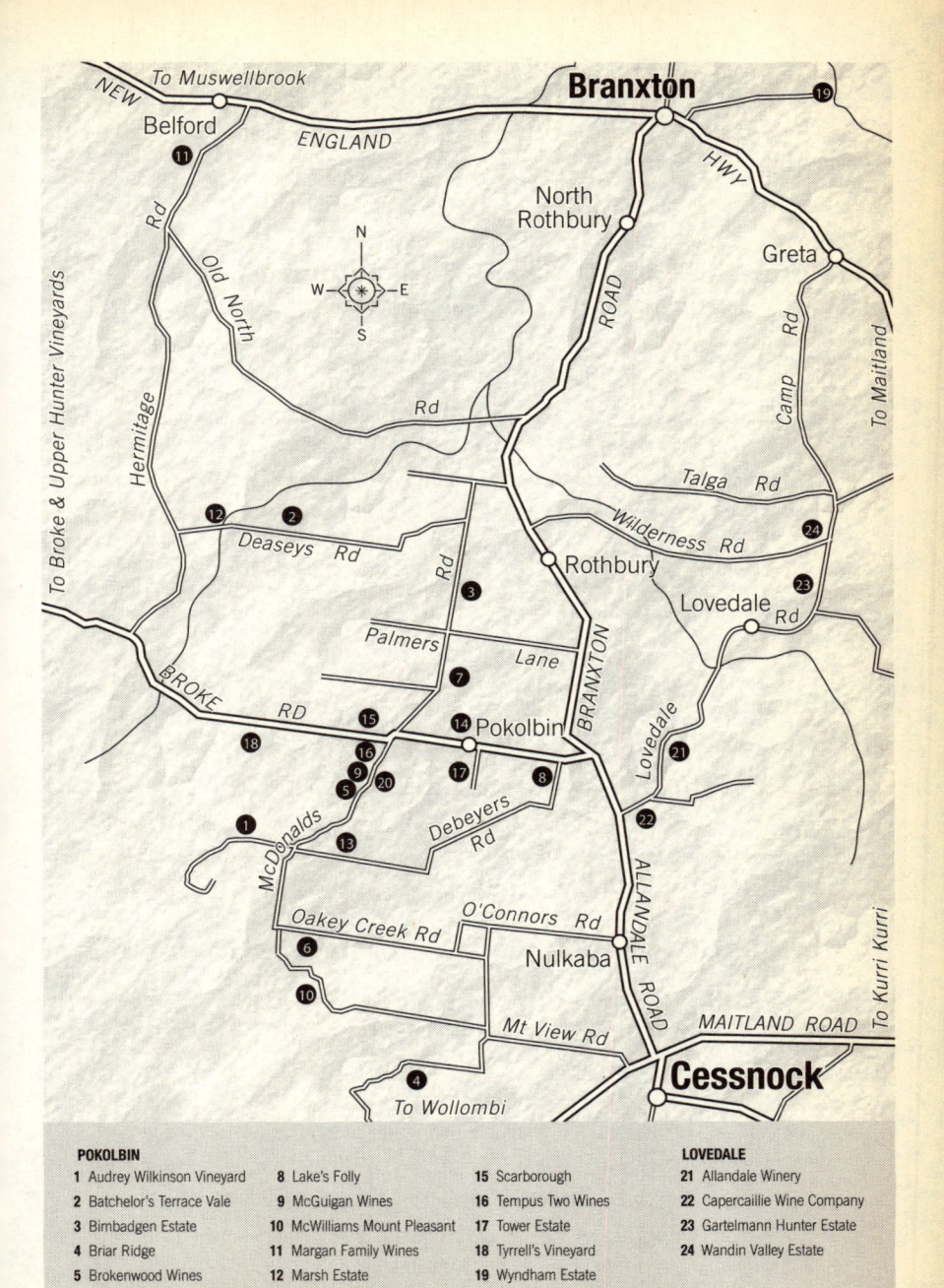

POKOLBIN
1 Audrey Wilkinson Vineyard
2 Batchelor's Terrace Vale
3 Bimbadgen Estate
4 Briar Ridge
5 Brokenwood Wines
6 Drayton's Family Wines
7 First Creek Wines
8 Lake's Folly
9 McGuigan Wines
10 McWilliams Mount Pleasant
11 Margan Family Wines
12 Marsh Estate
13 Poole's Rock Wines
14 Rothbury Estate
15 Scarborough
16 Tempus Two Wines
17 Tower Estate
18 Tyrrell's Vineyard
19 Wyndham Estate
20 Verona/Small Winemakers Centre

LOVEDALE
21 Allandale Winery
22 Capercaillie Wine Company
23 Gartelmann Hunter Estate
24 Wandin Valley Estate

LOWER HUNTER VALLEY 33

Wineries

Pokolbin

WM Mark Woods
CD 9 am–5 pm Mon–Fri, 9.30 am–5 pm Sun and public holidays

Audrey Wilkinson Vineyard
De Beyers Rd, Pokolbin
T 02 4998 7411 **F** 02 4998 7303 **E** wines@audreywilkinson.com.au
W www.audreywilkinson.com.au

This long-established estate, with superb sweeping views across the valleys, offers a small range of wines made from old vines. Grape varieties include Shiraz, Merlot, Chardonnay and Traminer, as well as Zinfandel. Specials are always available at the cellar door, sometimes including a quaffable Zinfandel blend and a Malbec—not a common variety in these parts.

WM Alain Leprince
CD 10 am–4 pm daily
P
BBQ

Batchelors Terrace Vale Wines
Deasys Rd, Pokolbin
T 02 4998 7517 **F** 02 4998 7814 **E** wines@terracevale.com.au
W www.terracevale.com.au

This family-owned winery was started in the early 1970s and has good facilities and fine wines made from Hunter grapes. The winery is set in pleasant country and enjoys views of the Brokenback Range. Try the Campbell's Orchard Semillon and the Unwooded Chardonnay. They also make reds—Cabernet Sauvignon, Shiraz and Merlot—a port and a fine dessert wine, Elizabeth Sauvignon Blanc.

WM Simon Thistlewood
CD 9.30 am–5 pm daily
R

Bimbadgen Estate
Lot 21, McDonalds Rd, Pokolbin
T 02 4998 7585 **F** 02 4998 7732 **E** office@bimbadgen.com.au
W www.bimbadgen.com.au

A wide range of wines is produced here, mostly in the medium and low price ranges but generally of a high quality. It includes the Hunter specialties Shiraz and Semillon, but also Chardonnay, Verdelho, Pinot Noir and a Cabernet blend in the cheaper range. Bimbadgen runs a club offering special events, wine discounts and priority access to activities at the winery—including various musical events. The winery's restaurant, Esca, has a fine reputation (see Food and Dining).

Briar Ridge

Mount View Rd, Pokolbin

T/F 02 4990 3670   **E** indulge@briarridge.com.au
W www.briarridge.com.au

The team at Briar Ridge has been making top Hunter wines for more than 25 years. The winery is located high on the slopes of Mount View, at the southern tip of the Hunter Valley viticultural area. Its hand-nurtured vines and low yields result in intensely flavoured, medal-winning wines that are distinctively Hunter in character. They include Semillon, Gewurztraminer, Chardonnay and Shiraz in two ranges, Premium and Signature. The views from the tasting room are a bonus.

Steve Dodd **WM**
10 am–5 pm **CD**
every day

Brokenwood Wines

McDonalds Rd, Pokolbin

T 02 4998 7559   **F** 02 4998 7893
E cellardoor@brokenwood.com.au   **W** www.brokenwood.com.au

Founded as a modest venture in the early 1970s by a group of hobbyists, this has become a highly successful winery with an enviable winemaking record. Notable successes include the Cricket Pitch range, Hunter Semillon, Sauvignon Blanc, Chardonnay and Graveyard Vineyard Shiraz, but all the wines are of consistently high quality and offer good value.

Ian Riggs, **WM**
Peter James
Charteris
10 am–5 pm **CD**
daily
First Sun of **GT**
each month
(book in advance)

Drayton's Family Wines

Oakey Creek Rd, Pokolbin

T 02 4998 7513   **F** 02 4998 7743

The Drayton name is legendary in the Hunter and has been associated with local winemaking since the late 1850s. It speaks of a long tradition of quality and value for money, now embodied in a range of full-flavoured, well-made wines. The Vineyard Reserve is a premium range that showcases varietal wines made with locally grown fruit; the Chardonnay is especially popular, as are the Merlot and Shiraz. The Hunter Valley range (try the Semillon) and New Generation range are also worthy bearers of the Drayton name, while the fortified wines—sherries, ports and Muscats—also have a strong following. The winery is set in pleasant grounds with views over vines, dams and wooded country.

Trevor Drayton **WM**
8 am–5 pm **CD**
Mon–Fri,
10 am–5 pm
weekends and
public holidays

P
BBQ

First Creek Wines

WM Greg Silkman
CD 9 am–5 pm Mon–Fri, 9.30 am–5 pm weekends and public holidays
P
BBQ
GT 12 noon daily
SCA

Cnr McDonalds and Gillards Rds, Pokolbin

T 02 4998 7293 **F** 02 4998 7294
E winemasters@firstcreekwines.com.au
W www.firstcreekwines.com.au

The whole range of First Creek wines is never less than well made and keenly priced; the Allanmere Durham Chardonnay represents particularly good value. The winery offers self-catering accommodation at Trinity Cottage (see Accommodation).

Lake's Folly

WM Rodney Kempe
CD 10 am–4 pm Mon–Sat

Broke Rd, Pokolbin

T 02 4998 7507 **F** 02 4998 7322 **E** folly@ozemail.com.au
W www.lakesfolly.com.au

Australia's first boutique winery, founded in 1963, is still making top wine, though it is no longer owned by the founder, Hunter Valley identity and wine visionary Dr Max Lake. Though the winery makes only a Cabernet blend and a Chardonnay—and only in small quantities sold from 1 April each year—the cellar door is part of Hunter mythology and is well worth a visit.

McGuigan Wines

WM Peter Hall
CD 9 am–5 pm daily
C

Cnr Broke and McDonalds Rds, Pokolbin

T 02 4998 7402 **F** 02 4998 7445 **W** www.mcguiganwines.com.au

The McGuigan family is well known in the Hunter and this winery complex attests to Brian McGuigan's success as a winemaker and businessman—and as a promoter of the Hunter Valley. The cellar door sells a wide range of wines at every price point, including specials and the Bin and Personal Reserve ranges, and the tasting facilities are among the best in the Hunter. There are also a cafe and, right next door, the Hunter Valley Cheese Company (see Food and Dining). But don't expect to have the place to yourself unless you go in the off-off season. McGuigan's reds, particularly the Old Vine Shiraz and Bin 4000 Cabernet Sauvignon, are good value for money, and the Bin 9000 Semillon is also excellent.

McWilliams Mount Pleasant Wines

Marrowbone Rd, Pokolbin
T 02 4998 7505 **F** 02 4998 7761 **E** mtpleasant@mcwilliams.com.au
W www.mcwilliams.com.au

Phil Ryan
10 am–4.30 pm daily

WM CD GT C

The Mount Pleasant vineyard was founded in 1921 by the legendary winemaker Maurice O'Shea. The historic estate is now owned by McWilliams family. The Mount Pleasant Elizabeth Semillon is a classic Australian wine and has received a record number of awards. Don't miss it. The rest of the range is also highly regarded, from the Philip Hunter Shiraz and Lovedale Semillon to the Rosehill Shiraz. The cellar door sells a number of special releases not available through the retail trade. As well as a cafe, there is a gift shop that stocks some local produce and gourmet items such as AC Butchery sausages and Poachers Pantry cold meats. The winery tours are well conducted and informative.

Margan Family Winery

Beltree, 266 Hermitage Rd, Pokolbin
T 02 6574 7004 **E** marganfw@hunterlink.net.au
W www.margan.com.au

Andrew Margan
10 am–5 pm daily

WM CD C

The emphasis here is on traditional Hunter Valley wines featuring intense flavours from low-yield vineyards. The Verdelho (top-notch), Semillon and Chardonnay lead the whites, and Shiraz, Cabernet Sauvignon and Merlot the reds. There's also a classy Botrytis Semillon if you're fond of stickies. The tasting centre has a cafe that serves light meals and coffee.

Marsh Estate

Deasys Rd, Pokolbin
T 02 4998 7587 **F** 02 4998 7884

Andrew Marsh
By appointment

WM CD

This small, unirrigated vineyard planted in the early 1970s uses only estate-grown fruit to produce top-quality wines that are rich, full-bodied and among the best in the Hunter. They include reds and whites—Semillon, Chardonnay, Cabernet Sauvignon and Shiraz—all available by appointment at the cellar door and via mail order.

Poole's Rock Wines

WM Patrick Auld
CD 9.30 am–5 pm daily
P
BBQ
SCA

Cnr McDonalds and Debeyers Rds, Pokolbin

T 02 4998 7356   **F** 02 4998 6866   **E** cellardoor@poolesrock.com.au
W www.poolesrock.com.au

Founded in 1895 by the pioneering Tulloch family, this winery was refurbished when David Clarke's Poole's Rock Wines took it over in 2002. The vineyard includes 8 ha of mature, drip-irrigated Shiraz—with some vines dating back to 1900. The ranges for sale include Poole's Rock, Cockfighters Ghost and Firestick. The winery has a cellar door and air-conditioned barrel store. Poole's Rock's original vineyard is in the Broke–Fordwich area and produces excellent Chardonnay and Semillon from the former Wollombi Vineyard. Cottage accommodation is available, but book ahead.

Rothbury Estate

WM Neil McGuigan
CD 9.30 am–4.30 pm daily
GT 10.30 daily
C

Broke Rd, Pokolbin

T 02 4998 7363   **F** 02 4993 3559   **W** www.beringerblass.com.au

Now part of the Beringer Blass group, the Rothbury Estate played an important role in raising the profile of the Australian wine industry and a visit to the historic winery can be a fascinating experience. Rothbury was originally started as a wine-tasting club by vigneron, show judge and luminary Len Evans and a consortium of directors that included Murray Tyrrell. Initially, the winery made only estate-grown Shiraz and Semillon that was sold exclusively to the club's membership list. But the outlets are now more numerous and the range has been expanded to include Chardonnay, Cabernet Sauvignon and, more recently, Merlot, as well as a Botrytis Semillon—all of them excellent. In addition to Rothbury wines, the cellar door offers tastings and sales of other Hunter wines and wines from other parts of New South Wales. The building, with its impressive barrel room, won an RAIA Blacket Award and is a Hunter landmark. It is surrounded by pleasant gardens and well-tended rose beds, and has a coffee house, Toby's, that serves good coffee and snacks.

Scarborough Wine Company

Gillards Rd, Pokolbin

T 02 4998 7563 **F** 02 4998 7786 **E** info@scarboroughwine.com.au
W www.scarboroughwine.com.au

Ian Scarborough **WM**
9 am–5 pm daily **CD**

This small family-owned vineyard, located on a hilltop, offers a terrific Hunter experience: the owners lead you through the tasting, helping you to get the most out of the wines, while you also admire the sweeping views. The principal wines are two Chardonnays, a refined Chablis-style and a richer Australian style, and an impressive Pinot Noir, a blend of several vintages. All three are well worth tasting—and buying, as the prices are very reasonable. The pleasant grounds are ideal for picnics.

Tempus Two Wines

Cnr Broke and McDonalds Rds, Pokolbin

T 02 4993 3999 **F** 02 4993 3988

Sarah-Kate Dineen **WM**
10 am–5 pm daily **CD**
C
R

The imposing modern winery of black and grey marble, with its fountains and sweeping lawns—the modern equivalent of a chateau winery—tells you immediately that this is a classy and well-funded operation. Run by Lisa McGuigan, it produces excellent wines under the Tempus Two and Roche Tallawanta labels using fruit sourced from all over Australia, including the Hunter. The tasting room converts to a lounge bar at night; in addition the complex houses a Japanese sushi restaurant (which also serves Thai dishes) and an espresso bar.

Tower Estate

Cnr Hall and Broke Rds, Pokolbin

T 02 4998 7989 **F** 02 4998 7919 **E** sales@towerestate.com
W www.towerestatewines.com.au

Dan Dineen **WM**
10 am–5 pm daily **CD**
SCA

Tower was founded by Len Evans and its philosophy is to produce very limited quantities of top-quality wines in classic styles using grapes from the Australian region that best suits the variety. Thus fruit is sourced from carefully selected vineyards in, among other areas, the Hunter, the Yarra Valley and the Adelaide Hills. The range includes Hunter Valley Semillon and Chardonnay, Pinot Noir and Cabernet Sauvignon. Luxurious accommodation and conference facilities are available.

Tyrrells Vineyards

WM Andrew Spinaze
CD 8 am–5 pm
Mon–Sat
GT

Broke Rd, Pokolbin

T 02 4993 7000 **F** 02 4998 7723 **E** admin@tyrrells.com.au
W www.tyrrells.com.au

Tyrrells is another Hunter Valley name that has been around for more than 100 years. It's widely accepted that this is where the Chardonnay revolution began, when Murray Tyrrell produced his Vat 47 Chardonnay in 1973. Since then, Australian wine drinking has never been the same, with Chardonnay sales consistently outstripping other white varieties. The winery is heritage-listed and the tours provide a highly informative introduction to the development of the local industry. Today, Tyrrells maintains consistent high quality across Chardonnay, Semillon and Shiraz as well as a range of blended wines. The wines are available at several price points and all represent good value. Note, however, that the perennially popular Long Flat labels are no longer owned by Tyrrells, but were sold to the Cheviot Bridge company.

Wyndham Estate

WM Brett McKinnon
CD 9.30 am–4.30 pm
daily
P
BBQ
GT 11 am daily or by appointment
R

700 Dalwood Rd, Dalwood, via Branxton

T 02 4938 3444 **F** 02 4938 3555 **W** www.wyndhamestate.com.au

One of the icons of the Hunter, this lovely estate set amidst the Dalwood Hills includes Australia's oldest continually operating winery. The wines come in the numbered Bin ranges and the premium Show Reserve range. Semillon, Chardonnay and Shiraz are strengths here, but Cabernet Merlot, Cabernet Sauvignon, Pinot Noir and Verdelho are also available. The estate is the venue for the annual Opera in the Vineyards weekend, held in October each year.

Lovedale

Allandale Winery

132 Lovedale Rd, Lovedale

T 02 4990 4526 **F** 02 4990 1714 **E** wines@allandalewinery.com.au
W www.allandalewinery.com.au

The winery and tasting room have a lovely hillside position with spectacular views over the Lovedale and Pokolbin vineyards to the Brokenback Range. The winery offers a small range of mid-priced wines of consistently good flavour and quality. They include a good-value Hunter Verdelho, Sauvignon Blanc and Chardonnay as well as a Méthode Champenoise sparkler and a Chardonnay Semillon Verdelho blend. Food and wine events are held throughout the year, including Strings in the Winery in August and Jazz at Budburst in October.

Bill Sneddon **WM**
9 am–5 pm **CD**
Mon–Sat,
10 am–5 pm Sun
P

Capercaillie Wine Company and Gallery

Londons Rd, Lovedale

T 02 4990 2904 **F** 02 4992 1886 **W** www.capercailliewine.com.au

Scottish wines—surely not! The name was actually 'inspired by the rare and majestic black woodlands grouse' of winemaker Alasdair Sutherland's native Scottish Highlands. The award-winning reds and whites are sourced from the Hunter and further afield: the Semillons, Chardonnay, Shiraz and Merlot are top quality, and there is also a stylish rosé. A tempting art and craft gallery shares space with the cellar door.

Alasdair Sutherland **WM**
9 am–5 pm **CD**
Mon–Sat,
10 am–5 pm Sun

Gartelmann Hunter Estate

Lovedale Rd, Lovedale

T 02 4930 7113 **F** 02 4930 7114 **E** sales@gartelmann.com.au
W www.gartelmann.com.au

The wines here range from Shiraz, Semillon, Chardonnay and Chenin Blanc to red and white sparklers and a very acceptable Merlot. The pleasant, shaded, park-like estate features a lake, barbecues and a picnic area. The choice of a magpie on the labels acknowledges the birds' help in keeping the vines free of insects.

Gary Reed **WM**
(contract)
10 am–5 pm daily **CD**
P
BBQ
By appointment **GT**

Wandin Valley Estate

WM Nicolas Paterson, Karl Stockhausen
CD 10 am–5 pm daily
P
C
SCA

Wilderness Rd, Lovedale
T 02 4930 7317 **F** 02 4930 7814
E sales@wandinvalley.com.au/accommodation

Known mainly for its Chardonnay, Wandin Valley Estate produces two ranges of white and red wines—the value-for-money Estate range and the Reserve range, which will reward cellaring—across several varieties and blends including Cabernet Merlot, Cabernet Malbec, Shiraz, Verdelho and Semillon as well as a rosé and a Muscat. The grounds are extensive and include self-catering villas (see Accommodation), a cricket pitch, tennis courts and picnic tables overlooking the vines.

Broke–Fordwich

Broke Estate/Ryan Family Wines

WM Jim Chatto
CD 11 am–5 pm weekends and public holidays, or by appointment

Wollombi Rd, Broke
T/F 02 6579 1065 **W** www.ryanwines.com.au

The delightfully rustic cellar door is housed in a slab cottage. The wines are offered in two ranges, the premium Broke Estate 'Hunter Classics' and the 'drink-now' Ryan label, and include Semillon, Chardonnay and Cabernet, and a sweet white, Lachryma Angelorum.

Catherine Vale Wines

WM John Hordern, Hunter Wine Services
CD 10 am–5 pm weekends and public holidays
P
BBQ

656 Milbrodale Rd, Broke
T/F 02 6579 1334 **E** finewines@catherinevale.com.au
W www.catherinevale.com.au

This is a small operation specialising in Semillon, Chardonnay, Verdelho and two light Italian reds—Dolcetto and Barbera. As well as a modern cellar door, it has two full-size bocce courts surrounded by lawns, for the use of visitors.

Elsemore's Caprera Grove

WM Monarch Winemaking Services
CD 10 am–5 pm weekends, Mon–Fri by appointment

657 Milbrodale Rd, Broke
T 02 6579 1344 **F** 02 6579 1355 **E** cjbe@hunterlink.net.au

This small olive grove and vineyard grows Chardonnay, Shiraz and Verdelho. Olives, jams and chutneys and other local products are sold, as well as artworks and pottery.

Elysium Vineyard

393 Milbrodale Rd, Broke

T 0417 282 746   **E** elysiumvineyard@bigpond.com

At this small winery, which specialises in producing award-winning Verdelho, there is an ironbark cottage set in beautiful gardens. Victoria Foster, the vigneron, also runs wines courses on weekend retreats in idyllic surroundings.

Wandin Valley Winery **WM**
10 am–5 pm **CD**
weekends, or by appointment

Hope Estate Winery

Cobcroft Rd, Broke

T 02 6579 1161   **F** 02 6579 1373   **E** info@hopeestate.com.au
W www.hopeestate.com.au

Good estate-grown wines are on offer here at fair prices. The winery, which started life as Saxonvale in the early 1970s, overlooks vineyards and the surrounding hills, and has one of the best views in the district. Semillon, Verdelho, Chardonnay, Shiraz and Merlot are made. If you join the Hope Club, you can order the wines at discount prices.

James Campkin **WM**
10 am–4.30 pm **CD**
daily

Krinklewood Vineyard

712 Wollombi Rd, Broke

T 02 9969 1311   **F** 02 9968 3435   **E** carla@krinklewood.com
W www.krinklewood.com

The varieties originally planted here were Chardonnay, Cabernet and Merlot, but the range now extends to Semillon, Verdelho, Mourvedre and Chambourcin. The wines are elegant—the rosé in particular is worth a try—and have won awards. The cellar door is surrounded by pleasant gardens and olive groves, and cheese platters are available.

John Hordern **WM**
(contract)
10 am–5 pm **CD**
weekends and public holidays

Mount Broke Wines

Adam's Peak Rd, Broke

T 02 6579 1314   **W** www.mountbrokewines.com.au

This family-owned vineyard produces a range of reds and whites, mostly at reasonable prices. The reds include River Bank Shiraz, Harrowby Cabernet Merlot and Black Pine Ridge Merlot. The Harrowby Verdelho is very well priced.

Monarch **WM**
Winemaking Services
11 am–4 pm **O**
weekends

Wine tours and activities

The following companies in Cessnock offer tours of the vineyards: Aussie Wine Tours (**T** 02 4991 1074), Trekabout Tours (**T** 02 4990 8277) and Grape Expectations (**T** 02 4991 1578 or 0405 155 456). The Vineyard Shuttle Service provides transfers between accommodation, wineries and restaurants (**T** 02 4998 7779).

Food and Dining

The Hunter has an abundance of restaurants and cafes. Standards are generally high and continue to improve with every passing year. However, some of the food is fussy and overpriced, and the service can be variable. If you find this to be the case, move on—there are always plenty of alternatives. Furthermore, a growing number of wineries offer barbecue and picnic facilities, so bringing your own food to accompany your purchases is yet another option.

Broke Village Store in Wollombi St, Broke, stocks a range of snacks and groceries as well as a small range of wines made by local producers (**T** 02 6579 1056). A fine range of food, including olives, tapenades, mustards, handmade breads, pickles and chutneys, as well as gourmet sausages and curries and a range of teas, coffee and soft drinks, can be purchased at the Australian Regional Food Store, which also has a cafe (see below). The building incorporates the Small Winemakers Centre, which stocks a wide range of wines from local producers (**T** 02 4998 7668 **E** poolside@hunterlink.net.au).

At the Hunter Valley Cheese Factory at the McGuigan complex (see Wineries) on McDonalds Rd, Pokolbin, you can take a look at the cheesemaking process through special viewing windows and taste handmade cheeses in various styles. You can also enjoy an antipasto plate on the terrace. The shop sells a range of breads, pates, dips and spreads as well as the cheeses (**T** 02 4998 7744 **F** 02 4998 7269 **E** cheesehuntervalley@bigpond.com **W** www.huntervalleycheese.com).

The Fordwich Grove Olive Farm Shop at 203 Fordwich Rd, Fordwich, sells olives and olive products from its 2000 trees. They include various olive oils infused with lemon and herbs, as well as chutneys, all of which can be tasted before you buy (**T** 02 6579 1179 **O** 10 am–5 pm weekends or by appointment).

Pokolbin

Australian Regional Food Store and Cafe, McDonalds Rd, Pokolbin **T** 02 4998 6800 **O** 10 am–5 pm daily. This establishment draws produce from all over Australia, and you'll find the prices of salads, platters and sandwiches in the cafe very reasonable. The cafe overlooks a pleasant garden and grassed area with a small lake. To accompany your choice of food, you can select wines by the glass or bottle.

Blaxlands, Broke Rd, Pokolbin **T** 02 4998 7550 **F** 02 4998 7802 **O** 11 am–late daily. Fine food and wine and a range of other drinks are served in a relaxed garden setting. The menu features specials and changes frequently.

Cafe Beltree, Margan Family Wines, 266 Hermitage Rd, Pokolbin **T** 02 6574 7216 **O** 10 am–5 pm. Enjoy lunch or coffee and cake in pleasantly casual surroundings adjacent to the cellar door. The blackboard menu changes daily.

Cellar Restaurant, Hunter Valley Gardens, Broke Rd, Pokolbin **T** 02 4998 7584 **F** 02 4998 7544 **O** 12 noon–3 pm daily for lunch, 6.30 pm–9 pm Mon–Fri, 6 pm–10 pm Sat. The modern Australian cuisine places emphasis on seasonal produce. A good selection of Hunter wines is available by the glass.

Esca, Bimbadgen Estate, Lot 21, McDonalds Rd, Pokolbin **T** 02 4998 4666 **O** Daily for lunch. Though it's not cheap, Esca does offer a special dining experience. It has stylish modern decor and views over the vineyards, as well as some of the best and most innovative modern Australian food in the Hunter, ranging from imaginative seafood dishes, featuring scallops, prawns and pan-roasted salmon, to game, quail and duck dishes and char-grilled local beef with Shiraz jus.

Splash Restaurant, Vineyards Estate, 555 Hermitage Rd, Pokolbin **T** 02 6574 7229 **F** 02 6574 7276 **E** splash@thevineyards.com.au **W** thevineyardestate.com.au/splash **O** 6.30 pm–10 pm Wed–Sun. This award-winning restaurant offers modern Australian/Asian/simply delicious cuisine with a focus on seafood. There is a wide-ranging wine list and house wines are available by the glass.

Lovedale

The Crocodile Cafe, Wandin Valley Estate, Wilderness Rd, Lovedale **T/F** 02 4930 7704 **O** 9.30 am–noon weekends, Wed–Sat for lunch and morning and afternoon teas. The blackboard menu features local produce and you can buy a range of Wandin Valley wines by the glass to accompany your meal.

Mojo's on Wilderness, Lot 82 Wilderness Rd, Lovedale **T** 02 4930 7244 **F** 02 4930 7725 **E** mojos@bigpond.com **W** www.mojos.com.au **O** 11.30 am–3 pm Thurs–Tues, 6.30 pm–10 pm Thurs–Mon, brunch from 10.30 am on Sun. Slightly off the beaten track, Ros and Adam Baldwin's stylish restaurant serves smart, light cuisine in a rural setting.

Broke

The Cow Cafe, Mount Broke Wines, Adam's Peak Rd, Broke **T** 02 6579 1314 **W** www.mountbrokewines.com.au **O** 11 am–4 pm weekends. This casual licensed cafe, with its open-air dining area, is fast gaining a following. The decor is idiosyncratic, the atmosphere is child-friendly and there is plenty of parking. The Asian-influenced modern Australian food and the views over the vineyards and surrounding hills are pretty good too. Wines are available in good-value tasting selections of both reds and whites. Try the Adam's Peak Chardonnay, Harrowby Cabernet Merlot and River Bank Shiraz.

Accommodation

The Hunter Valley offers a huge range of accommodation, from backpacker lodges to luxurious resorts and bed and breakfasts. Much of it is of high quality, but the cost can also be high. The requirement of a minimum two-night stay is widespread, especially at weekends, and the charges are often of the wounded bull variety. However, some operators are recognising that with tourism numbers down they may need to be a bit more flexible; rules are not always strictly applied and rates can be negotiated down, particularly midweek.

Pokolbin

Dingo's Retreat, Lot 11, McDonalds Rd, Pokolbin **T** 02 9449 1593 or 0417 692 942 **W** www.dingosretreat.com. This cute cottage is set in a pretty garden close to Pokolbin village.

Kurrajong Vineyard Cottages, 614 Hermitage Rd, Pokolbin **T** 02 6574 7117 **F** 02 6574 7006 **E** stay@kv.com.au **W** www.kv.com.au. These comfortable two-bedroom cottages provide an excellent base from which to explore the vineyards. They have fine views and the reasonable tariffs also include the use of a pool. The cottages are air-conditioned; all have CD players and barbecues and one has an outdoor heated spa. One of the best places to stay in Pokolbin.

Lovedale

Rothbury Escape, 310 Talga Rd, Rothbury, Lovedale **T** 02 4930 7011. Once known as Alleyn Court, these purpose-built units are comfortably furnished and have a pleasant communal kitchen, dining and barbecue area. Each unit has its own small terrace and looks over the countryside towards Pokolbin. Discount deals are available in off-peak periods.

Trinity Cottage, cnr McDonalds and Gillards Rds, Pokolbin **T** 02 4998 7293 **F** 02 4998 7294 **E** winemasters@firstcreekwines.com.au **W** www.firstcreekwines.com.au. This luxurious cottage at the Allanmere Winery at First Creek Wines is a tranquil self-contained retreat with fine views of the Brokenback Range.

Wandin Valley Estate, Wilderness Rd, Lovedale **T** 02 4930 7317 **F** 02 4930 7814 **E** sales@wandinvalley.com.au/accommodation. Luxurious accommodation is available in four villas with full kitchens, verandahs and woodland views (book ahead).

Broke

Cockfighters Ghost Vineyard Cottage, 331 Milbrodale Rd, Broke **T** 02 4998 7356 **F** 02 4998 6886 **E** cellardoor@poolesrock.com.au. This is the archetypal luxury 'cottage', providing peaceful valley views from the verandah, comfortable rooms (two bedrooms) and easy access to premium wines. Book ahead.

The Dairy, Tinonee Vineyard, 1273 Milbrodale Rd, Broke **T** 02 6579 1308 or 0409 913 355 **E** tonyrmears@msn.com.au **W** www.tinoneewines.com.au. The genuinely luxurious two-bedroom accommodation features spas, lounge and dining rooms, a barbecue and a fireplace for winter.

Starline Alpaca Farm Stay, 1100 Milbrodale Rd, Broke **T** 02 6579 1081. The five two-bedroom cottages here are all air-conditioned. Facilities include tennis courts, a spa and a pool. Children—and adults!—might also enjoy watching local wildlife, including kangaroos.

Travel Information

How to get there
By road The Hunter Valley is 2.5 hours by road from Sydney. Take the F3 Fwy and follow the signs to Cessnock from Freemans Waterhole. From there you can take Mount View and Marrowbone roads to Pokolbin. Alternatively, from Cessnock you can head north via Allandale Rd towards Rothbury. From Sydney you can also travel north via the Putty Rd to Wollombi, a slower but more scenic drive, and start your exploration of the Hunter at Broke.
By air Both Qantas's Aeropelican and Virgin Blue fly to Newcastle's Williamtown airport from Sydney, with services every hour at peak commuter times and less frequently at other times.
By train There are fast XPT services from Sydney to Newcastle Broadmeadow, with connecting services to Scone and Maitland. Special Hunter Valley excursion trains to explore the vineyards are run both by tour groups and State Rail.

Other attractions
Hunter Valley Gardens is a 300-ha tourist complex incorporating garden displays, accommodation and restaurants—there's even a chapel and an Irish pub, Harrigan's, which also has accommodation. Spectacular floral displays can be viewed in the spacious and immaculate novelty gardens throughout the year; the roses are best seen Sept–Oct (**T** 02 4998 7600).

The Hunter is famous for hot-air ballooning. Balloon Aloft, at Lot 1, Main Rd, North Rothbury, was one of the first balloon companies to be established. It has managed to stay, well, aloft and retain an admirable service and safety record. Flights take place every day, weather permitting, and the company can arrange accommodation and tours, too (**T** 1800 028 568 or 02 4938 1955 **F** 02 4938 3727
E balloons@balloonaloft.com
W www.balloonaloft.com).

For kids
Hunter Valley Gardens at Pokolbin has 300 ha of gardens and displays, but children will be especially enchanted by the Storybook Garden, which features models of favourite fairytale characters such as Alice in Wonderland at the Mad Hatter's Tea Party (**T** 02 4998 7600
W www.hvg.com.au).

Events
A wide range of events takes place throughout the year and individual vineyards often host musical entertainments, tastings and long lunches.
Mar–April: Hunter Valley Harvest Festival (theatre, concerts and festivities to celebrate the harvest)
May: Lovedale Long Lunch
Oct: Jazz in the Vines, Tyrrell's; Opera in the Vineyards, Wyndham Estate

Information
Hunter Valley Wine Country Visitor Information Centre, 111 Main Rd, Pokolbin **T** 02 4990 4477 **F** 02 4991 4518 **E** info@winecountry.com.au
W www.winecountry.com.au

Hunter Valley: Upper Hunter

There is one good reason why the Upper Hunter is home to so many vineyards and produces some of Australia's best wines: the region offers excellent winemaking conditions. The soils are fertile and well drained, and there is plentiful rainfall during the growing season. The summer months are usually hot and dry, allowing the fruit to reach optimum ripeness just before harvesting. Both rainfall and humidity levels are lower than in the Lower Hunter, so there is less risk of damage to the grapes. Furthermore, the Upper Hunter has five distinct soil types, making it suitable for growing a wide range of grape varieties.

The first vines were planted here in 1864 by German migrant Carl Brecht, on land that would later become part of Rosemount Estate. The vines grew well, but for several reasons, including an economic recession in the 1890s and the significant distance between the region and Sydney, the vineyards could not be sustained. Most of the vines were abandoned soon after the beginning of the twentieth century and it was not until the 1950s that a revival took place.

One of the first of the new generation of vineyards was planted by Penfolds in the 1950s (now Yarraman Estate). Bob Oatley planted more vines at Rosemount in the late 1960s and by the mid-1970s the area was experiencing a major expansion. The combined effects of the Chardonnay revolution and Australians' rediscovery of red table wines meant that the industry in the Upper Hunter subsequently enjoyed a period of sustained growth.

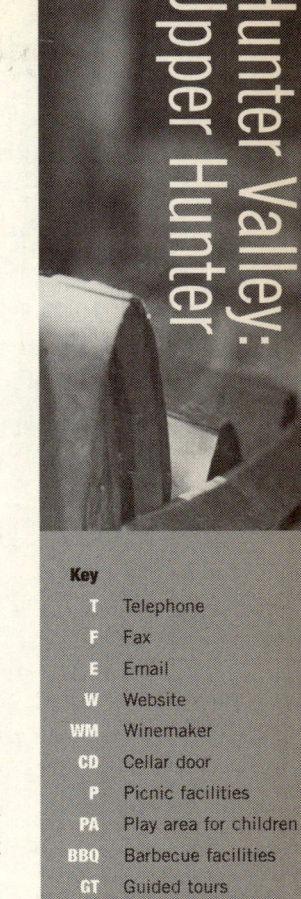

Key

T	Telephone
F	Fax
E	Email
W	Website
WM	Winemaker
CD	Cellar door
P	Picnic facilities
PA	Play area for children
BBQ	Barbecue facilities
GT	Guided tours
C	Cafe
R	Restaurant
O	Opening hours
B&B	Bed and breakfast
H	Hotel/Inn
M	Motel
G	Guesthouse
SCA	Self-catering accommodation

The Upper Hunter is centred on Denman, about an hour's drive north-west from the Lower Hunter wine region. Its quiet atmosphere, narrow roads and small wineries are especially appealing if you want to get away from the crowds. Overall it is much more relaxed than the Lower Hunter, where the pace can seem somewhat frenetic, the wineries over-commercial and the number of tourists at times overwhelming. Moreover, there are some very pleasant small towns that are well worth a visit. Historic Denman has some grand old buildings, including its pubs. The town of Muswellbrook also has some fine buildings and an intriguing history—it was the centre of the area terrorised by the bushranger Captain Thunderbolt.

What to buy

The Upper Hunter is known for its medium to full-bodied whites, including Semillon and Chardonnay; Verdelho is also being grown with great success as well as some more exotic varieties such as Gewurztraminer. Cabernet Franc, Shiraz, Pinot Noir and Cabernet Sauvignon blends are the most popular of the reds. And if you are a convert to the seductive, plummy qualities of Merlot and Chambourcin, you are in luck, too, for sizeable areas of these varieties have been planted in recent years as they have become more fashionable.

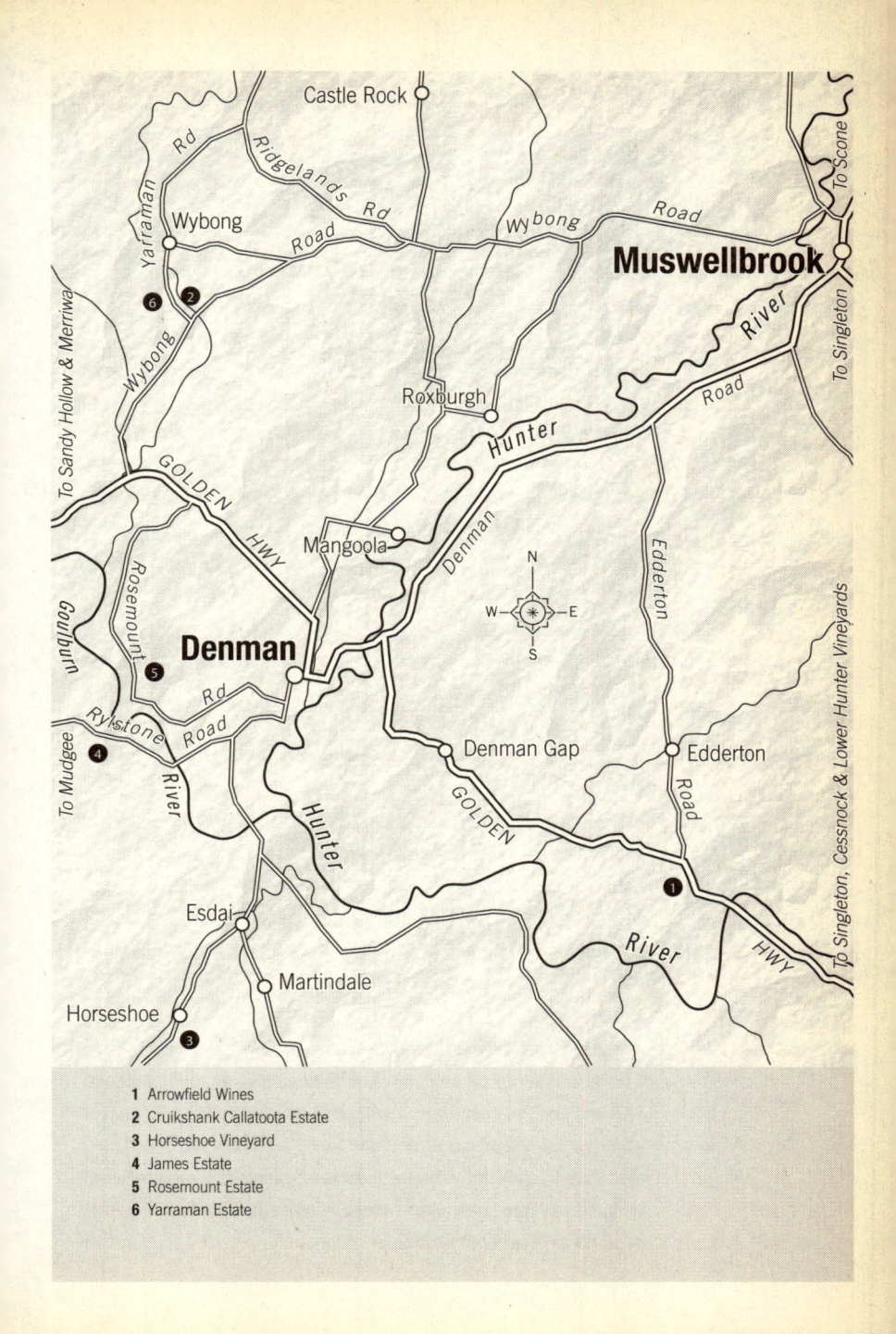

1 Arrowfield Wines
2 Cruikshank Callatoota Estate
3 Horseshoe Vineyard
4 James Estate
5 Rosemount Estate
6 Yarraman Estate

UPPER HUNTER VALLEY 51

Wineries

Arrowfield Wines

WM Tim Pearce
CD 10 am–5 pm daily
P
BBQ
SCA

Denman Rd, Jerrys Plains
T 02 6576 4041 **F** 02 6576 4144
E cellardoor@arrowfieldwines.com.au
W www.arrowfieldwines.com.au

This medium-sized winery is set on a hillside overlooking the Hunter River, and the beautiful picnic area and barbecue facilities have an awesome view over the valley—site of the famous Coolmore stud—and the surrounding mountain ranges. A good range of reds and whites is made here. Chardonnay, Cabernet and Shiraz, Merlot and Petit Verdot are included in the premium Show Reserve range and are all worth sampling. So, too, are the lower priced Arrowfield and Regional ranges, which include Verdelho, Sauvignon Blanc, Semillon Chardonnay, Cabernet Merlot and Chardonnay.

Cruikshank Callatoota Estate

WM John Cruikshank
CD 9 am–5 pm daily
P
BBQ

2656 Wybong Rd, Wybong
T 02 6547 8149 **F** 02 6547 8144 **E** johnc@nobbys.net.au
W cruikshank.com.au

A small family winery, Cruikshank uses only its own fruit and specialises in Cabernet Sauvignon, though some Shiraz, Cabernet Franc and Merlot are also grown. The Cabernet Rosé is well worth trying and there is also a port-style fortified wine. Food platters are available for a light lunch.

Horseshoe Vineyard

WM John Hordern
CD By appointment
10 am–4 pm
weekends and
public holidays

Horseshoe Rd, Horseshoe Valley via Denman
T 02 6547 3528 **F** 02 6547 3548 **E** horseshoe@hunterlink.net.au

This is a small family-owned vineyard which focuses primarily on white wines—Semillon and Chardonnay—though small amounts of Shiraz and Pinot Noir have also been planted. It's worth a visit for its scenic setting, tucked away on the edge of Wollemi National Park, as well as for the wines.

James Estate Wines

951 Bylong Valley Way (Rylestone Rd), via Denman
T 02 6547 5168 **F** 02 6547 5354 **E** info@jamesestatewines.com.au
W www.jamesestatewines.com.au

Originally known as Serenella, this winery is superbly located, overlooking the Goulburn River valley on the very edge of Wollemi National Park. The wines are top quality and very reasonably priced. They include Chardonnay, Semillon and the Compass label's crisp, dry Verdelho—one of the Hunter's best. An unusual and delicious European wine, a white Sylvaner, is also made here; it's particularly clean and aromatic. Of the reds, the Pinot Noir, Merlot and Reserve Shiraz are the most interesting.

Peter Orr **WM**
10 am–4.30 pm **CD**
daily
P
BBQ

Rosemount Estate

Rosemount Rd, Denman
T 02 6549 6450 **F** 02 6549 6499
E rosemountestateshv@southcorp.com
W www.rosemountestates.com

Rosemount has been one of the Hunter's great success stories, though times have been tough of late. The company has gone through major changes of management (it's now owned by Southcorp) and experienced export sales problems. Despite this, it still produces a huge variety of wines and standards have largely been maintained. The whites play a major role here, Rosemount having been at the forefront of the white-wine revolution of the 1970s. The Chardonnays (including the legendary Roxborough Chardonnay), Rieslings and Sauvignon Blancs (Diamond Label) are all made with locally sourced fruit. The Hunter reds are generally not as well regarded, but there are plenty of blended reds and varietals sourced from other regions, notably Orange and parts of South Australia, that are well made and offer good value for money. The restaurant serves à la carte dishes and daily blackboard specials that are reasonably priced.

Matt Koch **WM**
10 am–4 pm daily **CD**
Wed–Sun from **R**
10 am for
morning teas,
12 noon–2 pm
for lunch

WM Chris Mennie
CD 10 am–5 pm daily
P
BBQ
GT By appointment
SCA

Yarraman Estate

700 Yarraman Rd, Wybong
T 02 6547 8118 **F** 02 6547 8039 **E** info@yarramanestate.com
W www.yarramanestate.com

Established by Penfolds in the late 1950s as the famous Dalwood Estate, Yarraman Estate is the oldest vineyard in the Upper Hunter and one of the oldest in the whole of the Hunter Valley. Many of the vines are more than 40 years old and are therefore capable of producing fruit of high intensity and high-quality wines. The winery occupies a strikingly beautiful setting amid sandstone outcrops and, despite some recent changes of ownership, continues to produce a strong range. Its labels include Classic Hunter and Black Cypress, named in honour of the trees that surround the estate; the wines range from Semillon and Chardonnay and a flavoursome, spicy, dry Gewurztraminer to Cabernet Shiraz, Pinot Noir and Merlot. The winery's Chambourcin is said to have converted many white-wine drinkers to reds. Two cottages on the estate are available as holiday accommodation (see Accommodation).

Wine tours and activities

Craig Benjamin's Upper Hunter Tours operates tours of the local wineries as well as horse studs and scenic locations such as Barrington Tops National Park (**T** 02 6541 4211 **E** wine@maxnet.net.au **W** www.upperhuntertours.com.au).

Food and Dining

The area produces high-quality beef, poultry and game, as well as cheeses and olives, stone fruit and honey. Hunter Belle Cheeses of Muswellbrook is gaining a reputation for its prize-winning handmade cheeses (**T** 02 6541 5066). There are some good places for a snack and a coffee and for more formal dining, largely centred on the towns of Denman and Muswellbrook. A much wider range of eateries is available in the Lower Hunter (see *Hunter Valley: Lower Hunter*).

Denman Royal Hotel, Ogilvie St, Denman T 02 6547 2226 O 12 noon–3 pm for lunch, 6 pm–9 pm for dinner. This older-style refurbished pub has a pleasant dining room offering daily blackboard specials as well as an à la carte menu.

Noah's Bar and Grill, 91 Bridge St, Muswellbrook T 02 6543 2833. Located in the town centre, Noah's has a comfortable bar and dining room, as well as accommodation.

Philippe Brasserie, 155 Bridge St, Muswellbrook T 02 6542 5166. This long-established restaurant has a dedicated local following for its French-inspired dishes.

Verona Cellars Cafe, 75 Aberdeen St, Muswellbrook T 02 6541 4777 E veronacellars@hotkey.net.au O 9 am–5 pm daily, dinner Fri–Sat only. This cafe/restaurant and cellar door operation serves main meals and light lunches, including salads, chicken and fish, as well as the wines of Verona Estate and other local wineries.

Accommodation

There isn't a huge range of accommodation here, so you may want to consider returning to the Lower Hunter or Lovedale. However Denman and Broke provide some options, a number of which are well worth considering. Some have the advantage of being situated at relatively small wineries or very close to them.

Denman Hotel, 3 Ogilvie St, Denman T 02 6547 2207. This refurbished hotel provides budget accommodation in seven rooms. A light breakfast is included in the room rate.

Denman Motor Inn, 8 Crinoline St, Denman T 02 6547 2462 F 02 6547 2268. Located within walking distance of clubs and pubs, this comfortable motel is convenient for several local wineries and horse studs.

Dolwendee Farm Stay Cottages, 770 Golden Hwy, Denman **T/F** 02 6547 2199 **W** www.dolwendee.com.au. The cottages are set within a 200-ha property inhabited by farm animals, including alpacas, and native wildlife. The price includes breakfast, and special 'three-nights-for-the-price-of-two' deals are available. Good value and great for kids.

Yarraman Estate Cottages, 700 Yarraman Rd, Wybong **T** 02 6547 8118 **F** 02 6547 8039 **E** info@yarramanestate.com **W** www.yarramanestate.com. Rustic but comfortable self-catering accommodation is available at two tranquil cottages situated among the vineyards on Yarraman Estate (see Wineries). Choose between two and four bedrooms, sleeping four and eight respectively. Breakfast is included in the reasonable nightly tariff, and you can walk to the cellar door. Book ahead.

Travel Information

How to get there
By road Take the New England Hwy from the main Hunter region and travel via Branxton to Singleton, then follow the Golden Hwy (the Merriwa road) to Denman via Jerrys Plains. It takes about an hour to drive from the Lower Hunter.

Other attractions
The scenery around these parts is verging on the spectacular and the region borders true wilderness—remember to breathe the air before you head back to town. Some of the most dramatic country is protected within Wollemi National Park, home to the Wollemi Pine. A relic from the age of the dinosaurs, this tree species was unknown until 1994, when it was found growing in a remote ravine. The Endeavour Museum at Wollombi has many exhibits that explore the links to the town's colonial past. There are horse studs in the area and you can visit some, such as Coolmore, Arrowfield and Woodlands, by arrangement; contact Craig Benjamin (**T** 02 6541 4211).

For kids
Lake Liddell Recreation Area, between Muswellbrook and Singleton, has an animal sanctuary, as well as opportunities for fishing, swimming and waterskiing; there are also tennis courts, barbecues and toilets (**T** 02 6541 2010). Lake Glenbawn State Park has walking trails and good spots for fishing and canoeing (**T** 02 6543 7193

E glenbawn@hunterlink.net.au
W www.stateparks.nsw.gov.au/glenbawn).
Or you can visit Burning Mountain, near Wingen, about half an hour away, where a sulphur seam burns continuously. It is thought to have been ignited by lightning. A well-marked walking path leads to the mountain.

Events
Sept: Wollombi Festival
Oct: Upper Hunter Spring Festival, Denman

Information
Hunter Valley Wine Country Visitor Information Centre, 111 Main Rd, Pokolbin T 02 4990 4477
F 02 4991 4518
E info@winecountry.com.au
W www.winecountry.com.au
Muswellbrook Visitor Information Centre, 87 Hill St, Muswellbrook
T 1800 065 773 or 02 6541 4050
F 02 6541 4051
E visitorcentre@muswellbrook.org.au
W www.upperhunterwine.com.au

Mudgee

Key

T	Telephone
F	Fax
E	Email
W	Website
WM	Winemaker
CD	Cellar door
P	Picnic facilities
PA	Play area for children
BBQ	Barbecue facilities
GT	Guided tours
C	Cafe
R	Restaurant
O	Opening hours
B&B	Bed and breakfast
H	Hotel/Inn
M	Motel
G	Guesthouse
SCA	Self-catering accommodation

The wine region of Mudgee—a name that means 'nest in the hills' in the local Aboriginal language—comprises an undulating area of rich agricultural land surrounded by the forested and gently rounded hills of the western slopes of the Great Dividing Range. Its vineyards, covering 4500 ha, now spread out from the very edge of the town of the same name.

Mudgee was gazetted in 1838 and vine-growing dates back to the 1850s when Adam Roth, a German labourer who had worked with William Macarthur at his Camden vineyard west of Sydney, settled at and planted vines on a property that later became known as Craigmoor. A boom in vine planting followed, but by the 1890s the industry had faded due to harsh economic times in eastern Australia. Following World War I, Italian settlers including Thomas Fiaschi planted more vines, some of which still survive, but it was the German Roth and Kurtz families who kept the industry alive in the mid-twentieth century.

In the 1960s and 1970s, the modern industry began to take shape, as a result of a renewed interest in winemaking and the efforts of investors and winemakers. Among those who played an important role in this period were Ian MacRae of Miramar, Bob Roberts of Huntington and Gil Walquist of Botobolar, an early devotee of organic methods. The region has since experienced steady growth and is now recognised as a dependable producer of high-quality wines. Large areas of vines are owned by the major players, but the number of small growers and producers is increasing.

Most of the well-established local wineries are to be found in the area immediately to the north of Mudgee along Henry Lawson Drive and the Ulan–Cassilis Road. A loop starting along either road and crossing to the other leads you to the main cellar doors. The roads are well signposted, though some are still gravel. Recently, there has also been considerable winery development and vine planting in almost every direction, particularly towards Gulgong and along the Sydney Road to the south of the town.

What to buy

Mudgee is best known for its full-bodied Shiraz and Cabernet varietals and blends, though you will also find Pinot Noir and Merlot. Mudgee has had some Italian grapes for a long time, and many more Italian and Spanish varieties, such as Sangiovese, Barbera, Nebbiolo, Tempranillo, Garnacha and Graciano, have recently been planted in small quantities. Mudgee is also a producer of premium Chardonnay as well as Semillon, Sauvignon Blanc, some Riesling and, more recently, even a little Verdelho.

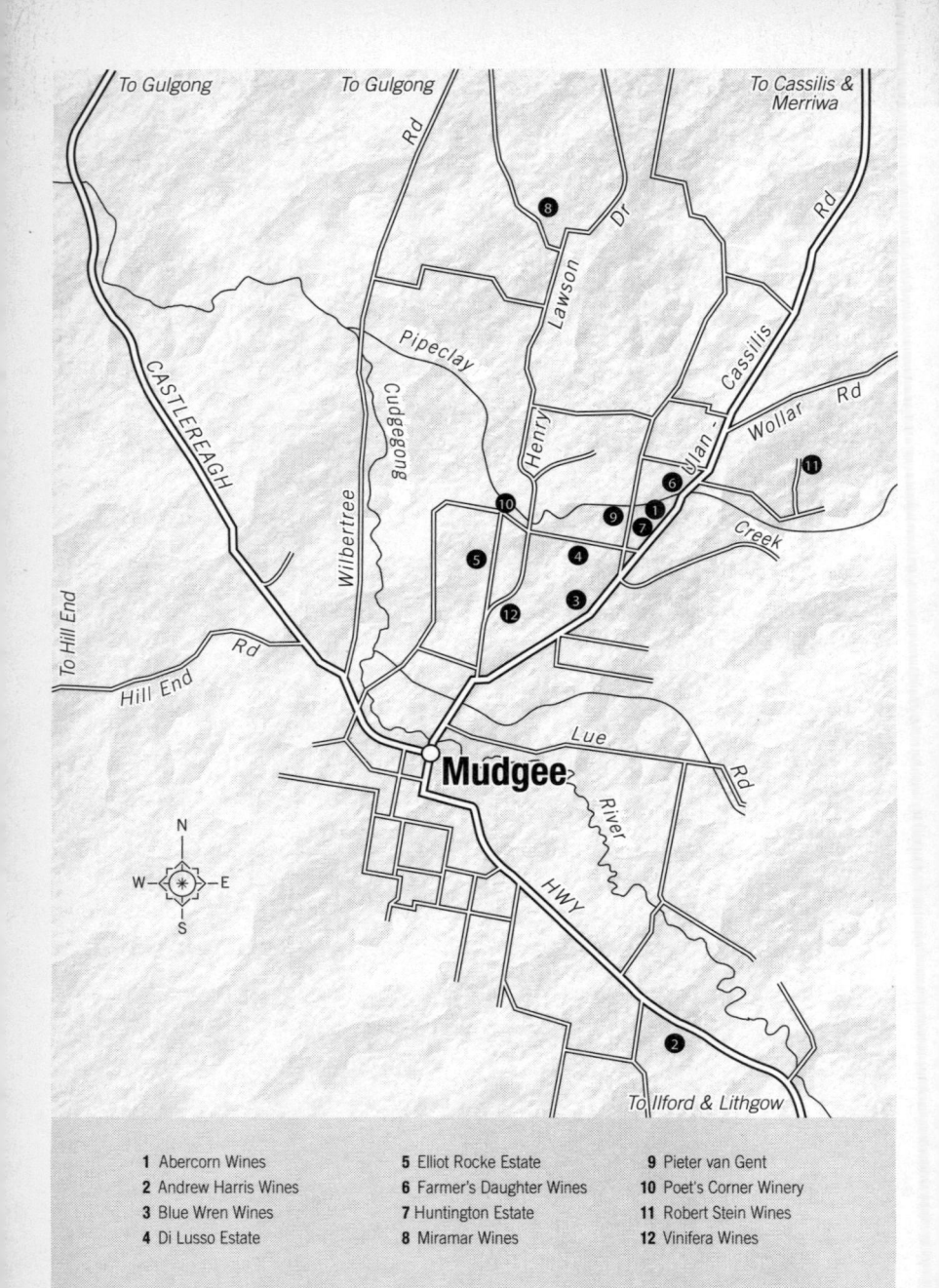

1 Abercorn Wines
2 Andrew Harris Wines
3 Blue Wren Wines
4 Di Lusso Estate
5 Elliot Rocke Estate
6 Farmer's Daughter Wines
7 Huntington Estate
8 Miramar Wines
9 Pieter van Gent
10 Poet's Corner Winery
11 Robert Stein Wines
12 Vinifera Wines

Wineries

Abercorn Wines

Cassilis Rd, Mudgee

T 02 6367 3106 **F** 02 6373 3108 **E** sales@abercornwine.com.au
W www.abercornwine.com.au

A trendy boutique vineyard with a smart new tasting room, Abercorn offers well-made and reasonably priced wines. The setting (next door to Huntington Estate) is pleasant, with a backdrop of the scenic Mudgee hills. Chardonnay (both basic unwooded and lightly oaked), Shiraz and Shiraz Cabernet are the staples here.

Tim Stevens **WM**
10.30 am–4.30 pm **CD**
Mon and Thurs–Sat,
10.30 am–3 pm
Sun

Andrew Harris Wines

Sydney Rd, Mudgee

T 02 6373 1213 **F** 02 6373 1296 **E** ahv@andrewharris.co.com.au
W www.andrewharriswines.com.au

This small family-owned enterprise produces premium wines that have a strong and growing reputation. They range from Chardonnay, Riesling and Semillon to Shiraz, Cabernet Sauvignon, Shiraz, Merlot and Petit Verdot. The reds are full flavoured and well made. The Reserve series is excellent and Vision (a blend of Shiraz and Cabernet Sauvignon) and Double Vision (a sparkling Shiraz) are both highly regarded. The atmospheric cellar door is in an old woolshed. There is also a cafe (see Food and Dining) and plenty of room for picnicking.

Frank Newman **WM**
9 am–5 pm daily **CD**
C

Blue Wren Wines

Cassilis Rd, Mudgee

T 02 6372 6205 **W** www.bluewrenwines.com.au

One of the most welcome recent additions and testament to Mudgee's increasing diversity, Blue Wren offers good wines, a stylish restaurant overlooking the vines (see Food and Dining), and a convenient position. The wines range from Chardonnay, Semillon and Verdelho through Shiraz, Cabernet Sauvignon and Merlot and have won several medals in the relatively short time the

Simon Gilbert **WM**
(contract)
10.30 am–4.30 pm **CD**
Mon–Sat,
10.30 am–3.30 pm
Sun
R

winery has been operating. Blue Wren operates a courtesy bus if you wish to be picked up from your accommodation and enjoy the wines to the full.

di Lusso Estate

WM Drew Tuckwell
CD 10 am–5 pm
Fri–Mon

Eurunderee Lane (off Henry Lawson Drive), Mudgee
T 02 6373 3125 **F** 02 6373 3128 **E** sales@dilusso.com.au
W www.dilusso.com.au

A relative newcomer to the Mudgee scene, di Lusso has had a splendid debut, creating an impressive and innovative range of wines. Owner Robert Fairall aims to produce 'Australian wines from Italian grapes', thereby continuing a long local association with Italian viticulture—wine pioneer Thomas Fiaschi founded the former Augustine vineyard next door, planting vines that now provide fruit for di Lusso's wines. The wide range of Italian varieties includes Pinot Grigio, Sangiovese (the grapes used to make the wines of Chianti and Brunello) Nebbiolo, Barbera, Aleatico and Picolit, a little-known grape from the Venice region used to make a delicious light dessert wine with a low alcohol level. Di Lusso also makes its own olive oil and figs (sold at the cellar door when available) and there are plans for a restaurant. After tasting the wines, I can't wait.

Elliot Rocke Estate

WM Simon Gilbert
(contract)
CD 9 am–4 pm daily
P
BBQ

Craigmoor Rd, Mudgee
T 02 6372 7722 **F** 02 6372 0680
E enquiries@elliotrockeestate.com.au
W www.elliotrockeestate.com.au

The old Seldom Seen vineyard has been reborn, with a smart cellar door and spacious grounds for picnics and barbecues. The wines are excellent and well made. The Semillon has always been well above average, and the Premium Chardonnay and Late Harvest Semillon also offer good value for money.

Farmer's Daughter Wines

791 Cassilis Rd, Mudgee
T 02 6373 3177 **F** 02 6373 3759 **E** fdwines@winsoft.net.au
W www.farmersdaughterwines.com.au

The red and white wines made at this family-owned winery are all produced with fruit from the adjacent vineyard. They include Semillon, Chardonnay, Cabernet Sauvignon, Merlot and Shiraz. The wines are good and reasonably priced. The winery has a large and welcoming barbecue area where you can cook your own meal and then retire to one of the umbrella-shaded picnic tables or the grassy surrounds to eat. It also has guest cottages and a gift shop.

Joe Lesnik **WM**
(contract)
9 am–5 pm daily **CD**
BBQ
C
SCA

Huntington Estate

Cassilis Rd, Mudgee
T 02 6373 3825 **F** 02 6373 3730

This long-established winery and cellar door operation is well known for its dependable whites and reds. Of the whites, the barrel-fermented Chardonnay, Semillon Chardonnay and Dry Semillon are the premium wines; of the reds, the straight Cabernet Sauvignon and Shiraz varietals and the Cabernet Sauvignon Merlot blend are top quality and terrific value for money. Sweet and dry rosés and a blended sweet white dessert wine are also available. The estate's annual chamber music festival, held in November each year, has grown greatly in popularity and tickets for it are now eagerly sought.

Bob Roberts **WM**
9 am–5 pm **CD**
Mon–Fri,
10 am–5 pm Sat,
10 am–3 pm Sun

Miramar Wines

Henry Lawson Drive, Mudgee
T 02 6373 3874 **F** 02 6373 3854 **E** miramar@hwy.com.au
W www.miramarwines.com.au

One of the modern pioneers of the Mudgee industry, Ian Macrae is acknowledged to be one of the region's best producers, offering terrific value for money. Chardonnay and Semillon are specialities, as is Shiraz. There is also a Riesling and a rosé named after Eurunderee, the village just down the road where Henry Lawson went to school.

Ian Macrae **WM**
9 am–5 pm daily **CD**

Pieter van Gent Wines

WM TBA
CD 9 am–5 pm
Mon–Sat, 11 am–4 pm Sun

141 Black Springs Rd, Mudgee

T 02 6373 3030 **F** 02 6373 3910 **E** pvgwinery@bigpond.com
W www.pvgwinery.com.au

This small-scale operation, founded by Pieter van Gent, has stood the test of time but has seen some change recently due to Pieter's retirement. The winery has always made quality table wines from Mudgee grapes—Chardonnay, Verdelho, Cabernet Merlot and Shiraz among others—but the specialty is fortified wines, from three types of port (including white port) to a Mudgee Oloroso and a Liqueur Muscat. Accommodation is available in a bushman's cottage on the property.

Poet's Corner Wines

WM James Manners
CD 10 am–4.30 pm
Mon–Sat and
10 am–4 pm Sun
and public holidays
P
BBQ
R

Craigmoor Rd, Mudgee

T 02 6372 2208 **F** 02 6373 4464 **E** info@poetscornerwines.com
W www.poetscornerwines.com

Poet's Corner is the current name for what was originally Craigmoor Estate, the Mudgee winery established in 1858 by Adam Roth. The winery is part of the Orlando–Wyndham group and is named after the hugely successful brand that sells in vast quantities worldwide. The old Craigmoor buildings have been renovated and now house the cellar door and separate restaurant facilities (see Food and Dining), which do a roaring trade. The cellar door sells all the ranges: Poet's Corner, Henry Lawson, Craigmoor and Montrose, the last being another winery situated about 10 km from Mudgee (not open to the public) that became part of the group and now makes a large proportion of its output. All the wines are very professionally made and good value for money over the full range of price points—hence their spectacular success. The cellar door hosts special events throughout the year, ranging from wine tastings to theatre evenings and even cricket matches.

Robert Stein Vineyard

Pipeclay Lane, Mudgee

T 02 6373 3991   **F** 02 6373 3709   **E** info@robertstein.com.au
W www.robertstein.com.au

Established in 1976, the Stein vineyards produce a range of premium red and white wines, with a focus on Shiraz and Cabernet Sauvignon and Semillon, Chardonnay, Riesling and Gewurztraminer. The vineyard also produces sweet white wines as well as a liqueur Muscat from black Muscat grapes. There is a motorcycle museum on the property, as well as open-air and sheltered picnic areas and free gas barbecues overlooking a lake backed by the Mudgee hills.

Michael Slater **WM**
10 am–4.30 pm **CD**
daily
P
BBQ

Vinifera Wines

194 Henry Lawson Drive, Mudgee

T 02 6372 2461   **F** 02 6372 6731   **E** vinify@winsoft.net.au
W www.viniferawines.com.au

Another newcomer to the Mudgee scene, Vinifera specialises in Spanish grapes such as Tempranillo and Gran Tinto as well as Chardonnay, Riesling, Semillon and Cabernet Sauvignon. The wines are well priced and the dessert wine, the Easter Semillon, offers outstanding value, though it's not made every year.

Tony McKendry, **WM**
Phillip van Gent
(contract)
10 am–5 pm daily **CD**
P
BBQ

Wine tours and activities

Mudgee Wine Tours at 14 Mulgoa Way, Mudgee, organises winery tours, as well as history and sightseeing tours by minibus—or by Harley Davidson motorcycle if you're game (**T** 02 6372 2367 or 0407 204 150   **E** info@mudgeewinetours.com.au **W** www. mudgeewinetours.com.au). For something out of the ordinary and if your time is limited, you can take a one-day Discovery Air tour by DC3 to Mudgee or Canowindra. It includes winery visits by minibus and a lunch accompanied by local wines (**T** 1800 246 747).

Food and Dining

In the space of a few years, Mudgee has been transformed from a sleepy rural town into a thriving community, whose successful wine industry is now complemented by a range of specialist food producers. Meat is good in Mudgee (particularly beef, venison and farmed rabbit), and you can also buy locally produced farmed fish (from Mudgee Fish), olives and honey, as well as jams, mustards, tapenades, nuts, pickles and chutneys. Many of these products can be obtained at Heart of Mudgee, a shop run by Clem and Vanessa Cox in one of Mudgee's oldest buildings (c. 1842) at 8 Court St, cnr of Short and Court Streets (**T** 02 6372 3224). Hampers containing a selection of foodstuffs are available and the shop also sells wine, gifts and craftware.

There's a Farmers' Market that takes place on the first Saturday of each month at the Anglican Church Hall at the corner of Church and March streets. And don't miss St Fillans Farmstead, on the Gulgong road, where you can buy fresh, handmade goat's cheeses and even see the goats being milked; call beforehand to check the milking times (**T** 02 6374 4260).

Two excellent self-guided tours around Mudgee bring together food and wine (and antiques if you wish). The first is the Gourmet Trail, which takes you through the wines and foods of the Hill End Road area, just 5 minutes from the centre of Mudgee; pitstops include Burnbrae Winery and Thistle Hill vineyard as well as the Mudgee Honey Haven and Figtree Retreat Olives. The second, the Mudgee Taste Trail, explores the Sydney Road side of Mudgee, taking in Melrose Park Deer Farm, where you can view deer and stock up on frozen, chilled or smoked venison as well as a selection of recipes for cooking venison (**T** 02 6373 1233). The tour takes in Offa Olives and Country Lane Antiques as well as two wineries, Clearview Estate and Woolshed Wines (there is also the Andrew Harris Winery). For details of both tours, consult the brochures available at the Mudgee Visitor Information Centre (see Travel Information).

Andrew Harris Wines, Sydney Rd, Mudgee   **T** 02 6373 1213   **F** 02 6373 1296   **O** 9 am–5 pm daily. The cafe at this winery offers light meals to accompany your tastings, including ploughman's lunches and cheese platters as well as tea, coffee and snacks all day.

Blue Wren Winery restaurant, Cassilis Rd, Mudgee T 02 6372 6205 O 10.30 am –4.30 pm daily for lunch, from 6.30 pm Wed–Sat for dinner. During good weather, the restaurant sets tables on a patio in the open air. There's also plenty of grass surrounding the patio for children to play on. Fresh local produce is used whenever possible and standard of the food is very high. The restaurant also has a children's menu.

Craigmoor Restaurant, Poet's Corner Wines, Henry Lawson Drive, Mudgee T 02 6372 2208 F 02 6373 4464 E info@poetscornerwines.com W www.poetscornerwines.com O From 10.30 am for coffee, 12 noon for lunch daily; from 6 pm Sat for dinner (bookings only). The restaurant is located in a large airy room overlooking the cellar door. It serves dishes to complement the wide range of wines on offer. There are daily blackboard specials and a kids' menu.

Deeb's Kitchen and B&B, Buckeroo Lane, Mudgee (off Cassilis Rd, near Huntington Estate) T/F 02 6373 3133 O Fri–Sun and public holidays for lunch, closed mid-Jan to mid-Feb. The kitchen conjures up light, tasty Mediterranean and Middle Eastern–influenced dishes. So popular has it become that the car park has recently been enlarged; Sunday lunch is especially busy, so book ahead. Bechora and Sybil Deeb also make tasty goat's and sheep's cheeses.

Eltons Cafe, 81 Market St, Mudgee T 02 6372 0772 O 8.30 am–late Fri–Sat, 8.30 am–6.30 pm Sun–Thurs. This unpretentious and stylish cafe is open every day for breakfast, lunch and coffees. The food is modern Australian with French, Asian and Italian influences. It's advisable to book for dinner.

Grapevine Restaurant, Lauralla Guesthouse, cnr Lewis and Mortimer Sts, Mudgee T 02 6372 4480 O 10 am–5 pm Wed–Sun. Grapevine offers an à la carte menu featuring modern Australian cuisine. Bookings are essential.

The Wineglass Bar & Grill, Cobb & Co Court, Mudgee T 02 6372 3417 O 9 am–late every day. Conveniently situated in the centre of Mudgee, this establishment offers modern Australian cuisine for lunch and dinner, as well as coffee and cakes all day long. In fine weather you can sit in the courtyard. A wide range of local and other Australian wines is sold by the glass, bottle or case.

Accommodation

There is a good selection of hotel, motel and bed and breakfast accommodation in the Mudgee region, and much of it is of a very high standard.

Bushman's Cottage, Pieter van Gent Wines, 141 Black Springs Rd, Mudgee **T** 02 6373 3030. This delightful self-contained cottage has been beautifully restored. It has its own kitchen and overlooks gardens.

Collits' Inn, Hartley Vale **T** 02 6355 2072 **F** 02 6355 2073 **E** info@collitsinn.com.au **W** www.collitsinn.com.au. If you fancy an overnight stop between Mudgee and Sydney, there is no better place to break your journey. The accommodation is either in the old inn or in cottages in the grounds. The restaurant serves great French food in an atmospheric dining room. Bookings essential.

Country Comfort Mudgee, Cassilis Rd, Mudgee **T** 02 6372 4500 **F** 02 6372 4525 **W** www.countrycomfort.com.au. Conveniently located, the motel has good facilities including a pool and a restaurant open every day.

Goulburn River Stone Cottages, 'Gleniston', Cassilis Rd, Ulan (50km from Mudgee) **T** 02 6373 4650 **E** info@stonecottages.com.au. **W** www.stonecottages.com.au. Two hand-built stone cottages in an idyllic bushland setting with abundant wildlife, open fires and solar hot water provide peaceful, self-contained and private rustic retreats in which to savour the local wines.

Ilkley Cottages, 644 Black Springs Rd, Mudgee (12 km from Mudgee) **T** 02 6373 3957 **F** 02 6373 3958 **E** carol@ilkleycottages.com.au. These self-contained cottages are set in pleasant countryside among vineyards and wineries. They have wood fires in winter and old-fashioned baths. The tariff also includes a country-style breakfast.

Mudgee Homestead Guesthouse, 3 Corumbene Rd, Mudgee **T** 02 6373 3786 **F** 02 6373 3086 **E** welcome@mudgeehomestead.com.au **W** www.mudgeehomestead.com.au. The rooms are comfortably furnished and there are common lounge and dining areas. Dinner is available, or you can opt for the 'room, afternoon tea and breakfast' rate. Guests will also enjoy the abundant wildlife and lovely country walks and views.

Travel Information

How to get there
By road Mudgee is a 3–4 hour drive from Sydney (260 kms). Follow the Great Western Hwy through the scenic splendour of the Blue Mountains (or take the Bells Line of Road from Windsor for a more leisurely drive). After Lithgow, turn right onto Hwy 86 to Mudgee via Cullen Bullen, Capertee and Windermere Dam, the source of much of the water used in Mudgee's vineyards.

By air There are two return flights a day from Sydney to Mudgee, with a flight time of 1 hour; the services are operated by Airlink (**T** 02 6884 2435).

By train From Sydney, take a train to Lithgow and then connect to a Countrylink (**T** 13 22 32) coach service to Mudgee.

Other attractions
Visit the nearby gold-rush town of Gulgong, whose heritage streetscapes and most famous son, poet Henry Lawson, were featured on Australia's first $10 note. The Henry Lawson Centre at 147 Mayne St has a fine selection of Lawson memorabilia and some fascinating displays relating to the life of one of Australia's best-loved poets (**T** 02 6374 2049). The Gulgong Pioneers Museum, 73 Herbert St, Gulgong, vividly brings to life the early period of European settlement. Displays include historic farm machinery, a re-creation of a settler's bedroom, tools and clothes belonging to early settlers, and a wealth of photographs (**T** 02 6374 1513).

For kids
At the Western Plains Zoo in Dubbo, north-west of Mudgee, animals roam in large enclosures sepa-rated from visitors by a system of moats (**T** 02 6882 5888). You can drive or walk around the zoo, but the best option is to cycle—bikes are available for hire. The zoo is among the world's leading breeders of black rhinos, Przewalski's horse and cheetahs. Overnight accommodation in comfortable tents is available at the zoo (book well ahead) or you can stay in town. Dubbo has a wide range of accommodation—contact the visitor centre for details.

Hill End, a former gold-mining town now managed by the National Trust, lies 74 km from Mudgee along the Hargraves and Hill End roads. About 23km of the route is unsealed and a little bumpy, but the trip is worth the effort. Interpretative displays and restored buildings make it easy to imagine the frenzied scenes of the gold-rush era. Kids and adults alike will also enjoy trying their hand at gold-panning in the creek beds adjacent to the town.

Events
Nov–Dec: Mudgee Festival of Art and Wine, Huntington Music Festival

Information
Mudgee Visitor Information Centre, 84 Market St, Mudgee **T** 02 6372 1020 **F** 02 6372 2853 **W** www.mudgee-gulgong.org

Orange

In the late nineteenth century, Orange was the scene of an economic boom following the discovery of gold at nearby Ophir in 1851, and it has long been the centre of an area blessed by abundant agricultural riches. The more recent growth of a cool-climate wine industry has seen many changes to the landscape, and the orchards and paddocks are now dotted with vines. There are now more than 30 vineyards in the region, many supplying large quantities of grapes to winemakers elsewhere, particularly the Hunter Valley.

The region is situated mainly between 600 and 900 m above sea level, and the soils and climate vary considerably. The soils within roughly a 12-km radius of Mount Canobolas are mainly well-drained clays that are fertile and make strong vine growth possible. The vineyards to the south of the mountain are considerably cooler than those to the north, due to the prevailing winds and aspect. Further away, the soils are lighter, with some pockets of terra rossa, mainly to the west of the region. Overnight temperatures are very cool during the growing season; spring rainfall is generally good, though dry summers make irrigation necessary through much of the growing season.

A combination of enthusiastic winemakers and fine wines, welcoming places to stay, and delicious food has made Orange a prime wine-touring destination, and there is a sense that the region will continue to grow rapidly in the provision of services as well as in the quality of its wines. There are several wineries on the road

Key

T	Telephone
F	Fax
E	Email
W	Website
WM	Winemaker
CD	Cellar door
P	Picnic facilities
PA	Play area for children
BBQ	Barbecue facilities
GT	Guided tours
C	Cafe
R	Restaurant
O	Opening hours
B&B	Bed and breakfast
H	Hotel/Inn
M	Motel
G	Guesthouse
SCA	Self-catering accommodation

into Orange from Sydney, but the bulk of the cellar doors are strung out along the Cargo and Cudal roads to the west of the town. These roads are linked by others, such as Borenore Lane, so a circuit is possible. The signposting in the whole area could be improved and some wineries are a bit hard to find.

What to buy

The region favours cool-climate reds and whites, including Chardonnay, Cabernet Sauvignon, Pinot Noir and Merlot. The Chardonnays and Sauvignon Blancs especially are gaining a reputation as well-made, flavoursome wines, offering good value for money. Cabernet Sauvignon, Merlot and Shiraz are also grown here and some more exotic varieties are being introduced on a limited scale, including Zinfandel, Viognier, Pinot Grigio and Gewurztraminer.

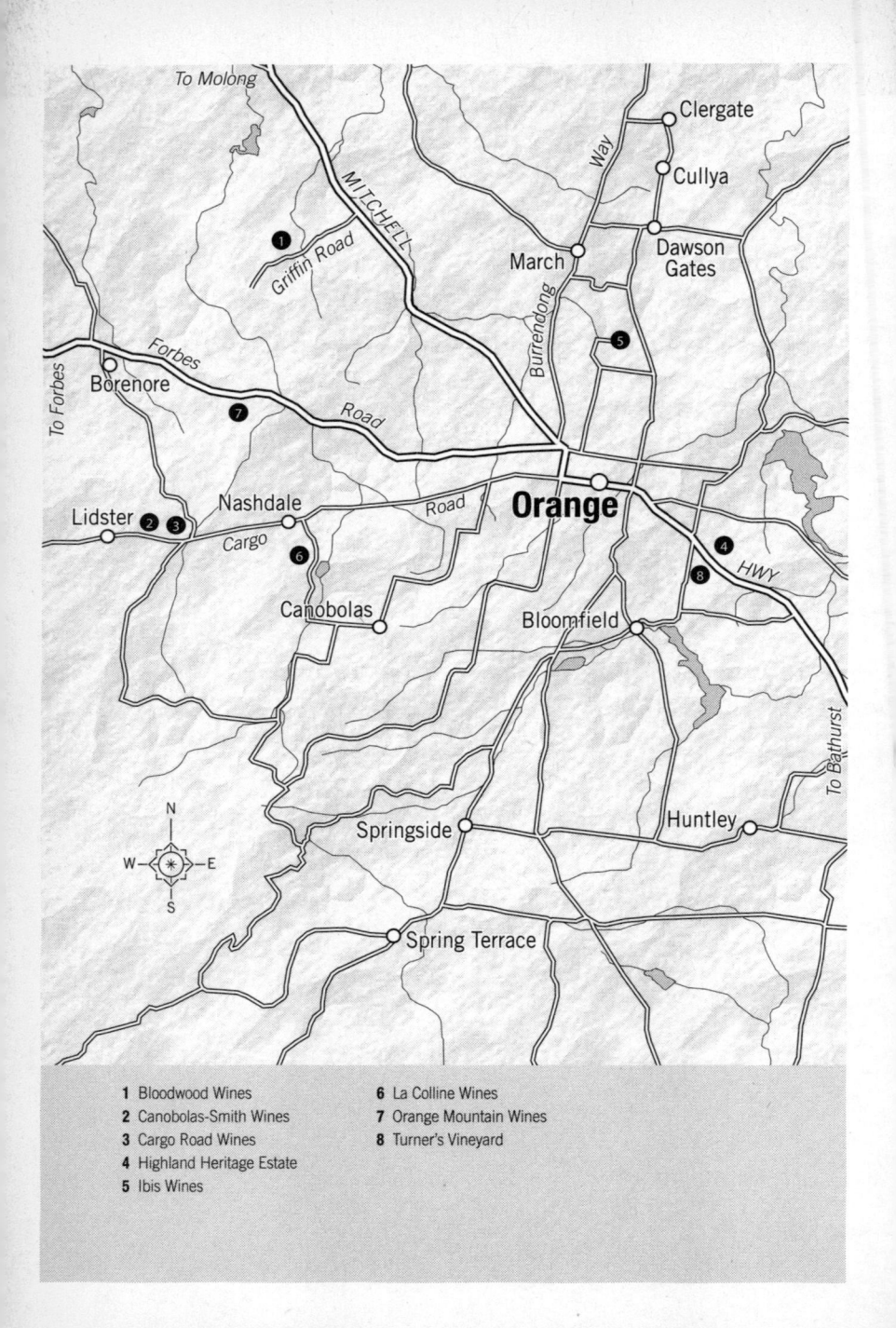

1 Bloodwood Wines
2 Canobolas-Smith Wines
3 Cargo Road Wines
4 Highland Heritage Estate
5 Ibis Wines
6 La Colline Wines
7 Orange Mountain Wines
8 Turner's Vineyard

Wineries

Bloodwood Wines

Lot 4, Griffin Rd (via Molong Rd), Orange
T 02 6362 5631 **F** 02 6361 1173 **E** sdoyle@bloodwood.com.au
W www.bloodwood.com.au

Stephen and Rhonda Doyle's wines are well made and stylish. Try Big Men in Tights, an unpretentious Malbec-based rosé, the delicious Bloodwood Riesling and the Schubert Chardonnay (named in honour of Max, of Grange Hermitage fame, not Franz!); of the reds, the Shiraz and Cabernet Sauvignon warrant attention. They also make a Merlot, a Pinot Noir and a sparkling white. All are seriously good wines without being at all solemn. The turn-off into the winery from Molong Rd is sharp, so take care!

Stephen Doyle **WM**
By appointment **CD**

Canobolas-Smith Wines

Boree Lane (off Cargo Rd), Lidster
T/F 02 6365 6113 **E** canobolas-smith@netwit.net.au

The Smith family is passionate about its wines. The premium cool-climate Chardonnay is excellent and there is also a Cabernet Sauvignon, Cabernet Franc and Shiraz blend known as Alchemy—a thumping good red. Also available are Pinot Noir, Grenache Shiraz, Méthode Champenoise Chardonnay (under the Shine label) and Late Harvest Riesling. Cellar-door customers can use the tennis court by prior arrangement, snacks and light meals are available, and main meals and functions can be booked. There are also fine views over the vineyard and wooded country beyond. A most pleasant place to visit.

Murray Smith **WM**
11 am–5 pm **CD**
weekends and
public holidays
C

Cargo Road Wines

Cargo Rd, Fernlidster
T 02 6365 6100 **F** 02 6365 6001 **E** cargo@ix.net.au

Cargo Road's Riesling, Sauvignon Blanc and Merlot are admirable. They also grow two less common varieties, Zinfandel and Gewurztraminer, the former producing an excellent light and spicy red, the latter an aromatic dry white. The winery also serves as a gallery for a number of local artists.

James Sweetapple **WM**
11 am–5 pm **CD**
weekends and
public holidays,
or by appointment
C

Highland Heritage Estate

WM John Hordern
CD 9 am–5 pm daily
R

Mitchell Hwy, Orange
T 02 6361 3612 **F** 02 6362 6138 **E** daquino@netwit.net.au
W www.highlandheritageestate.com

This is one of the oldest wineries in the Orange region, and its main production centre is now located in the Hunter Valley. The cellar door is housed in an old railway carriage and there is a good restaurant (see Food and Dining).

Ibis Wines

WM Phil Stevenson
CD 11 am–5 pm weekends and public holidays, or by appointment
P
BBQ

239 Kearneys Dr, Orange
T 02 6362 3257 **F** 02 6362 5779 **E** ibiswines@bigpond.com

Located just past the Botanic Gardens on the road north out of Orange, Ibis is a high-altitude vineyard that produces both whites and reds. Sample the Pinot Noir, which is excellent, and The Pagan, a blend of Pinot Noir and Cabernet. The range also includes Riesling, Merlot, Chardonnay and Sauvignon Blanc. One of the top family-owned wineries in the region.

La Colline Wines

WM Christophe Derez, Andrew Margan (contract)
CD 10 am–5 pm Wed–Sun, or by appointment
C

Lake Canobolas Rd, Nashdale
T 02 6365 3275 or 0427 635 275 **E** kuringai1@bigpond.com.au

This combined vineyard and orchard is delightfully sited on the side of Mount Canobolas. Two ranges of delicious wines are offered: La Colline consists of a Cabernet Franc Merlot and a Riesling; Fossil Creek Wines (sourced from Cowra Fruit) includes a Chardonnay and a Cabernet Merlot. The wines can be sampled with delicious food in the adjacent cafe-restaurant (see Food and Dining).

Orange Mountain Wines

WM Terry Dolle
CD 9 am–5 pm weekends and public holidays, or by appointment

Cnr Forbes Rd and Radnedge Lane, Borenore
T 02 6365 2626 **E** terrance@ix.net.au
W www.orangemountain.com.au

A relative newcomer to the region, Orange Mountain produces classics—Sauvignon Blanc and Cabernet Sauvignon—alongside its more unusual Viognier and Shiraz Viognier, both made with

Viognier grapes grown at the company's Manildra vineyard a few kilometres to the north-west. Make sure you taste the Shiraz Viognier, which sells out quickly on release. The wines are sold in two ranges, Orange Mountain and Manildra.

Turner's Vineyard

Mitchell Hwy, Orange
T 02 6369 1045 F 02 6369 1046 E TurnersVineyard@bigpond.com
W www.turnersvineyard.com.au

John Holmes **WM**
(contract)
12 noon–4 pm **CD**
weekends (wine also sold at motel 10 am–5 pm)

C
R
M

This 22-ha vineyard has a modern visitor complex on a hillside overlooking the Sydney Road, which includes a motel (see Accommodation) restaurant and cafe (see Food and Dining), and elegant function centre. The wine-tasting area also doubles as a museum of agricultural and winemaking equipment. The vineyard produces two ranges, the Turner's Vineyard range and the budget Summer Hill range.

Wine tours and activities

Wine tours of the local vineyards can be arranged with Reds & Whites (T 02 6362 2344 or 0418 688 550). A five-hour tour in a small group (maximum 10 people) includes pick-up and drop-off in Orange and takes in four vineyards in the area; a light lunch is provided.

Food and Dining

Quality meats are widely available, with venison fast becoming a regional speciality. Local seasonal vegetables are also excellent. On the second Saturday of each month a farmers' market is held at the Orange showground. On sale are fresh (including organic) vegetables, free-range eggs, smoked trout, breads, olives, mustards and pickles, as well as poultry and preserved meats, including venison and kangaroo. In season, you can pick your own berries at Huntley's

Berry Farm, 13 km from town on the back road to Blayney (**T** 02 6365 5282). Amanda's Hampers can provide gourmet picnics including sandwiches, cheese platters or a ploughman's lunch; you can even have one delivered to your accommodation (**T** 02 6360 4033).

Cafe at Cargo Road Wines, Cargo Road, Orange Cargo Rd, Fernlidster **T** 02 6365 6100 **F** 02 6365 6001 **E** cargo@ix.net.au **O** 11 am–5 pm weekends. This low-key cafe has a simple terrace overlooking the vineyard slopes. It offers light meals, coffee and cakes. Try the local venison pie or venison lasagne, or vegetarian ravioli.

Highland Heritage Estate Restaurant, Mitchell Hwy, Orange **T** 02 6361 3054 **F** 02 6361 3632 **E** heritage@netwit.au **O** 12 noon–2.30 pm Thurs–Sun (Fri–Sun in winter), from 6 pm Thurs–Fri for dinner. A well-run family restaurant that features à la carte dining and a menu that changes frequently depending on local seasonal produce. A good wine list including wines from local wineries is available and the view out over the vineyards is a bonus.

La Colline Cafe, Lake Canobolas Rd, Nashdale **T** 02 6365 3275 or 0427 635 275 **O** 10 am–5 pm Wed–Sun. An ideal place to unwind after a hard morning's sampling, this small, modern, stylish licensed cafe-restaurant is run by Philippe and Aline Proudhomme, originally from Auch in south-west France. The food is light and tasty, using local seasonal produce whenever possible. The blackboard menu lists daily specials.

Lakeside Cafe and Cellar, Lake Canobolas Rd, Orange **T** 02 6365 3456 **O** 10 am–3 pm Fri and Mon, 10 am–5 pm weekends. Relax here by the water in an attractive setting beneath Mount Canobolas. The cafe serves brunches, light lunches (omelettes, pastas, steak sandwich) and afternoon teas, and you can sample a range of local wines. Takeaway refreshments and picnic hampers are also available (though you must return the hampers!).

Lolli Redini, 48 Sale Street, Orange **T** 02 6361 7748 **O** From 9.30 am Wed–Mon for coffee, Mon and Wed–Fri for lunch, 10 am–3 pm weekends for brunch and lunch, from 6 pm Thurs–Sat for dinner. Simonn Hawke has established this local landmark eatery and has attracted a considerable following for her innovative modern Australian food.

The Old Convent, Convent Rd, Borenore T 02 6365 2420 O 10 am–4 pm weekends Josie Chapman serves good modern Australian cafe food that is deservedly regarded by locals as some of the best in the area. Bookings essential.

Old Mill Cafe, 12 Pym St, Millthorpe T 02 6366 3188 F 02 6366 3688 O 12 noon–2 pm daily for lunch, from 6 pm Wed–Sat for dinner. Owned by Janis Pritchard, a refugee from the coast, this is an ideal place for a relaxed country lunch, especially on the small terrace in summer. The blackboard menu changes regularly according to the availability of fresh seasonal produce. After your meal, stroll the streets of heritage-listed Millthorpe.

Selkirks, 179 Anson St, Orange T 02 6361 1179 O From 6.30 pm Tues–Sat. Michael Manners' acclaimed food is based on fresh local seasonal produce and the restaurant is regarded as fully deserving of its prestigious culinary awards. The wine list includes a range of local and other Australian wines, with a good selection available by the glass. Not to be missed, but book ahead.

Tonic, 30 Victoria St, Millthorpe T/F 02 6366 3811 O Thurs–Sat for brunch and dinner. Stylish, innovative, award-winning food is served up in this converted corner shop in the heritage village of Millthorpe. Locally produced ingredients include Cowra lamb and Mandagery Creek venison.

Turner's Bar & Grill, Turner's Vineyard, Mitchell Hwy, Orange T 02 6369 1045 F 02 6369 1046 O 12 noon–2 pm Fri for lunch, 6.30 pm Fri–Sat for dinner. The à la carte restaurant serves a range of good meat dishes from steaks, venison and chicken to lobsters, other seafood and salads. The cafe serves light meals as well as pastas and more substantial dishes. It has a kids' corner and a kids' menu. Excellent, reasonably priced food—and wines.

Accommodation

Acacia Grove B&B, 33 Neals Lane (off Cargo Rd), Orange **T** 02 6365 3336 **F** 02 6365 3000 **E** bnb@acaciagrove.com.au **W** www.acaciagrove.com.au. Comfortable, homely accommodation is offered in two private suites located in a country setting with pleasant rural views. Families are welcome.

Canobolas Cabins and the Mountain Tea House, Canobolas Rd, Orange **T** 02 6365 3471 **W** www.octec.org.au/mtcanobolas. Two comfortable, two-bedroom log cabins and a four-bedroom cabin are tucked away in a leafy setting at the base of Mount Canobolas. They feature open verandahs, log fires and have barbecues.

Parkview Hotel, 281 Summer St, Orange **T** 02 6361 7014. Situated in the centre of town, this recently refurbished hotel offers straightforward accommodation at reasonable rates.

Turner's Vineyard Lodge, Mitchell Hwy, Orange **T** 02 6369 1045 **F** 02 6369 1046. The modern and comfortable motel accommodation offers sweeping views over vines and the Lucknow Valley. Every room has internet access as well as television and there is an excellent restaurant (see Food and Dining).

Travel Information

How to get there
By road Orange is a 3.5 hour drive from Sydney (270 km). Take the Great Western Hwy via the Blue Mountains (or the more scenic Bells Line of Road) and then the Mitchell Hwy from Bathurst.

Other attractions
Don't forget that this is Banjo Paterson country—there's a memorial to him in the centre of Orange by the visitor centre, where you can listen to a 2-hour audio presentation on his life and work, including poems and stories. 'Banjo's' birthplace can be visited out on the Ophir Rd, 3 km from town, where there is a barbecue and picnic area.

You can play golf at the beautiful Duntryleague golf course, and if you want to tee off early you could stay at their accommodation (**T** 02 6362 3822). The top of Mount Canobolas offers fantastic views and is a great spot for a picnic—take the Cargo road out of town and turn left onto Ploughmans Lane then right at Canobolas Rd. The Golden Memories Museum at Millthorpe (**T** 02 6366 3079) explores the history of farming in the region. The complex has several historic buildings, including a blacksmith's shop, and a pioneers gallery. You can buy afternoon tea, and lunches can be prepared if booked in advance.

For kids
There's an excellent adventure playground in Orange, on Kearneys Dr near the Orange Botanic Gardens (**T** 1800 069 466). The walking trails around Lake Canobolas are splendid for older kids who like bushwalking. At Gunnadoo Gold Mine, at Ophir, 26 km from Orange, you can visit a working gold mine (bookings **T** 02 6366 0445). Also on Ophir Rd, 27 km from town (note that part of the road is unsealed), there is an obelisk that marks the official first discovery of gold in Australia. You can also go gold-fossicking (and camp) at the historic site on Summer Hill Creek in the Ophir Reserve—but avoid the old mines, which can be dangerous. The Orange Visitor Information Centre produces a list of 20 fun things for teenagers to do in Orange, ranging from tracking down a good pizza to finding a place to skateboard, rollerskate or go tenpin bowling.

Events
Apr: Food of the Orange District (F.O.O.D.) Week
Oct–Nov: Orange Reds and Whites Regional Winefest

Information
Orange Visitor Information Centre, Byng St, Orange, 2800 **T** 1800 069 466
W www.orange.nsw.gov.au
Orange Region Vignerons Association, PO Box 1363, Orange
W www.orangewines.com.au

Queensland

Granite Belt

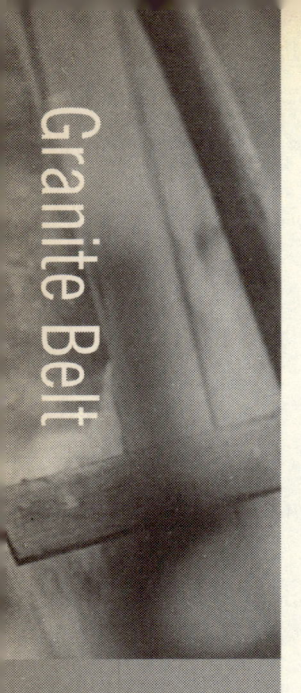

Key

T	Telephone
F	Fax
E	Email
W	Website
WM	Winemaker
CD	Cellar door
P	Picnic facilities
PA	Play area for children
BBQ	Barbecue facilities
GT	Guided tours
C	Cafe
R	Restaurant
O	Opening hours
B&B	Bed and breakfast
H	Hotel/Inn
M	Motel
G	Guesthouse
SCA	Self-catering accommodation

The Granite Belt region is Queensland's premium winegrowing area. It encompasses a wide area of rocky mountainsides, grassland and river flats and has two main centres, Stanthorpe and Ballandean. Both have a history of winegrowing dating from the end of the nineteenth century, when farmers first planted grapes before turning to other, more profitable crops. Some vines were planted after 1920 by Italian immigrants, but the modern industry did not begin to take shape until the 1960s, when a number of farming families, many also of Italian origin, began planting vineyards. Initially, this was simply to supply their own needs, but they soon realised there was potential for selling the wines to a wider market and began to expand their operations accordingly. Many other small wineries have been established since then.

The vineyards are scattered either side of the Severn River on the western edge of the Great Divide. The largest are to the south of Stanthorpe, with many clustered around Ballandean on the New England Highway to the west of Girraween National Park.

This is one of the highest winegrowing areas in Australia, much of the land planted being more than 800 m above sea level. Average temperatures are approximately 10 degrees cooler than the coastal areas to the east, and winters can be very cold, with snow possible and hail common in spring. Combined with highly variable soils, these conditions pose significant challenges for viticulture. Winemakers have responded by taking extra steps to shield vines—

protective nettings are widely used—and by trying out a wide range of grape varieties to find the most appropriate for each locality. The number of varieties planted has more than doubled in the last 10 years.

As winemakers hone their techniques and selections, the area is likely to undergo further development. Although variable, the quality of the wines surprises many visitors, some of whom have regarded the whole notion of Queensland wines with scepticism. They may just have to change their tune.

What to buy

The variety of wines on offer is increasing rapidly. Chardonnay, Sauvignon Blanc and Semillon are the most popular whites, Shiraz and Cabernet Sauvignon the most common reds. Other varieties include increasingly fashionable Merlot as well as Nebbiolo, Verdelho, Viognier and late-harvest Sylvaner (Ballandean). Wines made with these varieties have won acclaim at international shows.

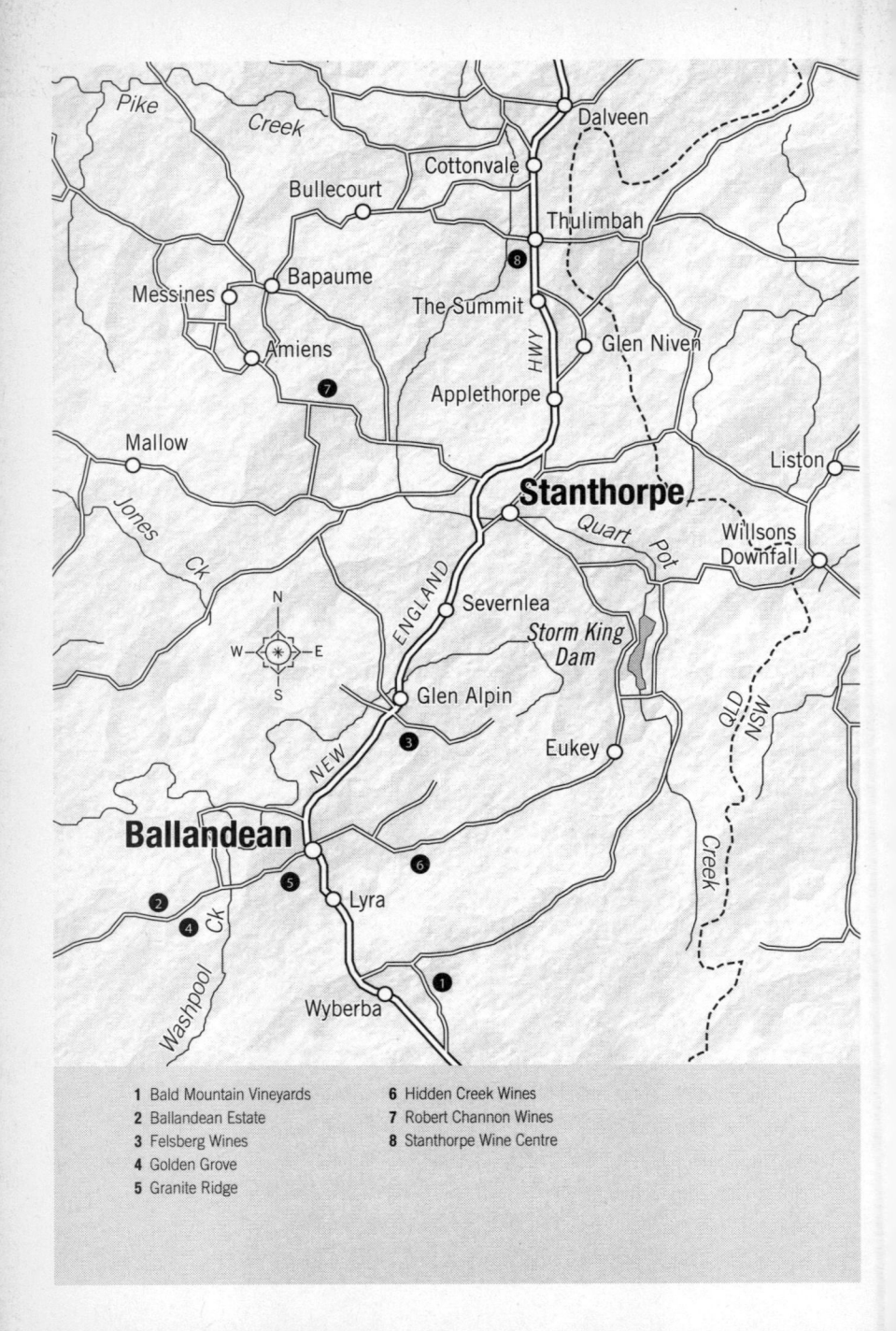

1 Bald Mountain Vineyards
2 Ballandean Estate
3 Felsberg Wines
4 Golden Grove
5 Granite Ridge
6 Hidden Creek Wines
7 Robert Channon Wines
8 Stanthorpe Wine Centre

Wineries

Bald Mountain Vineyards

Hickling Lane, Wallangarra
T 07 4684 3186 **F** 07 4684 3433 **E** baldmountain@halenet.com.au
These well-established, small-scale growers produce estate wines of high quality. Both the reds and whites are full of flavour, with Shiraz and Sauvignon Blanc being the pick of the range. The vineyard enjoys a tranquil rural setting at the base of Bald Mountain.

Simon Gilbert **WM**
(contract)
10 am–5 pm daily **CD**

Ballandean Estate

354 Sundown Rd, Ballandean
T 07 4684 1226 **F** 07 4681 1288 **E** info@ballandeanestate.com
W www.ballandeanestate.com
Ballandean was founded in 1931 by the Puglisi family, and is still run by them. Its wide range is generally of high quality and features some exceptional wines, such as the Sylvaner Late Harvest sweet dessert wine. The white table wines include an easy-drinking Semillon Sauvignon Blanc, a Chardonnay and a Classic White blend. Of the reds, the Shiraz is preferable to the Cabernet Sauvignon and Cabernet Merlot blends; for a lighter style, try the Nebbiolo. Ports and Muscats are also available. The winery, the largest in the area, has attracted tourism awards as well as wine awards. It has a friendly atmosphere and incorporates a popular cafe (see Food and Dining).

Dylan Rhymer, **WM**
Angelo Puglisi
9 am–5 pm daily **CD**
P
By appointment **GT**
C

Felsberg Wines

Townsends Rd, Glen Aplin
T 07 4683 4332 **F** 07 4683 4377 **E** felsberg@ozemail.com.au
A small, family-owned winery, Felsberg produces Chardonnay, Riesling, Gewurztraminer, Shiraz, Merlot and Cabernet Sauvignon. The reds are the best value, though the whites have a devoted following. Two meads round out the list. Situated at an altitude of 875 m, the winery enjoys fine views over the surrounding hills.

Otto Haag **WM**
9.30 am–4.30 pm **CD**
daily

Golden Grove Estate

WM Raymond Costanzo
CD 9 am–5 pm daily
P
BBQ
C Thurs–Sun for lunch

Sundown Rd, Ballandean
T 07 4684 1291 **F** 074684 1247

The quality of wines is improving here and the range has broadened from just Shiraz to include Chardonnay, Cabernet Sauvignon and Merlot. The winery sells barbecue picnic packs so that visitors can cook their own lunch to eat at tables in the spacious gardens. It also has an attractive cafe with an à la carte menu, where you can enjoy traditional Italian hospitality and a mix of Australian and Italian dishes, either inside or *al fresco* on the terrace.

Granite Ridge Wines

WM Dennis Ferguson, Juliane Ferguson
CD 9 am–5 pm daily, 1 pm–5 pm on Anzac Day
GT By appointment
B&B

Sundown Rd, Ballandean
T 07 4684 1263 **F** 07 4684 1250 **E** graniteridge@bigpond.com
W www.graniteridgewines.com.au

This is a family-owned winery producing a small range of reds and whites. All the winemaking is done on the premises. The reds range from a soft Merlot Cabernet blend to the bold Granite Rock Shiraz, though the blends change from year to year depending on yields. Sales of the Bilby red (Cabernet Sauvignon Merlot) and Bilby white (Sauvignon Blanc Chardonnay) contribute to the protection of this endangered species through a donation of a proportion of the sale price to the Queensland Environmental Protection Agency's conservation program. Comfortable chalet accommodation is available on the estate (see Accommodation).

Hidden Creek Wines

WM Jim Barnes
CD 11 am–3 pm Mon–Fri, 10 am–4 pm weekends
GT By appointment
C

Eukey Rd, Ballandean
T 07 4684 1383 **F** 07 4684 1385 **E** info@hiddencreek.com.au
W www.hiddencreek.com.au

The winery has a beautiful setting high on the side of the Severn Valley, on the edge of rugged Girraween National Park. The wines are made with grapes from old, organically grown vines, and include Shiraz, Cabernet Sauvignon, Merlot and the less common Nebbiolo, as well as Chardonnay and Verdelho. A cafe serves light meals and snacks made mainly with local ingredients and fresh produce.

Robert Channon Wines

Amiens Rd, Stanthorpe

T 07 4683 3260   **F** 07 4683 3109   **W** www.robertchannonwines.com
Fabulous lake and mountain views are one good reason to visit this small-scale winery; another is the award-winning range of wines, which includes Merlot, Shiraz, Cabernet Sauvignon and an especially good Verdelho. Monthly concerts are held here—and an annual family picnic and concert day in October.

Mark Ravenscroft **WM**
10 am–5 pm daily **CD**
11 am–4 pm daily **C**
for light lunches

Stanthorpe Wine Centre

291 Granite Belt Drive, The Summit

T 07 4683 2011   **F** 07 4683 2600   **E** stanwine@halenet.com.au
W www.summitestate.com.au

The Stanthorpe Wine Centre produces wines under the Stanthorpe Wine Company and Summit Estate brand names. The wines range from Chardonnay, Semillon, Verdelho and a Semillon Chardonnay blend to Cabernet Merlot, Pinot Noir, and Tempranillo. The Merlot Cabernet Shiraz blend is the leading red, though the Reserve Shiraz is also popular. A port and a liqueur Muscat are sold under the Happy Valley label and there is also a dessert wine, Golden Gleam. Popular with tour groups, the winery complex has a cellar door that retails the full range of wines as well as jams, chutneys and other local foods; a cafe and a pleasant vine-covered verandah overlooking the vineyards; and accommodation in the form of a bush cottage. The centre also runs wine-education courses and a wine club, whose members receive regular mailings including offers of discounts on wines and accommodation.

Paolo Rymer **WM**
9 am–5 pm daily **CD**
C
B&B

Wine tours and activities

Half-day and full-day tours are available during high season (late autumn to winter; check availability during the off season) with The Great Escape (**T** 07 4681 4761). Filipo's Tours offers one-day mini-bus tours by arrangement all year round (**T** 07 4683 5126).

Food and Dining

Fruit and vegetables are so plentiful and of such good quality here that, in season, tourist coaches stop for passengers to load up with fresh produce on what is known as 'the Fruit Run'. Apples and pears, stone fruits such as peaches, nectarines, plums and apricots, as well as a range of berries are all on offer, in cases or smaller quantities to suit. Olives, figs and persimmons are also grown in the area. Vegetables range from beans and broccoli through to squash and zucchini, and pretty much everything in between. Check what's in season when you arrive.

The New England Larder offers a choice of gourmet picnic and dinner hampers incorporating the best local ingredients (**T** 07 4683 4183). The hampers can be ordered the night before for delivery by 9 am the following day. If you are in the area for long enough, they also run cooking classes.

Eagle's Produce grows great vegetables and runs 'Seed to Salad' farm tours (**T** 07 4683 3351; see Giardino Cafe below). Mount Stirling Olives, at 200 Collins Rd, Glen Aplin, between Ballandean and Stanthorpe, sells a good range of home-grown olives from an old railway goods shed. You can also buy a range of cold-pressed olive oils, some infused with herbs, as well as other Mediterranean products. For a modest fee you can even take a tour through the olive grove and see how the olives are pressed (minimum of 10 visitors). Finally, if you're looking for anything handmade, home-grown or home-cooked, you'll probably find it at the Market in the Mountains, held monthly at the Stanthorpe Civic Centre.

Barrel Room Cafe, Ballandean Estate Wines, 354 Sundown Rd, Ballendean **T** 07 4684 1226 **F** 07 4681 1288 **E** info@ballandeanestate.com **W** www.ballandeanestate.com **O** 11 am–3 pm daily for lunch, 9 am–5 pm daily for coffee and cakes. Fine Italian fare is served in the atmospheric barrel room of the popular Ballandean winery.

Beverley Vineyard Restaurant, Beverley Rd, Severnlea (4 km from the New England Hwy junction) **T** 07 4683 5100 **O** 11 am–3 pm for lunch, 7.30 pm–late for dinner (bookings essential). The restaurant is housed in a beautifully restored colonial cottage. The menu changes according to what seasonal produce is obtainable, but the style is generally French. A children's menu is available.

Customs House Cafe, 66 Rockwell St, Wallangarra (10 minutes south of Ballandean) **T** 07 4684 3488. The fine old double-fronted timber cottage that houses this cafe was built around 1885 and was for many years the state border customs post. The pleasant, casual cafe serves light, fresh meals and top-quality cakes and coffee. There are blackboard specials and a kids' menu. Good value.

Giardino Cafe and Farm Tours, 212 Bapaume Rd, Amiens **T** 07 4683 3351 **F** 07 4683 3235 **E** eagles@halenet.com.au. At this family business you can enjoy lunch made with crisp, home-grown Eagle's Produce vegetables, try a local wine (cellar-door prices), or make use of the fully licensed bar. Breakfast (try the Sicilian breakfast—poached eggs topped with parsley and pepato cheese, drizzled with extra virgin olive oil, and served with crusty bread), morning tea, lunch and afternoon tea are all served in the cafe. Cakes and Italian sweets are made on the premises. Popular with tours, and deservedly so.

Lots of Goodies Country Kitchen, Lot 1, Granite Belt Drive, Thulimbah **T** 07 4685 2001. Browse the antiques and collectibles while enjoying a light lunch or a cup of coffee.

Vineyard Cafe, New England Hwy, Ballandean **T** 07 4684 1270 **E** admin@vineyard-cottages.com.au **W** www.vineyard-cottages.com.au. The cafe's simple, fresh fare matches quality ingredients—Italian pasta, New England trout and locally produced lamb and beef—with Granite Belt wines. See also Accommodation.

Accommodation

The Granite Belt has a decent range of accommodation, from pubs and motels to some of the best bed and breakfasts in Australia. However, in season lodgings are often booked for weeks ahead so it's wise to make a reservation in advance of any visit.

Accommodation Creek Cottages, Sundown Road, Ballandean **T** 07 4684 1144. This clean and comfortable country-style accommodation consists of two self-contained one-bedroom cottages and a two-bedroom cottage, all set within a garden on a rural property. Hotplates, a microwave and barbecue are all provided. Breakfast can be included in the tariff or you can take your own.

Fergies Hill Spa Cottage, Granite Ridge Wines, Sundown Rd, Ballandean **T** 07 4684 1263 **F** 07 4684 1250 **E** graniteridge@bigpond.com. This self-contained cottage located in the grounds of the Granite Ridge winery offers two-bedroom, two-bathroom accommodation, a spa, log fire and numerous other creature comforts.

Vineyard Cottages, New England Hwy, Ballandean **T** 07 4684 1270 **W** www.vineyard-cottages.com.au. Seven luxuriously appointed cottages, all with verandas, are set within splendid gardens. There is also a cafe (see Food and Dining).

Travel Information

How to get there
By road Accessible in under 3 hours by road from Brisbane (213 km), the Gold Coast and the northern New South Wales towns of Byron Bay and Ballina, the area is just over 800 km from Sydney via the New England Hwy and just over the border from Tenterfield. From Victoria and South Australia, travel via the Newell Hwy.
By air Qantas and Virgin Blue both fly to Brisbane, Coolangatta and Ballina (NSW). Rex Regional Express also flies to Lismore (NSW).

Other attractions
There are several national parks in the area worth visiting, most notably Boonoo Boonoo Falls National Park, the hide-out of the bushranger Captain Thunderbolt (see below), the unspoilt wilderness of Sundown National Park, and Girraween National Park. Girraween has abundant bird life (146 species) as well as wombats, possums, quolls and kangaroos. There are numerous walking trails and camping is permitted. Barbecues, picnic areas and toilets are located near the Bald Rock Information Centre (**T** 07 4684 5157). Across the border at the old School of Arts in Tenterfield is the stylish new Henry Parkes Museum, which celebrates a visit to the area by the 'Father of Federation' (**T** 02 6736 3592).
Tenterfield is also known as the birthplace of singer-songwriter Peter Allen, whose grandfather's saddlery, made famous in Allen's song 'Tenterfield Saddler', still stands in the main street.

For kids

For picnics, swimming and fishing, try Storm King Dam, 5 minutes out of Stanthorpe on the Eukey Rd. The bushranger, Captain Thunderbolt, who roamed the New England tablelands, had one of his hide-outs at Pozieres near Stanthorpe, in a rock formation now known as Donnelly's Castle (take the Amiens Road turnoff at Thulimbah and follow the signposts). You can explore the rock formation, enjoy great views from the lookout and stop for a snack at the adjacent picnic tables.

Events

Feb–Mar: Apple and Grape Harvest Festival (**E** info@appleandgrape.org)
Oct: Spring Wine Festival

Information

Stanthorpe Visitor Information Centre, 28 Leslie Parade, Stanthorpe
T 07 4681 2057 **F** 07 4681 1200
E sdtastan@flexi.net.au
W southerndownsholidays.com.au

South Australia

Adelaide Hills

In common with many other Australian wine-growing areas, the Adelaide Hills was first planted with vines in the 1840s. Over the next 60 years, a thriving industry developed, but by the beginning of the twentieth century winemaking in the area was at a low ebb due to poor yields, difficult terrain and the public's preference for rich, high-alcohol reds from warmer regions such as the Barossa and the Hunter.

Not until the boutique winemaking revolution of the 1970s and 1980s did the region recover. During that period, small producers and hobby winemakers from Adelaide replanted vines and began to make good wines. Prominent among them were Tim Knappstein, Geoff Weaver and, especially, Brian Croser. Their contribution to the re-emergence of the Adelaide Hills as a wine region of international significance cannot be underestimated.

Since then, the local industry has been transformed and nowadays the Adelaide Hills has a well-deserved reputation as one of Australia's premium cool-climate regions. Conditions are said to be similar to those in Burgundy, France, and some wineries are more than 400 m above sea level.

The Adelaide Hills is one of the prettiest wine regions in the country, with much of the area consisting of undulating hills dotted with vineyards and eucalypts. Visitors usually drive from Adelaide to Hahndorf via the Onkaparinga River crossing at Clarendon. Located at the heart of the wine region, Hahndorf is Australia's oldest German settlement and has classified heritage

Key

T	Telephone
F	Fax
E	Email
W	Website
WM	Winemaker
CD	Cellar door
P	Picnic facilities
PA	Play area for children
BBQ	Barbecue facilities
GT	Guided tours
C	Cafe
R	Restaurant
O	Opening hours
B&B	Bed and breakfast
H	Hotel/Inn
M	Motel
G	Guesthouse
SCA	Self-catering accommodation

buildings, shops and bakeries. From here, a circuit via Verdun, Balhannah, Woodside, Lobethal, Lenswood, Ashton and Crafers takes you past most of the vineyards as well as richly varied landscapes of forests, orchards and grazing and farming country. Detours allow visitors to enjoy spectacular views of the Mount Lofty Ranges from Mount Barker and the picturesque village of Bridgewater, by Cox's Creek.

What to buy

First and foremost, this is Sauvignon Blanc country, though Chardonnay, Semillon, Pinot Noir and Cabernet Sauvignon are also mainstream varieties. Less widespread but also producing some good results are Riesling, Pinot Gris, Viognier and Zinfandel. Visitors will also find some Italian varieties, such as Sangiovese and Barbera, as well as some rare German varieties including Lemberger and Trollinger. Last but not least, Shiraz is becoming more common in the region.

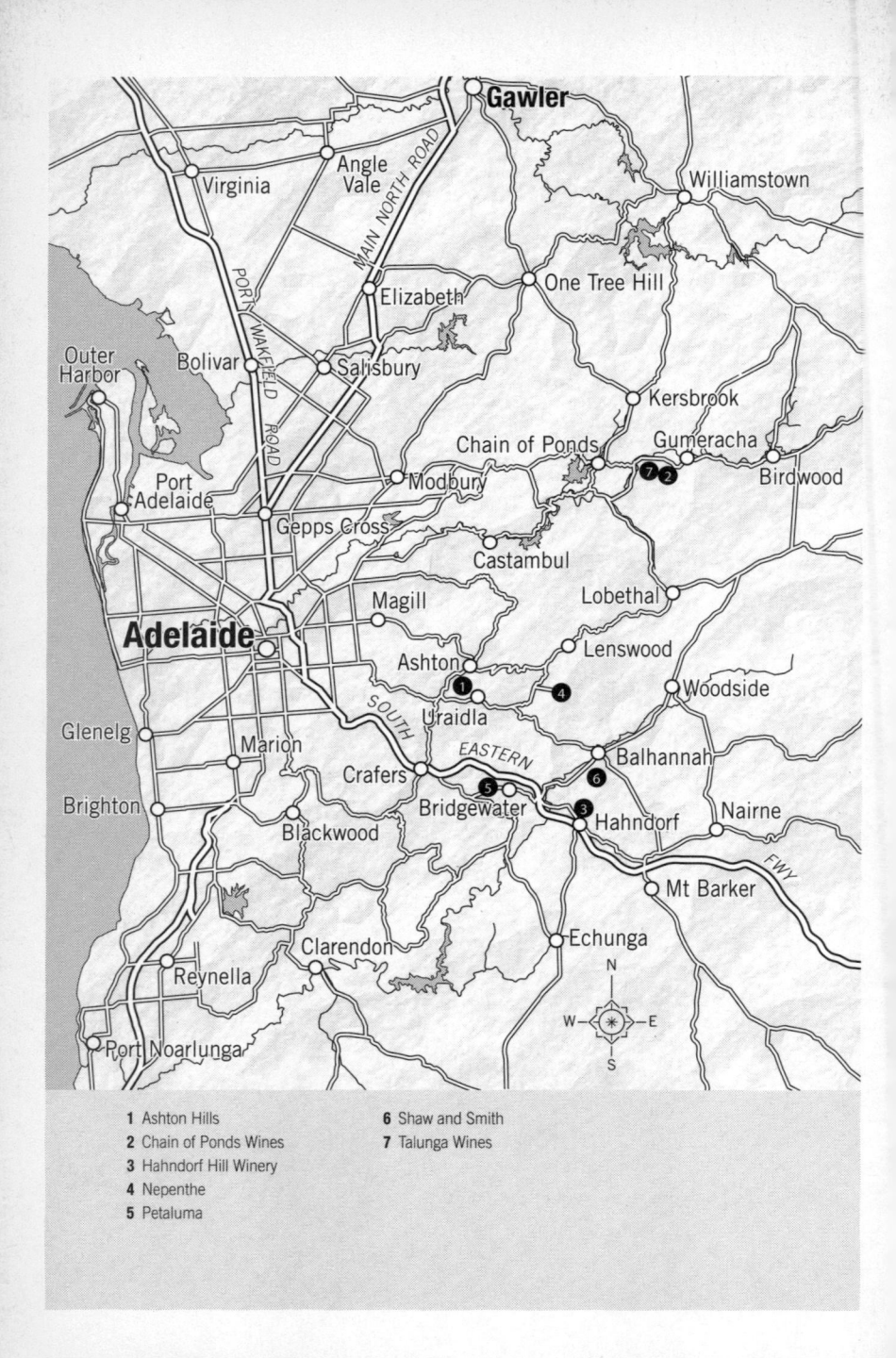

1 Ashton Hills
2 Chain of Ponds Wines
3 Hahndorf Hill Winery
4 Nepenthe
5 Petaluma
6 Shaw and Smith
7 Talunga Wines

Wineries

Ashton Hills

Tregarthen Rd, Ashton
T/F 08 8390 1243

Located in an elevated position just below Mount Lofty, this tiny, resolutely independent, family-owned vineyard produces a small range of delicious, mainly white wines. 'Cool' and 'climate' are the operative words and the Riesling, Chardonnay, Pinot Noir and sparkling Pinot Noir (Salmon Brut) are the specialities, though a red blend of Merlot, Cabernet Franc and Malbec is also available. A second label, Galah Wines, is reserved for earthier reds.

Stephen George **WM**
11 am–5 pm **CD**
Sat–Sun and public holidays, or by appointment

Chain of Ponds Wines

Adelaide–Mannum Rd, Gumeracha
T 08 8389 1415 **F** 08 8389 1877 **E** admin@chainofponds.com.au
W www.chainofponds.com.au

Chain of Ponds is a small, family-owned winery founded in 1985. It offers a range of fine wines and an Italian restaurant, The Balcony (see Food and Dining). The wines are Italian-influenced too, featuring Sangiovese and Barbera as well as Pinot Noir, Semillon, Riesling, and Shiraz. Blends called Novello Bianco and Novello Rosso are available at very reasonable prices.

Neville Falkenberg **WM**
11 am–4 pm daily **CD**
12 noon–3 pm **R**
G

Hahndorf Hill Winery

Lot 10, Pains Road, Hahndorf
T 08 8388 7512 **F** 08 8388 7618
E cellardoor@hahndorfhillwinery.com.au
W www.hahndorfhillwinery.com.au

This newish winery occupies a lovely setting close to the centre of Hahndorf and produces a small range of interesting wines. It includes Chardonnay and Shiraz, and also two unusual and rare German varieties: Trollinger, which makes a refreshing rosé, and Lemberger, which yields a light, fruity red. 'Taste the Hills' platters of local produce are available to accompany weekend tastings.

Geoff Weaver **WM**
(contract)
10 am–5 pm daily **CD**

Nepenthe

WM Peter Leske
CD 10 am–4 pm daily

Jones Rd, Balhannah

T 08 8388 4439 **F** 08 8388 0488 **E** cellardoor@nepenthe.com
W www.nepenthe.com.au

The Tweddell family started this vineyard in 1994 and the wines have grown steadily in quality and reputation since then. An impressive array of grape varieties is grown in the three vineyards, Nepenthe, Charleston and Lanswood. The white wines include Chardonnay, Pinot Gris, an excellent Sauvignon Blanc, and Semillon. Of the reds, the best is probably the Cabernet Sauvignon, though Pinot Noir, Cabernet Franc, Tempranillo, Malbec and Zinfandel are also of interest and have good potential.

Petaluma

WM Brian Croser
CD 10 am–5 pm daily
PA
R

Mount Barker Rd, Bridgewater

T 08 8339 3422 **F** 08 8339 5311
E bridgewatermill@petaluma.com.au **W** www.petaluma.com.au

Petaluma is housed in the exceptionally beautiful Bridgewater Mill, which has a wonderful restaurant (see Food and Dining) and tasting room, and lies in a scenic part of the Torrens Ranges. Petaluma's history in achieving legendary status within Australia and contributing significantly to the country's enviable international reputation is well known. Brian Croser established Petaluma in 1976 with the aim of producing Australian sparkling wine of the highest quality and his success was such that the French champagne house Bollinger acquired a controlling interest in 1985. Petaluma went on to acquire a number of other local labels, including Knappstein, Michelton and Stonier. It is now owned by Lion Nathan, the New Zealand brewing group, and has two main labels, Petaluma and Bridgewater Mill, and two Adelaide Hills vineyards, at Piccadilly Valley and Mount Barker. The wines range from the Croser sparkling wine and top-quality Chardonnay, Riesling and Viognier to Pinot Noir, Merlot and Shiraz. They are not cheap, but the quality is consistently high.

Shaw & Smith

Lot 4, Jones Rd, Balhannah
T 08 8398 0500 **F** 08 8398 0600 **E** info@shawandsmith.com
W www.shawandsmith.com

Martin Shaw **WM**
10 am–5 pm **CD**
Mon–Fri,
11 am–5 pm
weekends

Cousins Martin Shaw and Michael Hill Smith started modestly in 1989, making just Sauvignon Blanc, still their best-known wine, and Chardonnay, but have since expanded their repertoire to include Shiraz, Merlot, Riesling and Pinot Noir. The elegant winery is set in beautiful country, with views to Mount Lofty. The wines can be tasted in a flight by the glass or by the bottle, and are served with specially selected cheeses and appropriate guidance.

Talunga Wines

Adelaide Rd, Gumeracha
T 08 8389 1222 **F** 08 8389 1233

Vince Scaffidi **WM**
10.30 am–5 pm **CD**
Wed–Sun and
public holidays
R

Talunga has been described as a little piece of Tuscany in the Adelaide Hills, though the owners, the Scaffidi family, actually have Sicilian origins. The wines are a classic mixture of French and Italian varieties, including Chardonnay, Sauvignon Blanc, Semillon and Verdelho, as well as Cabernet Sauvignon, Cabernet Franc, Pinot Noir, Merlot, Shiraz, Sangiovese, Grenache and Nebbiolo. The restaurant serves tasty Italian dishes at reasonable prices.

Food and Dining

A large part of the success of the Adelaide Hills as a food and wine region is due to its great produce. In season, strawberries, apples, pears, cherries and a range of seasonal vegetables are produced here. Add cheeses, bread and olives, salmon and venison, and some of the best meats in Australia, and you get some idea of the goods on offer. Great coffee and tempting lunchtime treats are also served at many cafes and wineries.

Willabrand Figs, whose produce is available at Glen Ewin Estate, Lower Hermitage Rd, Houghton, makes fresh figs in season as well as dried figs treated in a number of mouthwatering ways—dipped in Belgian chocolate, brandy or liqueur, for example (**T** 08 8380 5657). The Bird in Hand Winery and Olive Grove at Woodside stocks a range of olives and olive oils as well as a selection of local wines (**T** 08 8389 9488). During the picking season (Oct–May), you can pick your own strawberries at a number of strawberry farms including Beerenberg Jams' Strawberry Farm on Mount Barker Rd (**T** 08 8388 7272).

The Udder Delights cheese factory at 15/1 Adelaide–Lobethal Rd, Lobethal, makes a range of goat's cheeses that should not be missed (**T** 0413 000 790); the cheeses are also available at Blessed Cheese at McLaren Vale (see *McLaren Vale*). For sheer indulgence you can't go past Stephen Down's Cocolat at 83 Main Rd, Balhannah, for a wonderful range of chocolate-based cakes and desserts (**T** 08 8388 4666).

Hahndorf in particular has some excellent food. Pecas Fine Olive Oils in Hahndorf Grove makes some of the best Frantoio olive oil in Australia (**T** 08 8270 5780). Hahndorf Venison in River Rd, Hahndorf, wholesales some of the finest meats in South Australia, inspired by a long European tradition, including venison and Fleurieu prime kid, which can be bought in bulk quantities (**T** 08 8388 7347).

There's no such thing as a country town without a bakery around here, and the Hills area is lucky enough to have many a good bakehouse where you can buy a crusty loaf to combine with some traditional mettwurst, pate or salad for a picnic. The Matisse Bakery at Shop 14–15, 23 Main St, Hahndorf, makes a variety of breads ranging from pain au levain, walnut and poppyseed bread, and French baguettes to fig and fennel bread and ciabatta. Other good bakeries include Ottos at Hahndorf, Millies at Mount Barker and the Lobethal Bakery at Lobethal.

The Adelaide Hills is home to a number of country markets, and some are particularly good for food. The Heart of the Hills Market is open every weekend and on public holidays at the Onkaparinga Woollen Mills, Lobethal (**W** www.marketsatheart.com). Battunga Growers Market is held at the Old Uniting Church camp at 2 Marriott St, Macclesfield (10 am–3 pm Sun). The Adelaide Hills Country Market takes place at Gumeracha Town Hall (10 am–3pm first Sun of each month **T** 08 8389 1393). Hahndorf Market is held at St Michael's Lutheran Church grounds on the fourth Sat of each month, (9 am–12 noon fourth Sat of each month **T** 08 8388 7386).

For further information on food in the Hills, take a look at www.adelaidehillsfood.com.au.

The Balcony, Adelaide–Mannum Rd, Gumeracha **T** 08 8389 1415 **F** 08 8389 1877 **E** admin@chainofponds.com.au **W** www.chainofponds.com.au **O** 12 noon–3 pm weekends and public holidays. The name of this Italian restaurant reflects its elevated location and outstanding views. The food displays European, specifically Tuscan, 'slow food' influences, which ensure that freshness and flavours are retained right through the range of meats, pastas and vegetables.

Lunch on the Pond, Lower St Vigeans, 9 Laurel Rd, Stirling **T** 08 8339 1137. Dine on a lovely timber deck projecting out over a 120-year-old lily pond—a memorable experience. The price of a two- or a three-course lunch includes a tour of the extensive heritage garden. Local produce is used year-round and BYO is permitted for a small charge. Morning and afternoon teas are also available. Only small numbers of people can be accommodated, so book in advance to avoid disappointment.

Maximilian's, Main St, Verdun **T** 08 8388 7771 **O** 11.30 am–4.30 pm Wed–Sun. This restaurant offers unusual Swiss-French cuisine and a selection of local wines. Dishes include garlic snails, prawns Florentine, duckling in cherry sauce, boned trout in champagne sauce, and special schnitzels, as well as the signature dessert, toffee strawberries.

Petaluma's Bridgewater Mill, Mount Barker Rd, Bridgewater **T** 08 8339 3422 **F** 08 8339 5311 **E** bridgewatermill@petaluma.com.au **W** www.petaluma.com.au **O** 12 noon–2.30 pm. The charming restaurant opens onto a deck that overlooks the gardens surrounding the old mill building. Modern Australian food prepared under the inspired direction of Le Thu Thai includes duck terrine, pigeon carpaccio, roast Kangaroo Island chicken breast with beetroot confit, and beef fillet with mushroom fricassee.

Piccadilly Restaurant, Mercure Grand Mount Lofty House, 74 Summit Rd, Mount Lofty, Crafers **T** 08 8339 6777 **W** www.mtloftyhouse.com.au **O** From 7.30 am daily for breakfast, from 12.30 pm Sun for lunch, from 6.30 pm daily for dinner. Innovative international food is served in a relaxed dining-room atmosphere.

Summit Restaurant, Summit Rd, Mount Lofty, Crafers **T** 08 8339 2600 **O** From 9 am daily for breakfast, from 12 noon daily for lunch, from 6 pm Wed–Sun for dinner. Treat yourself to a meal looking out over the surrounding hills. There's a cafe and a fully licensed à la carte restaurant which, at 727 m above sea level, enjoys some of the finest views in the area.

Accommodation

Chain of Ponds Vineyard Cottage, Main Rd, Gumeracha **T** 08 8339 1415 **W** www.babs.com.au/vineyard. Set amid vines and gardens, this self-contained cottage is fully equipped with a kitchen, spa, log fire, heating throughout, outdoor patio and barbecue area. It can accommodate up to four couples in a group.

Mercure Grand Mount Lofty House, 74 Summit Rd, Mount Lofty, Crafers **T** 08 8339 6777 **W** www.mtloftyhouse.com.au. This small, beautifully restored and extended country hotel has terrific views, food (see Food and Dining) and wines. Special packages are available for midweek bookings.

Warrawong Earth Sanctuary, Stock Rd, Mylor **T** 08 8370 9197. This wildlife sanctuary (see Other attractions) has bush-tent accommodation. You can experience an interpretative walk after dark, enjoy a two-course dinner at the restaurant, then wake in the morning to the sounds of the Australian bush in full cry—unforgettable.

Travel Information

How to get there
By road Take the South Eastern Fwy (M1) from Adelaide towards Murray Bridge, then turn off at Hahndorf, a run of about 30 minutes in all.

Other attractions
Mount Lofty Botanic Gardens at Crafers gardens have several walking trails that take visitors up and down seven valleys dedicated to particular plant groups, including magnolias and rhododendrons. The deciduous trees form a magnificent display in autumn, there are spectacular views from the summit of Mount Lofty, and you can picnic beside the lake.

The Cedars, the former home of Sir Hans Heysen in Heysen Rd, Hahndorf, has remained virtually unchanged since the 1930s; it has a grace and charm that speaks of an earlier time (**T** 08 8388 7277). The award-winning Warrawong Earth Sanctuary on Stock Rd, Mylor, is home to an amazing array of Australian wildlife including bettongs, bilbies and other threatened species. You can browse in the native-plant nursery and even stay overnight (see Accommodation).

For kids
Youngsters can feed, cuddle and play with animals ranging from rabbits to goats at the Hahndorf Farm Barn on Mount Barker Rd, Hahndorf (**T** 08 8388 7289). Miniature models of German trains are on display at German Model Train Land, 47 Main St, Hahndorf (**T** 08 8388 7953). At Melba's Chocolate Factory, 22 Henry St, Woodside, visitors can wander through five production rooms and watch a traditional range of sweets being made on historic machinery; samples and entry are free (**T** 08 8389 7868).

Events
Feb, last weekend: The Hills Harvest Festival (tastings and sales of wines and regional produce at venues throughout the hills **T** 1300 305 577).

Information
Adelaide Hills Visitor Information Centre, 41 Main St, Hahndorf
T 1800 353 323 **F** 08 8388 1319
E tourism@adelaidehills.com.au
W www.visitadelaidehills.com.au
Adelaide Hills Wine Region Inc.
T 1300 305 577

Barossa Valley

The Barossa Valley was one of the first parts of Australia to be planted with vines and is regarded by many as the cradle of the Australian wine industry. First settled by the English in the 1830s, it was subsequently populated by German and Polish (Silesian) refugees in the 1840s, mainly Lutherans escaping religious persecution. It was named by Colonel Light, the founder of Adelaide, after a battle site in Spain—Barrosa—and subsequently misspelt.

The German and Polish settlers were used to drinking wine with their meals and it was natural for them to plant a few vines. By 1842, grapes were growing all around Bethany, a settlement that was laid out according to a traditional Silesian village plan, known as a Hufendorf, with small farm buildings fronting the main road and the farmland stretching back from the road in long, narrow strips. A number of villages such as Tanunda and Langmeil followed the same pattern. The villagers took pride in their winemaking skills and by the late 1840s their wines were being exhibited at local agricultural shows in Tanunda and elsewhere.

During the latter part of the nineteenth century, as occurred in other Australian wine regions, a number of family names gradually came to prominence. In the Barossa, these were generally German names such as Henschke, Seppelt and Gramp. The industry expanded toward the end of the century, partly as a result of its ability to supply large quantities of the robust red wines that could survive shipping to the growing market in Britain. The difficulties

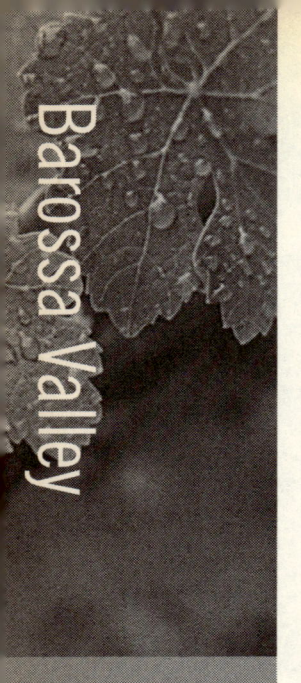

Key

T	Telephone
F	Fax
E	Email
W	Website
WM	Winemaker
CD	Cellar door
P	Picnic facilities
PA	Play area for children
BBQ	Barbecue facilities
GT	Guided tours
C	Cafe
R	Restaurant
O	Opening hours
B&B	Bed and breakfast
H	Hotel/Inn
M	Motel
G	Guesthouse
SCA	Self-catering accommodation

created by a lack of shipping and a degree of anti-German sentiment during World War I were only temporary setbacks, and the industry continued to grow again in the 1920s. However, the Depression was a more significant blow and conditions did not improve until after World War II. From the 1950s on, other winemakers of German origin, including Max Schubert, Peter Lehmann and Wolf Blass, were prominent in reviving and developing the local industry and gaining the international reputation that it enjoys today.

The vineyards of the Barossa are spread along the valley between Lyndoch in the south and Nuriootpa in the north, with the largest group clustered around Tanunda. Arriving from Adelaide, you can easily access the majority of cellar doors off the Barossa Valley Highway (B19), which runs from Lyndoch through Rowland flat to Tanunda. Most of the wineries are well signposted along this route and on circuits on the western side of the Highway, via Seppeltsfield Road, and to the east, via Bethany and Basedow roads. Further north, the road from Nuriootpa to Angaston also takes in several wineries, as well as the famous Maggie Beer Farm Shop.

What to buy

The Barossa is red wine country. Shiraz and Cabernet Sauvignon are the traditional strengths, though Grenache, Mourvedre, Merlot and even Pinot Noir are gaining ground. In addition, the warm, dry summer climate of the Barossa is ideal for the production of the ripe fruit needed for fortified wines. Ports, Muscats and Tokays are made by many of the wineries and are usually available for tasting.

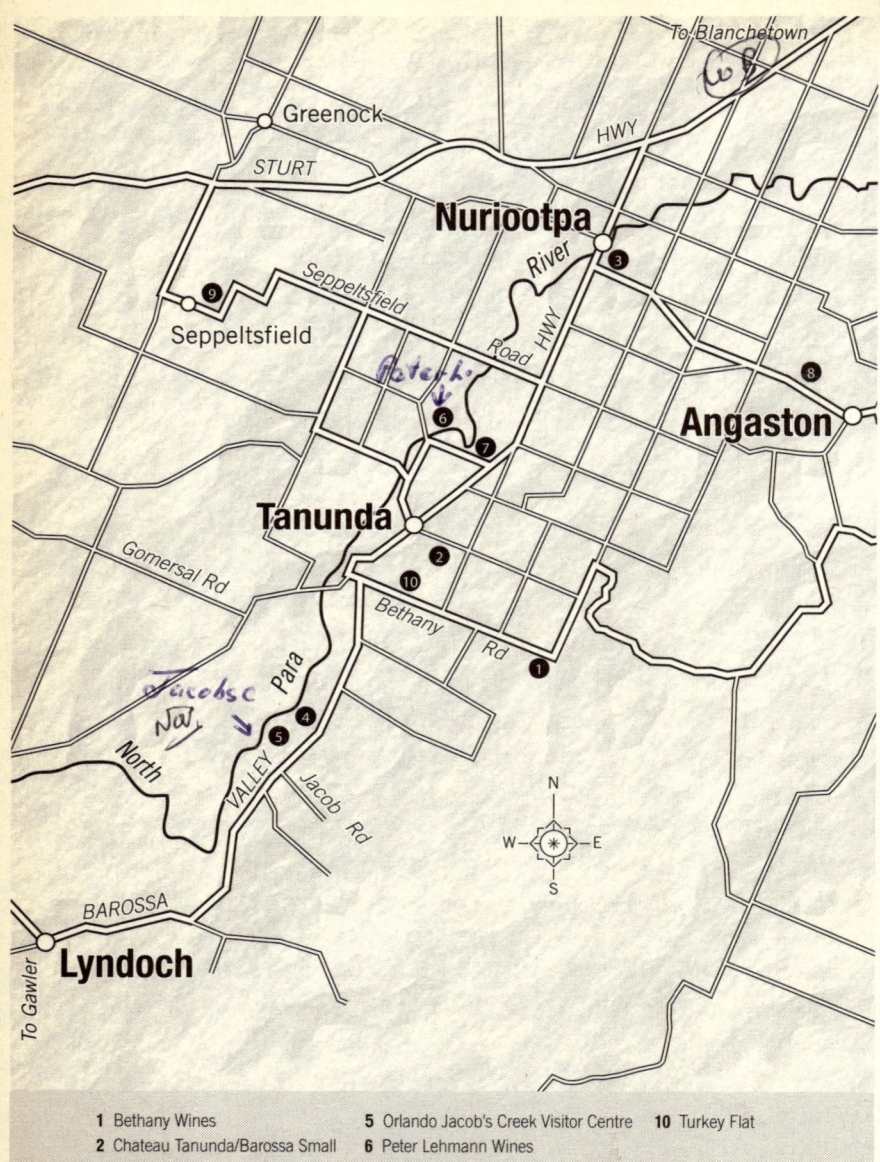

1 Bethany Wines
2 Chateau Tanunda/Barossa Small Winemakers Centre
3 Elderton Wines
4 Grant Burge Wines
5 Orlando Jacob's Creek Visitor Centre
6 Peter Lehmann Wines
7 Richmond Grove
8 Saltram Wines
9 Seppelts Wines
10 Turkey Flat

Wineries

Bethany Wines

Bethany Rd, Tanunda

T 08 8563 2086 **F** 08 8536 0046 **E** bethany@bethany.com.au
W www.bethany.com.au

The wines produced here are excellent and represent a tradition that goes back more than 150 years. They include Riesling and Chardonnay, but it is the Grenache, Cabernet Sauvignon, Merlot and Shiraz that have established Bethany's reputation. Late Harvest Riesling, port and white port are also available. The winery enjoys superb views over the Barossa Valley, and the cellar door sells a variety of local produce.

Robert Schrapel, Geoff Schrapel **WM**
10 am–5 pm Mon–Sat, **CD**
1 pm–5 pm Sun
P
BBQ

Chateau Tanunda

Basedow Rd, Tanunda

T 08 8563 3888 **F** 08 8563 1422 **E** info@chateautanunda.com
W www.chateautanunda.com

Recently and tastefully renovated, this classic bluestone building, dating from the 1890s, contains the winery and a stylish cellar door and function centre, as well as the Barossa Small Winemakers Centre. The centre promotes the wines of 25 winemakers, mostly small, family-owned wineries with modest production levels. The list of Chateau wines includes Riesling and Chardonnay, Pinot Noir and Shiraz, sold under the Chateau Tanunda and The Chateau labels. The cellar door also sells wines from Cowra Estate, Chateau Tanunda's sister operation in New South Wales, including the Eagle Rock label. The tasting room has good coffee and a range of regional cheeses. Gardens, a croquet lawn and a cricket pitch flank the building (check the website for information on functions and events—and how to enlist for cricket matches!) and the fine views of the Barossa Ranges complete a very pleasing picture. Accommodation is also planned, so check before you visit.

Ralph Fowler **WM**
10 am–5 pm daily **CD**

Elderton Wines

WM Richard Langford
CD 8.30 am–5 pm Mon–Fri, 11 am–4 pm weekends and public holidays

3–5 Tanunda Rd, Nuriootpa

T 08 8568 7878 **F** 08 8568 7879
E elderton@eldertonwines.com.au **W** www.eldertonwines.com.au

Owned by the Ashmead Family, this estate has some of the oldest vines in the Barossa Valley. The wines have won many awards, including the Jimmy Watson trophy (for the 1992 Cabernet Sauvignon). They range from big, flavoursome reds with plenty of oak and tannin (Shiraz, Cabernet Sauvignon) to medium-bodied and lighter whites (Unwooded Chardonnay, Verdelho, Sauvignon Blanc, Riesling) and also encompass Sparkling Shiraz, Cabernet Rosé and Botrytis Semillon.

Grant Burge Wines

WM Grant Burge
CD 10 am–5 pm daily

Barossa Valley Way, Jacob's Creek

T 08 8563 3700 **F** 08 8563 2807 **W** www.grantburgewines.com.au

Established in 1988, Grant Burge Wines has become one of the top-ten privately owned wine companies in Australia. A fifth-generation winemaker committed to the Barossa Valley, Burge has developed one of the most extensive networks of premium-quality vineyards in Australia. The wines range from fine Pinot Noir-based sparkling wine through Riesling, Sauvignon Blanc, Semillon and Chardonnay to Shiraz, Cabernet Sauvignon and the latest success, Merlot. There are also reserve wines, ports and Muscats. The iconic brands are the Shadrach Cabernet Sauvignon and Meshach Shiraz, though the 2002 Hillcot Merlot has also drawn much praise. A sister operation at Krondorf Rd, Tanunda, called Barossa Vines, occupies a beautiful setting and operates a cafe offering light meals at lunchtime (**T** 08 8563 7675). Grant Burge has also recently opened a separate outlet for his fortified wines at Illaparra Cellar Door, 161 Murray St, Tanunda (**T** 08 8563 3500).

Orlando

Barossa Valley Way, Rowland Flat

T 08 8521 3000 **F** 03 8521 3003 **W** www.jacobscreek.com.au

The stylish, modern, spacious and well-sited Jacob's Creek Visitor Centre at Orlando has interactive displays that tell the story of Johann Gramp, the founder of the original vineyard, as well as the history of the winery and its notable successes. The brand is famous around the world and although it is now owned by the French Pernod-Ricard group it is still viewed as an icon of the Australian wine industry. The wines are sold in three product ranges, at price points ranging from less than $10 to more than $50, so there is something for everyone here. The high quality and consistency of the output in large measure explains its outstanding success, with the Reserve range offering particularly good value. Wine tastings tailored to your preferences are available in a separate area from the main tasting room. Special events are held regularly at the centre, so it's worth checking the website before your visit. The winery also has good views of the Barossa Ranges.

Philip Laffer **WM**
10 am–5 pm daily **CD**
GT
11.30 am–2.30 pm **R**
daily

Peter Lehmann Wines

Para Rd, Tanunda

T 08 8563 2500 **F** 08 8563 3402

A legend in the Barossa, Lehmann is a winemaker of firm convictions and for many years has produced a range of reasonably priced, exceptional wines that reflect the true spirit and *terroir* of the Barossa. The Stonewell Shiraz is a classic, the straight Barossa Shiraz is a good, easy-drinking 'house red', and Clancy's, a blend of Shiraz, Cabernet Sauvignon and Merlot, is a bargain and deservedly popular. The cellar door serves platters of local produce, including smoked meats from Linke's, a Nooriootpa butcher's shop (see Food and Dining), local bread, olives, pickles and relishes—an ideal for lunch for two.

Andrew Wigan **WM**
9.30 am–5 pm **CD**
Mon–Fri,
10.30 am–4.30 pm
weekends and
public holidays

P

Richmond Grove

WM Steve Clarkson
CD 10 am–5 pm Mon–Fri, 10.30 am–4.30 pm weekends
P

Para Road, Tanunda

T 08 8563 7303 **F** 08 8563 7330 **E** lodgee@orlando.com.au
W www.richmondgrovewines.com

Ernst Gottlieb Hoffman established this winery on the banks of the North Para River in 1897 on a fertile mixed farm and orange grove inherited from his father. The restored winery and cellar door now occupy park-like surroundings. The range consists of premium wines made with grapes sourced from Australia's leading viticultural regions. It includes a great Barossa Shiraz and excellent Barossa and Watervale Riesling, as well as Chardonnay, Cabernet Sauvignon and Semillon made with fruit from outside the valley. The winery hosts many musical events throughout the year, including the Barossa Music Festival in October.

Saltram

WM Nigel Dolan
CD 9 am–5 pm daily
R
GT

Salters Gully, Nuriootpa Rd, Angaston

T 08 8564 3355 **F** 08 8564 2209
E cellardoor@saltramestate.com.au **W** www.saltramwines.com.au

Saltram is enjoying a renaissance under Nigel Dolan's careful guidance and the wines are better than they have been for years. Try the Mamre Brook Shiraz or the Pepperjack Barossa Grenache Shiraz Mourvedre. The other wine that has been a steady performer is the Metala Shiraz Cabernet.

Seppelts Wines

WM James Godfrey
CD 10 am–5.00 pm Mon–Fri, 11 am–5 pm weekends and public holidays
GT 11 am, 1 pm, 2 pm, 3 pm Mon–Fri; 11.30 am, 1.30 pm, 2.30 pm weekends and public holidays
BBQ
P

1 Seppeltsfield Rd, Seppeltsfield

T 08 8568 6217 **F** 08 8562 8333 **E** seppelt.bv@cellar-door.com.au
W www.seppelt.com.au

The House of Seppelt has a rich heritage, with over a century and a half of experience of winemaking in the Barossa. Its historic winery, located at Seppeltsfield, is a national treasure and well worth a visit. The buildings are beautifully maintained and are surrounded by immaculate gardens. The cellar door offers structured tastings that take half an hour and include a sampling of five Seppelt premium wines accompanied by complimentary cheese and crackers (minimum of 10 people required). The wines include

Cabernet Sauvignon and Chardonnay, but the main interest here is fortified wines. Seppelt has a particularly strong tradition in this field and a number of vineyards, all mature and low-yielding, produce the principal varieties for fortified wines: Grenache, Shiraz, Mourvedre and Touriga. The broad range includes sherries (Amontillado, Oloroso, Fino) as well as Muscat and Tokay from Rutherglen, and port, of which the DP 90 Tawny Port is regarded by the company as its flagship wine, 'the standard by which all other Australian tawnies are judged', according to winemaker James Godfrey. At the top of the range, costing around $1000 a bottle, is the 100-year-old Para Liqueur tawny port.

Turkey Flat

Bethany Rd, Tanunda
T 08 8563 2851   **F** 08 8563 3610   **E** turkeyflat@bigpond.com
W www.turkeyflat.com.au

Peter Schultz **WM**
11 am–5 pm daily **CD**

This family-owned winery produces an unusual but delicious rosé—a blend of Turkey Flat's own old-vine Grenache, Cabernet Sauvignon, Shiraz and Dolcetto—a blended Semillon Marsanne white, and some terrific reds. The Turkey Flat Grenache is light, spicy and smooth; the Shiraz is a big, fruit-driven wine with lots of oak. There is also a classy Cabernet Sauvignon.

Wine tours and activities

Barossa Valley Tours offer regular scheduled tours or can tailor an itinerary to suit your needs (**T/F**   08 8563 3248   **E** info@barossavalleytours.com   **W** www.barossavalleytours.com). Small groups only.

Food and Dining

There is so much good food in the Barossa that the visitor is spoilt for choice. The shopping in Nuriootpa, Tanunda and Angaston is good, with cheeses, olives, smoked meats, and gourmet produce of many kinds always available—great for picnics. Linke's Bakery Tearooms at 40 Murray St, Nuriootpa, features homemade cakes and bread, the likes of which are hard to find elsewhere (**T** 08 8562 1129). Linke's Butcher's shop at 48B Main Rd, Nuriootpa, is a Barossa institution, selling a fascinating range of smoked mettwurst, chicken, sausages, bacons and other meats (**T** 08 8562 1143). The Maggie Beer Farm Shop at Pheasant Farm Shop, Nuriootpa, is also a delight. It has a cafe (see below) and sells food and wine and all manner of good things—try the mushroom pate as well as the meaty ones and don't forget the desserts. Victoria Glaetzer's Barossa Valley Cheese Shop in Murray St, Angaston, is becoming a must-visit for cheese enthusiasts. Brie, feta and a curd cheese are among the delights on offer (**T** 08 8564 3636 **O** Wed–Sun).

The Barossa Farmers Market is held on Saturday at the Vintners Sheds, next to Vintners Restaurant, on the corner of Angaston and Stockwell Rds, Angaston (7:30 am–11:30 am).

The 'Butcher, Baker and Winemaker Trail' leaflet, available from the Tourist Information Centre, is a handy guide to the best that the Barossa has to offer. There is also a regularly updated list of food suppliers and shops on www.barossafood.com.

Jacob's Restaurant, Jacob's Creek Visitor Centre, Barossa Valley Way, Rowland Flat **T** 08 8521 3000 **O** 10 am–4 pm daily, lunch 12 noon–3 pm. The visitor centre restaurant serves international cuisine with an emphasis on local produce such as Barossa olives, oysters from the Yorke Peninsula, Mount Compass lamb, and fish fillets from the St Vincent Gulf. There are also pizzas and salads as well as local cheeses and desserts, and a huge range of wines by the glass to accompany your meal. The restaurant has a pleasant outlook over the vines and the red gums lining the banks of the famous creek.

Maggie Beer Farm Shop, Pheasant Farm, Pheasant Farm Rd, Nuriootpa **T** 08 8562 4477 **F** 08 8562 4757 **E** farmshop@maggiebeer.com.au **W** www.maggiebeer.com.au. Specially prepared platters are served for lunch between 12.30 and 2.30 pm. Pheasant Farm Beer Brothers wines are available.

Salters, Saltram, Salters Gully, Nuriootpa Rd, Angaston   T 08 8564 3344
F 08 8564 2209   O 12 pm–3 pm for lunch, from 6 pm Thurs–Sat for dinner. Under the guidance of chef Vince Trotta, Salters serves Italian-influenced fare incorporating locally sourced produce. The lunchtime specials represent particularly good value.

Vintners' Bar and Grill, Nuriootpa Rd, Angaston   T 08 8564 2488. This dining landmark specialises in Barossa wines and local food. The menu features top-quality meat, ranging from barbecued beef to kangaroo steaks, but also includes a range of Asian and Mediterranean dishes, salads and seafood.

Accommodation

Barossa Weintal Resort, Murray St, Tanunda   T 08 8563 2303   F 08 8563 2279
E reservations@accommodationbarossa.com   W www.barossa-weintal.com   An ideal base for tours of the Barossa, Weintal offers various bars and restaurants, standard rooms and luxury spa suites. Check for midweek and other specials, such as rates including three-course dinners and breakfasts.

Langmeil Cottages, 89 Langmeil Rd, Tanunda   T 08 8563 2987. These self-contained cottages are situated in a tranquil part of the historic town of Tanunda. The rates are reasonable, the location is good and there is even a pool.

Novotel Barossa Valley, Golf Links Rd, Rowland Flat   T 08 8524 0000
W www.barossanovotel.com.au. A quintessential wine-region resort, the Novotel offers top-class accommodation and a range of recreational facilities including golf, archery and, for the more adventurous, mountain-bike tours.

Whirlwind Farm, Samuel Rd, Nuriootpa   T 08 8562 2637. A comfortable, country-style home located 5 minutes from the centre of Nuriootpa, the farm offers tranquil accommodation and a cooked or continental breakfast. Pets by arrangement only.

Travel Information

How to get there
By road The Barossa valley is approximately 75 km (about 1 hour) from Adelaide. Take the Main North Road and follow the signs to Gawler, then turn off to Lyndoch, Tanunda and Nooriootpa.

Other attractions
Don't miss the view from Mengler's Hill, which takes in the broad valley floor with its vines and villages, olive groves, fruit trees and churches. The orderly vegetation gives the Barossa a European look that contrasts with many Australian landscapes. Lyndoch Lavender Farm, cnr Hoffnungstal and Tweedies Gully Rds, Lyndoch, grows 60 different varieties of lavender (**T** 08 8524 4538).

For kids
Barossa Kiddypark, at the corner of Magnolia St and Menge Rd in Tanunda, is paradise for kids and may be hard for parents to escape from! The park's attractions range from dodgem cars and merry-go-rounds to fun parlours and a wildlife park (**T** 08 8563 2868). Story Book Cottage & Whacky Wood in Oak St, Tanunda (look for the Tin Man on the Barossa Hwy), is a good place for kids to unwind—either by looking at Story Book Cottage's 60 displays of dolls and illustrated children's stories or by pondering the devilish puzzles and giant games of Whacky Wood (**T** 08 8563 2910). Lyndoch Recreation Park, Barossa Valley Way, Lyndoch, has a well-maintained sports oval, tennis courts, a children's playground and shaded areas for barbecues and picnics (**T** 08 8563 8451). There's an authentic Aussie feel to the show at Norm's Coolies Performing Sheepdogs, Gomersal Rd, Tanunda (**T** 08 8563 2198), and Norm Keast is the genuine (country) article. 'Get behind!'

Events
Jan–Mar (date varies): Barossa under the Stars (concert at Novotel Barossa Valley **W** barossaunderthestars.com.au)
Easter Mon, odd-numbered years: Barossa Vintage Week Festival (music, food and festivities)
Oct, long weekend: Barossa Music Festival (music and food events at a number of wineries)
Nov: Para Road Wine Path festival at Para Rd wineries, including Peter Lehmann Wines, Langmeil, Richmond Grove (sample the wines while listening to music and eating the best of local produce)

Information
Barossa Wine and Visitor Information Centre, 66–68 Murray Street, Tanunda
T 08 8563 0600 **F** 08 8563 0616
E info@barossa-region.org
W www.barossa-region.org **O** 9 am–5 pm Mon–Fri, 10 am–4 pm Sat–Sun
South Australian Visitor and Travel Centre **T** 1800 655 404
W www.southaustralia.com

Clare Valley

The Clare Valley is one of the prettiest of Australia's wine regions. Nestling amid gently undulating wooded hills, golden fields, and extensive vineyards are attractive towns with historic buildings and intriguing architecture, ranging from the famous 'Kapunda lace' balcony ironwork of the town of the same name through Martindale Hall outside Mintaro to the impeccable wine cellars and historic church of St Aloysius at Sevenhill. The combination of these attractions and top-class food and wine make the Clare Valley an ideal wine-touring region.

Vines were planted here as far back as 1852, by John Horrocks, an early English settler after whom Mount Horrocks was named. He used cuttings he imported from South Africa to make the Clare's first wines, but his life was tragically cut short in a shooting accident and it was left to others to develop the valley's viticulture. Among them was an Irishman, Edmund Gleeson (a name honoured by Brian Barry's label Gleeson's Ridge), who named the town and valley after his birthplace in County Clare, Ireland.

One of the earliest wineries, Sevenhill, was established by Jesuits who had fled persecution in Europe in 1848 and emigrated to Australia. They were producing wine by the mid-1850s. By 1853, another settler, a Cornishman called Francis Treloar had planted vines in the area that was to become Watervale, and in 1895 JH Knappstein and others established the Stanley Wine Company. A period of expansion followed under the guidance of enthusiasts including Herman Buring, Carl Sobels and the Birks family

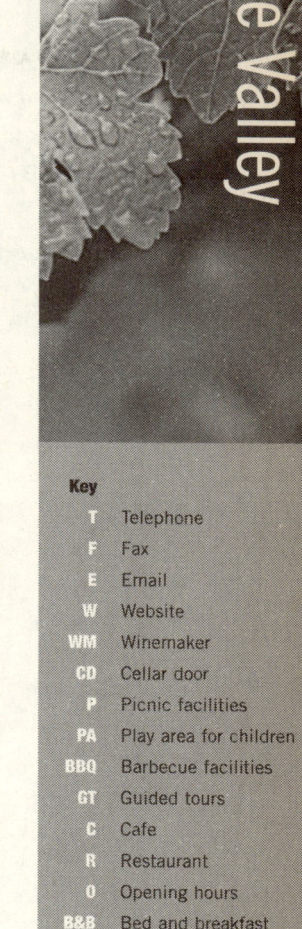

Key

T	Telephone
F	Fax
E	Email
W	Website
WM	Winemaker
CD	Cellar door
P	Picnic facilities
PA	Play area for children
BBQ	Barbecue facilities
GT	Guided tours
C	Cafe
R	Restaurant
O	Opening hours
B&B	Bed and breakfast
H	Hotel/Inn
M	Motel
G	Guesthouse
SCA	Self-catering accommodation

of Wendouree. After the good years of the 1920s, not many companies survived the Great Depression of the 1930s. However, from the 1950s and 1960s onwards a number of small firms were established, among them Jim Barry and Taylors. Since then, and particularly since the 1980s and 1990s, there has been a steady growth in the number of boutique wineries producing wines of very high quality and using an ever-growing range of grape varieties.

The Clare Valley is a warm region and generally experiences hot, dry summers, but it also enjoys cooling afternoon breezes. These temper the worst effects of the heat and allow a longer, slower ripening of the fruit, and producing a depth of flavour normally associated with a cooler climate. Winters are wet and cold. Some areas, such as Polish Hill River, are higher and therefore cooler than others, and more suited to grape varieties like Riesling. There is a great diversity of vineyard sites and aspect.

What to buy

The Clare Valley produces a huge range of wines and offers some of the best value in the country. Both reds and whites are made, and both are good. For climatic reasons, Riesling has long been regarded as the area's speciality, particularly in the Polish Hill River and Watervale areas. Semillon, Chardonnay and Sauvignon Blanc are among the most successful of the other whites. Of the reds, Cabernet Sauvignon and Shiraz have traditionally predominated, but more recently a range of other varieties has been grown, including Merlot, Pinot Noir, Sangiovese, Malbec and Grenache.

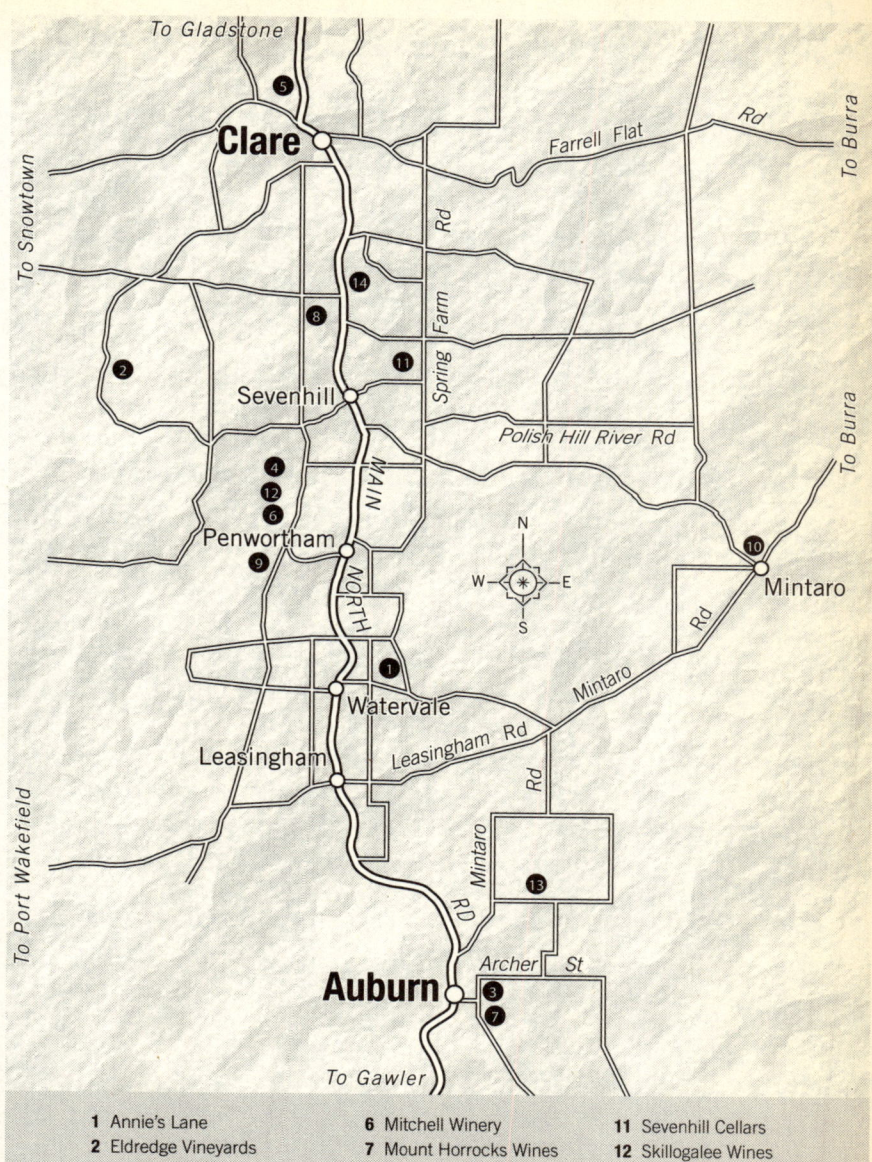

1 Annie's Lane	**6** Mitchell Winery	**11** Sevenhill Cellars
2 Eldredge Vineyards	**7** Mount Horrocks Wines	**12** Skillogalee Wines
3 Grosset Wines	**8** Neagles Rock Vineyard	**13** Taylor's Wines
4 Jeanneret Wines	**9** Penna Lane Wines	**14** Tim Adams Wines
5 Jim Barry Wines	**10** Reilly's Wines	

CLARE VALLEY 117

Wineries

Annie's Lane

WM Caroline Dunn
CD 8.30 am–5 pm
Mon–Fri, 11 am–
4 pm weekends
and public holidays
P

Quelltaler Rd, Watervale
T 08 8843 0003 **F** 08 8843 0096
E grant.thomas@beringerblass.com.au
W www.beringerblass.com.au

A historic stone winery, which as Quelltaler produced some of the Clare Valley's earliest wine successes, Annie's Lane is now part of the Beringer Blass group. The winery complex boasts an art gallery and conference facilities and a good picnic area, and you can also buy gourmet foods and olive oil at the cellar door. Many of the wines are well made and good value. Try the screw-capped Riesling, the Copper Trail Shiraz (not cheap but terrific value), and the silky, smooth Clare Valley Cabernet Merlot.

Eldredge Vineyards

WM Leigh Eldredge
CD 11 am–5 pm daily
C

Spring Gully Rd, Sevenhill
T/F 08 8842 3086 **E** bluechip@capri.net.au

This is a small family-run winery producing some sensational wines. The Watervale Riesling is particularly good value, but the range also includes Semillon Sauvignon Blanc, Mourvedre Shiraz Grenache and Cabernet Sauvignon, as well as Shiraz, a sparkling white and a tawny port. The cellar door is housed in a cottage set among vines and bushland and has a stone-floored tasting room. There is also a cafe (see Food and Dining).

Grosset Wines

WM Jeffrey Grosset
CD 10 am–5 pm
Wed–Sun until
wines are sold out

Manoora Rd, Auburn
T 08 8849 2175 **F** 08 8849 2292 **E** info@grosset.com.au
W www.grosset.com

If you are lucky enough to arrive in springtime, Grosset's old stone winery is a good place to start your Clare cellar-door touring—wines go on sale from the first weekend in September and are in great demand. Grosset specialises in Riesling and Chardonnay.

The Rieslings (the flavoursome Watervale Riesling or the flinty Polish Hill) are seriously good wines, as is the Gaia blend (Cabernet Sauvignon, Cabernet Franc and Merlot). Grosset also makes Piccadilly Pinot Noir and Chardonnay—both top Clare wines.

Jeanneret Wines

Jeanneret Rd, Sevenhill
T 08 8843 4308   **F** 08 8843 4251   **E** jwines@bigpond.com
W www.ascl.com/j-wines.com

This family-owned winery makes small quantities of Riesling, Chardonnay, Cabernet Sauvignon, Shiraz, and Grenache. The Shiraz and Riesling are well made and well priced. Jeanneret is one of the few winemakers to produce a sparkling Grenache. The winery has a charming picnic area in a pretty lakeside setting. The tasting area is in a cellar beneath the original Jeanneret house.

Ben Jeanneret **WM**
11 am–5 pm **CD**
Mon–Fri,
10 am–5 pm
weekends and
public holidays
P
Book in advance **GT**

Jim Barry Wines

Craigs Hill Rd, Clare
T 08 8842 2261

An iconic Clare Valley winery, Jim Barry Wines was founded in 1959 and produces a great range of flavoursome wines. Both the Watervale Riesling and the Shiraz are very popular. The Lodge Hill range offers top value at moderate prices, whereas the Armagh Shiraz is a beauty in a higher price range. The winery's cellar door set-up is relatively modest but has plenty of atmosphere and some very good wines, with the emphasis on quality and reasonable prices.

Mark Barry **WM**
9 am–5 pm **CD**
Mon–Fri,
9 am–4 pm
weekends and
public holidays

Mitchell Winery

Hughes Park Rd, Sevenhill
T 08 8843 4258   **F** 08 8843 4340   **E** jmitchell@mitchellwines.com

This small family-owned winery is located in one of the most beautiful parts of the Clare Valley and the cellar door is housed in a quaint old stone apple shed. The wines are traditional Clare styles with good cellaring potential; choose from Riesling, Semillon, Cabernet Sauvignon, Shiraz and Grenache.

Andrew Mitchell **WM**
10 am–4 pm daily **CD**
until sold out

Mount Horrocks Wines

WM Stephanie Toole
CD 10 am–5 pm weekends and public holidays only
C See Food and Dining

Curling St, Auburn

T 08 8849 2243   **F** 08 8849 2265   **E** sales@mounthorrocks.com
W www.mounthorrocks.com

This outlet was named in honour of the explorer and vine-grower John (JH) Horrocks rather than the mountain, which lies some distance away. It occupies the renovated Auburn railway station building (the trains stopped running a long time ago), though Stephanie Toole actually makes her highly regarded wines at her husband Jeffrey Grosset's winery (see page 118). The elegant whites and reds range from stunning Semillon and intense Riesling through to Shiraz, Cabernet Sauvignon and Cabernet Merlot, as well as dessert wines.

Neagles Rock Vineyard

WM Steve Wiblin
CD 10 am–5 pm daily
R

Lot 1, Main North Rd, Clare

T 08 8843 4020   **F** 08 8843 4021   **E** nrv@neaglesrock.com
W www.neaglesrock.com

This friendly winery has a cellar door and cafe operation with delightful views and a casual atmosphere. The small family-owned winery makes a small range of premium quality wines at reasonable prices—the Riesling, Sauvignon Blanc, Chardonnay, Cabernet Sauvignon, Shiraz, Grenache and Sangiovese are all worth tasting and offer good value. And if you feel in the mood, you can have a go at petanque after lunch.

Penna Lane Wines

WM Ray Klavins
CD 11 am–5 pm Fri–Sun
BBQ
C

Lot 51, Penna Lanes, Penwortham

T 08 8843 4364   **F** 08 8843 4349

The wines here are better than good—and some are trophy winners. Riesling is the main focus, though Semillon, Shiraz and Cabernet Sauvignon are also produced. The cellar door is located in a rustic old dairy and the setting is suitably bucolic. There's an outside area where seating is available, and a range of homemade (and home-grown) chutneys, pickles and dressings is on sale at the cellar door. The cafe serves light lunches—including home-made soups in winter—at very reasonable prices.

Reilly's Wines

Burra Rd, Mintaro

T/F 08 8843 9013 **E** cellar@reillyswines.com **W** www.reillyswines.com
This winery is named after Hugh Reilly, an Irish shoemaker who arrived in the Clare in 1856 and lived in the building that now houses the cellar door. Reilly's has a limited range, but the wines are good and the cellar door also sells some terrific local food produce including an olive oil pressed from wild olives. The Watervale Riesling is a favourite here, but don't overlook the Cabernet Sauvignon. If you like sparkling reds, you shouldn't pass up the chance to try the Grenache, which has a vibrant crimson colour and rich berry aromas. And if you want to come back for more, you can stay the night (see Accommodation).

Justin Ardill **WM**
10 am–5 pm daily **CD**
10 am–4 pm daily **R**
for lunch; Mon, Wed, Sat, Sun for dinner

SCA

Sevenhill Cellars

College Rd, Sevenhill

T 08 8843 4222 **E** sales@sevenhillcellars.com.au
W www.sevenhillcellars.com.au
The oldest winery in the Clare Valley, this establishment is still run by members of the Jesuit order, which founded the vineyard in 1851. It's well worth a visit for its historic atmosphere—the stone, vaulted cellars are wonderful—as well as the wines. Riesling, a Chenin Blanc Chardonnay Verdelho blend (St Aloysius), Grenache, Cabernet Shiraz and others are available. The proud claim for the wines is that they are '100% Clare'—made only with valley-grown fruit. The grounds are beautiful and you can use the picnic tables or hire bikes to tour the estate or travel the Heritage Trail of historic buildings in Sevenhill.

Brother John May, **WM**
Tim Gniel
9 am–5 pm **CD**
Mon–Fri,
10 am–5 pm
weekends and
public holidays

P

Skillogalee Wines

Trevarrick Rd, Sevenhill

T 08 8843 4311 **F** 08 8843 4343 **E** skilly@chariot.net.au
W www.skillogalee.com
This tiny winery and restaurant are set in a pretty and secluded area to the west of Sevenhill. The restaurant and cellar door area share an old settler's cottage. The gardens are delightful and the wines have excellent flavour and offer good value. The winery also has self-catering cottages set in adjacent bushland (see Accommodation).

David Palmer **WM**
10 am–5 pm daily **CD**
12 noon–3 pm **R**
for lunch

SCA

Taylor's Wines

WM Adam Eggins, Helen McCarthy
CD 9 am–5 pm Mon–Fri, 10 am–5 pm Sat and public holidays, 10 am–4 pm Sun

Taylor's Rd, Auburn

T 08 8849 2008 **F** 08 8849 2240 **E** sales@taylorswines.com.au
W www.taylorswines.com.au

Founded in the late 1960s, Taylor's is a family-owned vineyard and winery that has grown from modest beginnings to become the largest landholder in the Clare Valley. It draws on grapes from numerous vineyards with varying microclimates and elevations, allowing it to produce all kinds of wines, from Riesling to Shiraz. These are sold at value-for-money prices under several labels, ranging from the modestly priced Promised Land label through the Taylors Estate and Jaraman mid-priced lines to the premium St Andrews label—all available for tasting at the cellar door. Taylors Shiraz has won much acclaim in recent years, but make sure you also try the Cabernet Sauvignon and Merlot, too.

Tim Adams Wines

WM Tim Adams
CD 10.30 am–5 pm Mon–Fri, 11 am–5 pm weekends and public holidays

Warenda Rd, Clare

T 08 8842 2429 **F** 08 8842 3550 **E** tim@timadamswines.com.au
W www.timadamswines.com.au

Established in 1986, this is a highly successful operation with an immaculate, low-key cellar door and tasting room. Adams worked with the legendary Mick Knappstein for a number of years and draws on more than 25 years of winemaking experience. As you would expect, therefore, these are top-quality, distinctive wines. They also offer excellent value and display the intense varietal flavours associated with the Clare. In particular, the Semillon and Riesling are well above average. Also available are Grenache, Shiraz and Cabernet Sauvignon—try the Fergus Grenache Cabernet Shiraz blend, the Aberfeldy Shiraz, and Botrytis Riesling.

Wine tours and activities

Clare Valley Experiences offers individually tailored wine itineraries or you can join a package that includes accommodation and restaurant bookings as well (**T** 08 8843 4169 **W** www.visitclarevalley.com.au). One of the best ways to see the Clare Valley is to hop on a bicycle; half- or full-day hire and drop-off and pick-up can be arranged through Clare Valley Cycle Hire (**T** 08 8842 2782).

Food and Dining

The Clare Valley produces some excellent food and has a number of good restaurants. It has always grown good fruit and vegetables, but has recently gained a reputation as a supplier of more specialised products, including olives, honey, sundried tomatoes, fine lamb from Burra and local rabbit and venison. Many of these delicacies, as well as saltbush lamb, saltbush sausages and a range of bacons and hams, can be sampled at McPhees Meats and Fine Foods of Clare (T 08 8842 2818). Valley of Armagh olive estate in Clare sells olives—the Spanish Manzanilla olives are delicious—olive oils, vinegars and honey (T 08 8842 1237). Tasting and sales of olive oils also take place at the Patly Hill & Terrace Gallery, St Georges Terrace, Armagh, which also sells kitchen-garden produce and preserves (T 08 8842 3557). In Penwortham, it's worth stopping by Morrison's, at the corner of Main North and Morrison roads, for jams, pickles, chutneys and a range of fresh seasonal vegetables (T 08 8843 4232 O 8.30 am–5 pm Wed–Mon morning). Mouthwateringly good food is also provided by the award-winning London Hill catering team of Philip Scarles and Amanda Waldron, who make handmade gourmet produce—jellies, chutneys, mustards and relishes—and gourmet picnic baskets for sale through various outlets (T 08 8843 4360).

Coleman's Restaurant at Kilikanoon, Penna Lane, Penwortham T 08 8843 4377 F 08 8843 4368 O 11 am–5 pm Fri–Sun and public holidays. This cellar-door cafe serves generous portions of traditional fare, including steak sandwiches, hamburgers and grills; there are also blackboard specials, coffee and cakes.

Eldredge Vineyards, Spring Gully Rd, Sevenhill T/F 08 8842 3086 E bluechip@capri.net.au O 12 noon–3 pm for lunch on weekends and public holidays. The cafe adjoins the cellar door area and has a pleasant jarrah deck from which visitors can look out over a dam and vines.

Mount Horrocks Wines, Curling St, Auburn T 08 8849 2243 F 08 8849 2265 E sales@mounthorrocks.com W www.mounthorrocks.com O 12 noon–3 pm weekends and public holidays. The cafe at Mount Horrocks winery (see Wineries) offers delicious light lunches at very reasonable prices. Soups, terrines and salads all feature here, and at least one vegetarian dish is usually available. Local produce is used and the menu changes frequently, depending on the season. Plunger coffee, cakes and shortbread are available at other times.

Salt 'n' Vines Bar and Bistro, Kirrihill Estates, Wendouree Rd, Clare **T** 08 8842 1796 **F** 08 8842 1702 **O** Thurs–Sun for lunch and dinner. This popular restaurant has a wide verandah overlooking the surrounding vines and countryside. It serves an eclectic selection of dishes, ranging from a steak sandwich with caramelised onions, bacon and fries to grain-fed yearling rump steak with mushroom sauce. Seafood is also on offer, including oysters, prawns from the Spencer Gulf, King George whiting and grilled Atlantic salmon.

Tatehams at Auburn, Main North Rd, Auburn **T** 08 8849 2030 **F** 08 8849 2260 **W** www.bnbbookings.com/tatehams **O** Wed–Sun for lunch and dinner. The emphasis at this elegant restaurant is on traditional French Alsace cooking. The fare includes schnitzels and a range of pancakes, as well as more substantial dishes. Guests sit at long wooden tables on the highly polished floors and candles are lit for dinner. Tatehams has its own vineyard and wines are available. Accommodation is also available (see Accommodation).

Accommodation

Clare Valley Motel, 74A Main North Rd, Clare **T** 08 8842 2799 **F** 08 8842 3121 **E** clarevalleymotel@internode.on.net. This modern, comfortable and central motel has a good restaurant and swimming pool. Some rooms have spas.

Oldfields B&B, Young St, Mintaro **T** 08 8843 9038. Oldfields offers bed and breakfast in a range of heritage-listed stone cottages. Choose from the Settler's Cottage, the Chapel or the Coach House, all of which date from the mid-nineteenth century and have been lovingly restored.

Reilly's Country Retreat, Burra Rd, Mintaro **T/F** 08 8843 9013 **E** cellar@reillywines.com **W** www.reillyswines.com. Operated by Reilly's Wines (see Wineries), the retreat consists of three cottages: the Antique Shop, Priest's Cottage and Pulford's. Ranging from one to three bedrooms, they offer creature comforts such as open fireplaces, queen-sized beds and colour TVs—as well as peace and quiet.

The Rising Sun Hotel, Auburn **T** 08 8849 2015. Auburn is one of the oldest settlements in the Clare Valley and the Rising Sun one of the oldest pubs. It has recently been refurbished and accommodation is offered in 10 self-contained units, four of which have been converted from stables to provide luxurious mews accommodation.

Skillogalee House and Windamere Cottages, Skillogalee Wines, Trevarrick Rd, Sevenhill **T** 08 8843 4311 **F** 08 8843 4343 **E** skilly@chariot.net.au **W** www.skillogalee.com. Comfortable self-catering accommodation is available at Skillogalee in three fully equipped two-bedroom cottages, all within walking distance of the cellar door and restaurant. The cottages are popular, so book ahead.

Tatehams at Auburn, Main North Rd, Auburn **T** 08 8849 2030 **F** 08 8849 2260 **W** www.bnbbookings.com/tatehams. This heritage-listed building that was once a general store now contains four guest rooms, two of which are located in a converted stable at the back of the building. All have been thoughtfully converted and tastefully decorated. There is also a restaurant (see Food and Dining).

Watervale and Rosebrae Cottage B&B, Watervale **T** 08 8843 0046 **W** www.gwynn-jones.com.au/watervalecottage. These charming self-contained sandstone cottages are conveniently located and set within vineyards. One was originally built as a Methodist Manse. They are well appointed, with air-conditioning, TVs, CD players, fully equipped kitchens and queen-sized beds.

Travel Information

How to get there
By road The Clare Valley is about 134 km (90 minutes' drive) north of Adelaide. Take the A20 to Gawler from the centre of Adelaide and then the Main North Rd (A32) to Tarlee via Roseworthy. After Tarlee, take the B82 to Rhynie and then Auburn, the first town in the Clare Valley.

Other attractions
You can walk or cycle along part of the well-signposted Riesling Trail, a cycle track that was once an old railway line and now links the villages of Auburn, Leasingham, Watervale, Penwortham and Sevenhill. Quarry Hill Lookout offers a great view of the Polish Hill Valley, taking in vines and farming country alike.

The heritage mining towns of Auburn and Mintaro repay exploration. Auburn was the birthplace of the poet CJ Dennis, a fact celebrated by a birdbath and drinking fountain in the town centre. It is also famous for the Rising Sun Hotel, which dates from 1849 and is still a popular place for a drink (see Accommodation). Departing from Hallett, the Dare's Hill Circuit drive offers a hint of the true Outback, taking you through saltbush and pastoral areas that have long since become marginal or abandoned.

For kids
Geralka Rural Farm, on Hwy 83, off the Main North Rd between Clare and Spalding offers rides and farm tours (**T** 08 8845 8081). Maynard Pioneer Park in Clare (near Knappstein Wines) has shady picnic spots, barbecues and swimming pool.

Events
May, third weekend: Clare Gourmet Weekend (food events at wineries and other venues)

Information
Clare Valley Visitor Information Centre, 229 Main North Rd, Clare
T 08 8842 2131 **F** 08 8842 1117
E ask@clarevalley.com.au
W www.clarevalley.com.au

Coonawarra

Coonawarra's limestone ridge of *terra rossa* soil is perhaps the most famous strip of vineyard earth in Australia and produces some of the best Cabernet Sauvignon and Shiraz in the country. How could you not take the notion of *terroir* seriously when you take a look at the Coonawarra's red, hot, flat, well-drained land and then sample its powerful and startlingly distinctive wines?

The first person to plant grapevines in Coonawarra (before it was known by that name) was William Wilson, a Scottish gardener. Not long after arriving in South Australia in 1850, he planted a small plot to the north of the town of Penola as part of a modest garden he had established. But it was another Scot, John Riddoch, a retired politician with considerable landholdings, who formulated a plan for the area that included the establishment of extensive vineyards. In 1891, Riddoch began building the cellars that are now part of Wynns Coonawarra Estate. However, the industry languished after the turn of the century and throughout the First World War, the Depression and the Second World War. Only when the Wynn family purchased Riddoch's cellars and vineyards in 1951, believing the soil and climate offered a unique combination for growing grapes for table wine, did the industry begin to turn around. In the 50 or so years since then, the combined efforts of many talented grape growers and winemakers have ensured that Coonawarra has steadily increased production of wines of a truly unique style and quality. They are now acclaimed as some of Australia's finest wines, and among the best in the world.

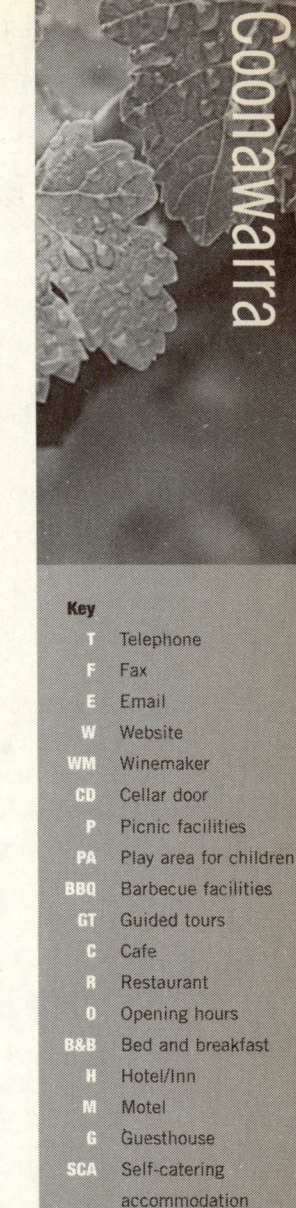

Key

T	Telephone
F	Fax
E	Email
W	Website
WM	Winemaker
CD	Cellar door
P	Picnic facilities
PA	Play area for children
BBQ	Barbecue facilities
GT	Guided tours
C	Cafe
R	Restaurant
O	Opening hours
B&B	Bed and breakfast
H	Hotel/Inn
M	Motel
G	Guesthouse
SCA	Self-catering accommodation

Coonawarra is the most southerly of South Australia's winegrowing regions and lies only 60 km from the cooling influences of the Southern Ocean. Its small, cigar-shaped tract of *terra rossa* is only 20 km long and 1.5 km wide. The thin layer of red soil and the underlying well-drained, porous limestone encourage low-yielding intensely flavoured fruit.

The centre of Coonawarra is very compact, and cellar door visits are accomplished by staying on the Riddoch Highway. The wineries are for the most part clearly signposted, accessible and have plenty of parking, but many do not offer much shade in summer. The towns of Penola and Naracoorte are close by and both offer good services. Located about 80 km north of Coonawarra, but often regarded as part of the same region, is the tiny wine-producing area of Padthaway.

What to buy

Coonawarra reds are renowned for their flavour and complexity, due in large part to the long, cool growing period which allows the fruit to ripen slowly. Though Cabernet Sauvignon and Shiraz are the characteristic wines of the Coonawarra, other red varieties are cultivated, too, including Merlot, Malbec, Cabernet Franc, Petit Verdot and Pinot Noir. Chardonnay, Riesling and some Sauvignon Blanc are also grown in the area, and though the quantities are small the resulting wines can be very good indeed.

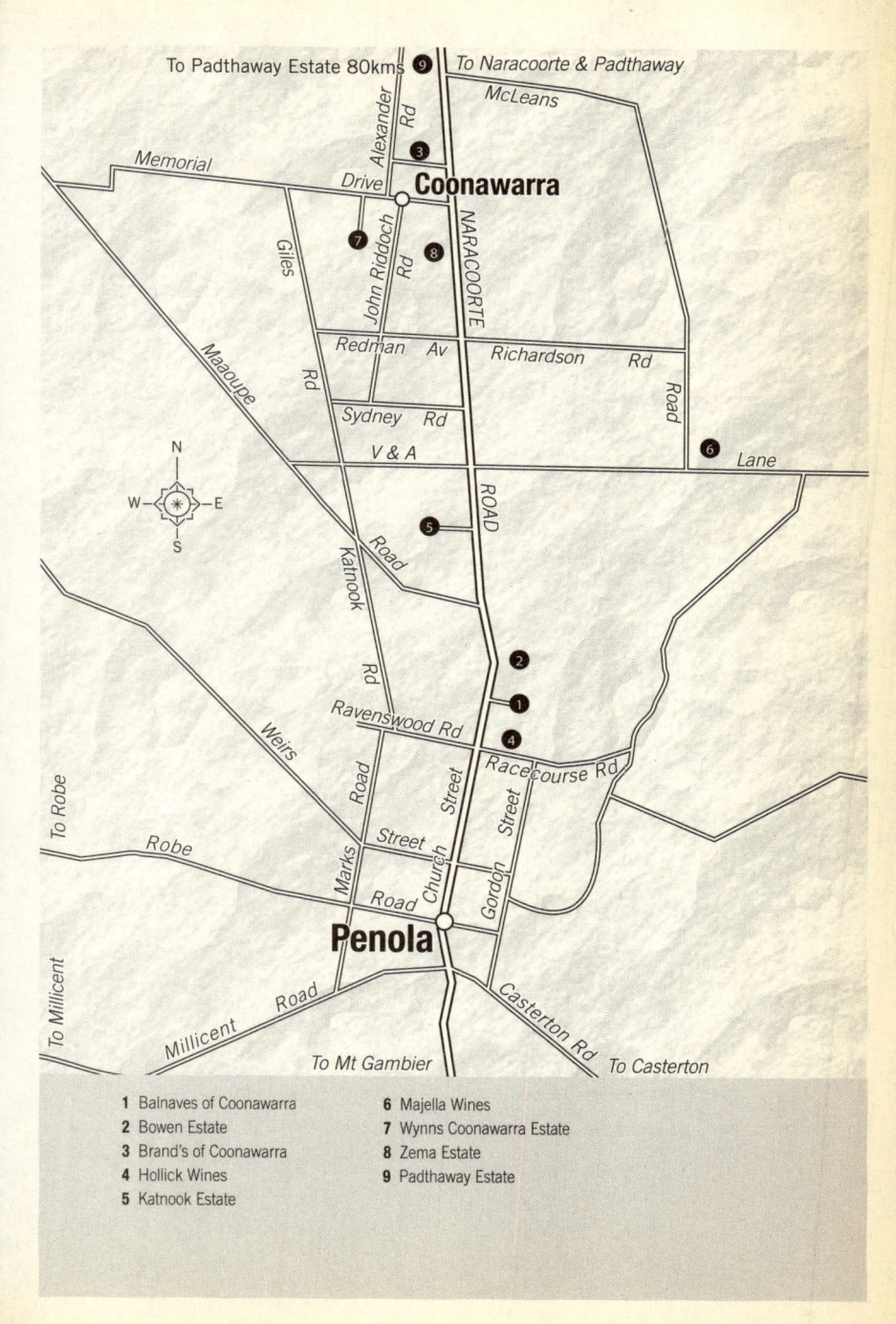

1 Balnaves of Coonawarra
2 Bowen Estate
3 Brand's of Coonawarra
4 Hollick Wines
5 Katnook Estate
6 Majella Wines
7 Wynns Coonawarra Estate
8 Zema Estate
9 Padthaway Estate

COONAWARRA 129

Wineries

Coonawarra

Balnaves of Coonawarra

WM Peter Bissell
CD 9 am–5 pm Mon–Fri, 10 am–5 pm weekends and public holidays
GT

Riddoch Hwy, Coonawarra

T 08 8737 2946 **F** 08 8737 2945
E kirsty.balnaves@balnaves.com.au **W** www.balnaves.com.au

The Bowen family have been growing vines for almost 30 years and they have been producing top-class wines since 1990. The best known is the Cabernet Sauvignon, but they also make Merlot, Cabernet Franc and Shiraz. The Blend (Merlot and Cabernet Franc) is a smooth and satisfying wine and there is a terrific Chardonnay. The cellar door overlooks a trout-filled pond and is surrounded by a pretty rose garden—a calming sight before or after the serious business of tasting wines.

Bowen Estate

WM Doug Bowen, Emma Bowen
CD 10 am–5 pm daily

Riddoch Hwy, Riddoch Hwy, Coonawarra

T 08 8737 2229 **F** 08 8737 2173
E bowenest@coonawarra.mtx.net.au

The winery has a charming rustic tasting room with an earth floor and wooden storage racks, and makes consistently good, big Coonawarra reds that are as characteristic of the area as anything else you'll find. They include Cabernet Sauvignon, Shiraz and a blend. The full-bodied Chardonnay and Riesling are both well worth buying. Top quality, hand-crafted wines.

Brand's of Coonawarra

WM Jim Brand
CD 8 am–5 pm Mon–Fri, 10 am–4 pm weekends and public holidays

Riddoch Highway, Coonawarra

T 08 8736 3260 **F** 08 8736 3208
E brands_office@mcwilliams.com.au **W** www.mcwilliams.com.au

Now part of the McWilliams group, Brand's produces some of the best Coonawarra reds year after year. Classic Coonawarra Cabernet Sauvignon, Shiraz and Merlot are the backbone of the range, which also includes Riesling, Chardonnay and a Sparkling Cabernet Sauvignon.

*(handwritten top: Barrels Cat   * Black Market $45   Reserve Chardonnay $79)*

Hollick Wines ✓

Ravenswood Lane, Coonawarra

T 08 8737 2318 **F** 08 8737 2952 **E** admin@hollick.com
W www.hollick.com

This family-run winery offers award-winning wines at reasonable prices. It produces a broad range of high-quality reds and whites—Cabernet Sauvignon, Shiraz, Merlot (including sparkling), Pinot Noir; Chardonnay, Riesling, Sauvignon Blanc and Semillon. It also makes limited quantities of less common varietals and blends from grapes such as Tempranillo and Sangiovese, grown in both Coonawarra and Wrattonbully, where the climate is slightly warmer and grapes ripen two weeks earlier than in Coonawarra. The Sangiovese Cabernet blend, Hollaia, and the Tempranillo are very promising. The fabulous new cellar door and the restaurant, Upstairs (see Food and Dining), are musts for all visitors to Coonawarra.

Ian Hollick, **WM**
David Norman
9 am–5 pm daily **CD**
R

Katnook Estate ✓

Riddoch Hwy, Coonawarra

T 08 8737 2394 **F** 08 8737 2397 **E** katnook@wingara.com.au
W www.katnookestate

Housed in a stone woolshed built by John Riddoch in 1896, Katnook inherited a century-old winegrowing tradition as well as a historic building. The emphasis here is on producing the finest estate-grown fruit and expressing the Coonawarra's distinctive characters. The premium Odyssey and Prodigy labels attract premium prices, but there are less expensive wines that offer good value in the lower-price Katnook and Riddoch ranges, such as the the Katnook Merlot and Riddoch Cabernet Merlot. Chardonnay, Riesling and Semillon are also available and the Sauvignon Blanc is multi-award-winning. The expansive lawn is ideal for picnics.

Wayne Stehbens **WM**
9 am–4.30 pm **CD**
Mon–Fri,
10 am–4.30 pm
Sat and public
holidays,
12 noon–4.30 pm
Sun
P
BBQ

Majella Wines

Lynn Rd, Coonawarra

T 08 8736 3057 **F** 08 8736 3057 **E** prof@penola.mtx.net.au
W www.majellawines.com.au

The Lynn family expanded from grazing into viticulture in the late 1960s and became highly successful contract grape growers before producing their own first vintage in 1991. They now make some of the best wines in Coonawarra, with Shiraz, Cabernet

Bruce Gregory **WM**
10 am–4.30 pm **CD**
daily

Sauvignon and Riesling being the specialities. Others include the Malleea, a Cabernet Shiraz blend that has won a steady stream of medals across the country, and the Sparkling Shiraz, which is made only in small quantities and sells out quickly. The smart, modern tasting room offers pleasant views over trees and vines.

Wynns Coonawarra Estate

WM Sue Hodder
CD 10 am–5 pm daily
P

Memorial Drive, Coonawarra
T 08 8736 2225 **F** 08 8736 2228 **E** wynns.cwe@cellar-door.com.au
W www.wynns.com.au

The famous triple-gabled winery and surrounding vineyards, established in the 1890s by John Riddoch, are still the foundation of this estate. Rescued from obscurity and ruin when it was purchased by Samuel Wynn and his son David in 1951, it is now owned by Southcorp. The labels of Wynns Coonawarra Estate bottles are emblazoned with the legend 'The estate that made Coonawarra famous' and indeed the wines produced here over the last six decades have included some excellent and deservedly famous wines. Among these are the flagship Coonawarra Estate John Riddoch Cabernet Sauvignon and the Michael Shiraz, a top-of-the-range Coonawarra created in 1955 and named by David Wynn in memory of his young son, who had died the previous year; it remains one of Coonawarra's benchmark wines. The other wines are not to be missed either, and range through excellent reds such as the Coonawarra Black Label Cabernet Sauvignon, Estate Shiraz and Cabernet Shiraz Merlot blend to full-flavoured Chardonnay and Riesling.

Zema Estate

WM Tom Simons
CD 9 am–5 pm daily

Riddoch Hwy, Coonawarra
T 08 8736 3219 **F** 08 8736 3280 **W** zemaestate@zema.com.au

Owned and operated by the Zema family, this winery produces a fine range of full-flavoured wines. Reasonably priced and made entirely from Coonawarra fruit, they include the top-quality Zema Estate Cabernet Sauvignon and Zema Estate Shiraz, and a blend called Cluny made from Cabernet Sauvignon, Merlot, Cabernet Franc and Malbec, which is terrific value. Zema also makes and sells its own delicious olive oil.

Padthaway

Padthaway Estate
Riddoch Hwy, Padthaway
T 08 8765 5555 **F** 08 8765 5554
E enquiries@padthawayestate.com **W** www.padthawayestate.com

Based around a beautiful old homestead built in 1882, the vineyards here are small, but the estate produces some good wines. They include the Eliza Sparkling Pinot Noir Chardonnay, Padthaway Estate Cabernet Sauvignon and Unwooded Chardonnay, and the Elgin Estate Merlot.

Ulrich Grey-Smith **WM**
10 am–4 pm daily **CD**
B&B

Wine tours and activities

Limestone Coast Discovery Tours, located at 7 Pine Avenue, Naracoorte, operates tours of Coonawarra and Padthaway, as well as visits to Naracoorte Caves, Wonambi Fossil Centre and to the coast to sample local seafood (**T** 08 8762 4111 or 0407 350 076 **F** 08 8762 3942 **E** taxi@rbm.com.au **W** www.limestonecoasttours.com.au).

Food and Dining

Plenty of good food is available in Coonawarra and Penola. For bread and a range of picnic items, try the Windara Bakery in Penola (**T** 08 7372 2215). Meek's Butchers at 66 Church St, Penola, sells a fine range of local meats, including smoked hams and bacon, as well as barbecue packs including gourmet sausages (**T** 08 8737 2330). Monthly farmers' markets take place from time to time: contact the visitor information centre (see below) for details.

Pipers of Penola, 58 Riddoch St, Penola **T** 08 8737 3999 **F** 08 8737 3666 **E** pipers@thelimestonecoast.com **O** From 6 pm Mon–Sat. Pipers offers fine dining with an emphasis on local produce. Dishes range from local grass-fed beef and lamb to Ceduna oysters, Limestone Coast fish and locally farmed trout and salmon. The restaurant is licensed and has a good selection of local wines.

Redfingers Cafe Bar & Grill, Memorial Dr, Coonawarra **T** 08 8736 3006 **F** 08 8736 3061 **O** From 10 am Wed–Mon (9 am on Sun). Set in the old Coonawarra schoolhouse building, this cafe-style restaurant serves grills, casseroles, focaccias, pastas and salads. The daily specials can include crepes, pies, lamb shanks, seafood and seasonal vegetables. A range of local wines is available by the glass and a shaded outdoor courtyard area under ancient peppercorn trees completes the picture.

Upstairs, Hollick Wines, Ravenswood Lane, Coonawarra **T** 08 8737 2318 **F** 08 8737 2952 **E** admin@hollick.com **W** www.hollick.com **O** From 10 am for coffee, from 12 noon for lunch, 6.30 pm–late Fri–Sat for dinner; closed last two weeks of Aug. The first winery restaurant to be established in Coonawarra, Upstairs is a favourite with locals and visitors alike. Extensively refurbished, it serves up imaginative modern Australian cuisine made with local produce such as lamb, seafood and seasonal vegetables. Hollick wines, as well as a carefully selected list of other local and imported wines, are available, several by the glass. Diners can also savour the lovely views over the vineyards and take a peek into the barrel room to see the winemakers going about their business.

Accommodation

Chardonnay Lodge, Riddoch Hwy, Coonawarra **T** 08 8736 3309 **F** 08 8736 3383 **E** chard@coonawarra.limestonecoast.net. Situated in the heart of Coonawarra, the lodge provides a good base for exploring the wineries. The dining room is comfortable and spacious, the food consistently good, and the wine list extensive, including up to 100 Coonawarra wines. The accommodation ranges from standard rooms through to deluxe suites with spas (and fancy taps!).

Cobb & Co Cottages, 2 Portland St, Penola **T** 08 9737 2526 **F** 08 8737 2926 **W** www.cobbnco.com. These comfortable cottages occupy a convenient location—opposite the Mary McKillop schoolhouse, adjacent to a restaurant, near Petticoat Lane, and a two-minute walk from the centre of Penola.

Punters Corner Vineyard Retreat, **T** 08 8737 2007　**F** 08 8737 3138　**E** punters@coonawarra.lscst.net　**W** www.punterscorner.com.au. The stylish accommodation at Punters Retreat is self-catering, though breakfast provisions are included in the price. Bicycles are available, and it's easy to ride to the wineries.

Padthaway

Padthaway Estate Historic Homestead, Riddoch Hwy, Padthaway **T** 08 8765 5555 **F** 08 8765 5554　**E** enquiries@padthawayhomestead.com.au　**W** www.padthawayhomestead.com.au. Accommodation at this winery (see Wineries) is divided into deluxe rooms in the homestead (some with ensuite, spa and balcony access) and comfortable rooms (with shared facilities) in the old shearers' building.

Travel Information

How to get there

By road Coonawarra is about 3 hours from Adelaide via the Princes Hwy and Mount Gambier, and about 5 hours from Melbourne via Hamilton.

By air O'Connor Airlines (**T** 08 8723 0666) flies from Melbourne to Mount Gambier three times a day Mon–Fri and twice a day at weekends. It also operates four flights a day from Adelaide to Mount Gambier Mon–Fri, and one a day on weekends. Flights take approximately 1 hour. Rex Regional Express (**T** 13 17 13) flies direct from Melbourne to Mount Gambier three times a day Mon–Fri and twice a day at weekends. It also operates four flights a day from Adelaide Mon–Fri and two a day on weekends. Flights take around 65 minutes. From Mount Gambier, it's a 30-minute car ride to Coonawarra.

Other attractions

The John Riddoch Interpretive Centre at 27 Arthur St, Penola, has a fascinating collection of photographs and documents relating to the history of the area (**T** 08 8737 2855). There are a number of wonderful buildings in Coonawarra, including Yallum Park. One of the best-preserved Victorian houses in Australia, this two-storey mansion has large verandas and a garden incorporating trees from all over the world (**T** 08 8737 2435 **O** By appointment).

Situated close to the original Josephite schoolhouse established by Sister Mary McKillop, the Interpretive Centre at the corner of Portland St and Petticoat Lane has fascinating displays and artefacts relating to the life of Australia's first nominee for sainthood.

Some date back to 1867, when the school was founded (**T** 08 8737 2092 **O** 10 am–4 pm daily). The schoolhouse itself, also in Portland St, is open to the public, too. Penola also has a number of early cottages, including Sharam Cottage, now owned by the National Trust, and Sarah's Cottage at Julian St West, which operates as a bed and breakfast (**T** 0407 719 030).

For kids
Toffee and Treats of Penola at 51 Church St, Penola, is an old-fashioned sweetshop selling homemade and imported sweets, toffee and milkshakes, including the most delicious macadamia toffee. Weight-watchers will be relieved to hear that it also sells a range of sugar-free sweets (**T** 08 8737 2717).

The Penola Memorial Park in Riddoch St, Penola, has a children's playground.

Events
Feb: Coonawarra Lazy Days of Summer Festival (six wineries celebrate summer; child-friendly drinks and food available **W** www.coonawarra.org)
May: Penola–Coonawarra Festival, an arts festival incorporating music, art shows and food and wine events
Oct: Coonawarra Cabernet Celebration

Information
Penola–Coonawarra Visitor Information Centre, 27 Arthur St, Penola
T 08 8737 2855 **F** 08 8737 2251
W www.wattlerange.sa.gov.au or www.limestonecoast.com
Coonawarra Vignerons **T** 08 8737 2392
F 08 8737 2433
E cvacga@limestonecoast.net
W www.coonawarra.org

McLaren Vale

The Fleurieu Peninsula has a number of wine-producing areas, including Langhorne Creek and Currency Creek, but by far the most important, in terms of the scale and diversity of production, is McLaren Vale. This region was the site of some of the state's earliest vineyards, which were planted by John Reynell, an early English settler, in 1838. Reynell's success encouraged others to follow. A period of rapid growth occurred after 1845, when a number of prominent Adelaide doctors, including Dr Christopher Rawson Penfold, planted vineyards in the belief that the wine would aid the recovery of their patients. In 1861, two other doctors, a Dr Alexander and a Dr Kelly—who also believed in the medicinal properties of wine—formed the Tintara Vineyard on land that is now part of McLaren Vale. But the company failed to prosper and in 1876 was sold to another Englishman, Thomas Hardy, whose name, along with Dr Penfold's, has been synonymous with the Australian wine industry ever since.

In the late nineteenth century, a steadily increasing number of growers planted vines and developed winemaking and exporting businesses, while often relying on mixed farming for their living. By the early 1900s, McLaren Vale was established as a significant wine-producing area, known principally for its high-alcohol fortified red wines, which commanded strong sales in the United Kingdom. As occurred elsewhere in Australia, there was a lull in production during the Depression and the Second World War, but after the war another period of growth saw the

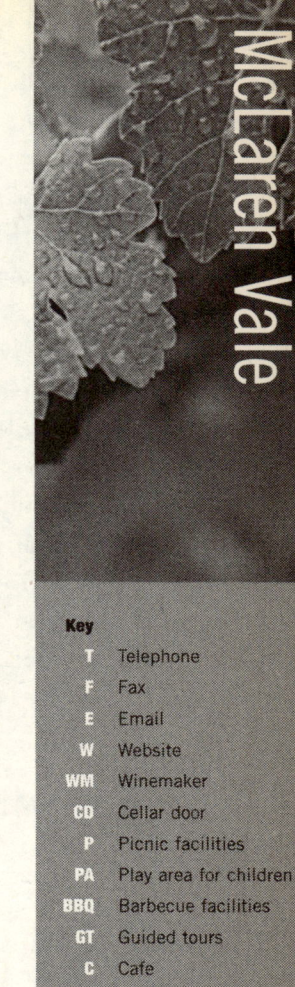

Key

T	Telephone
F	Fax
E	Email
W	Website
WM	Winemaker
CD	Cellar door
P	Picnic facilities
PA	Play area for children
BBQ	Barbecue facilities
GT	Guided tours
C	Cafe
R	Restaurant
O	Opening hours
B&B	Bed and breakfast
H	Hotel/Inn
M	Motel
G	Guesthouse
SCA	Self-catering accommodation

district, and in particular McLaren Vale, flourish again. However, it was not until Australian wine drinkers began to favour lighter styles of red and white wines in the 1960s and 1970s that the basis for today's hugely successful and diverse McLaren Vale wine industry was established. This was due in part to the introduction of a number of new grape varieties, including Chardonnay, Sauvignon Blanc, Merlot and others, all of which grew well in the region.

The McLaren Vale region runs from the outer southern suburbs of Adelaide in the north to Willunga in the south and from Kangarilla in the east to the coast of the Gulf of St Vincent in the west. The main towns in the area, apart from McLaren Vale itself, are Willunga and Aldinga Beach. The winegrowing area is large and climatically diverse, and has a great variety of aspects, elevations and soil types. All of this means that it can produce good wine from almost any grape variety. Because rainfall is low, irrigation is widely required, but the Onkaparinga River provides a ready source of water for this purpose.

What to buy

McLaren Vale is better known for its red wines than its whites. The main varieties have traditionally been Shiraz, Cabernet Sauvignon and Grenache, although Tempranillo, Merlot and Sangiovese have recently been gaining in popularity. Among the whites, Chardonnay, Semillon and Sauvignon Blanc have been prominent alongside Viognier and Marsanne.

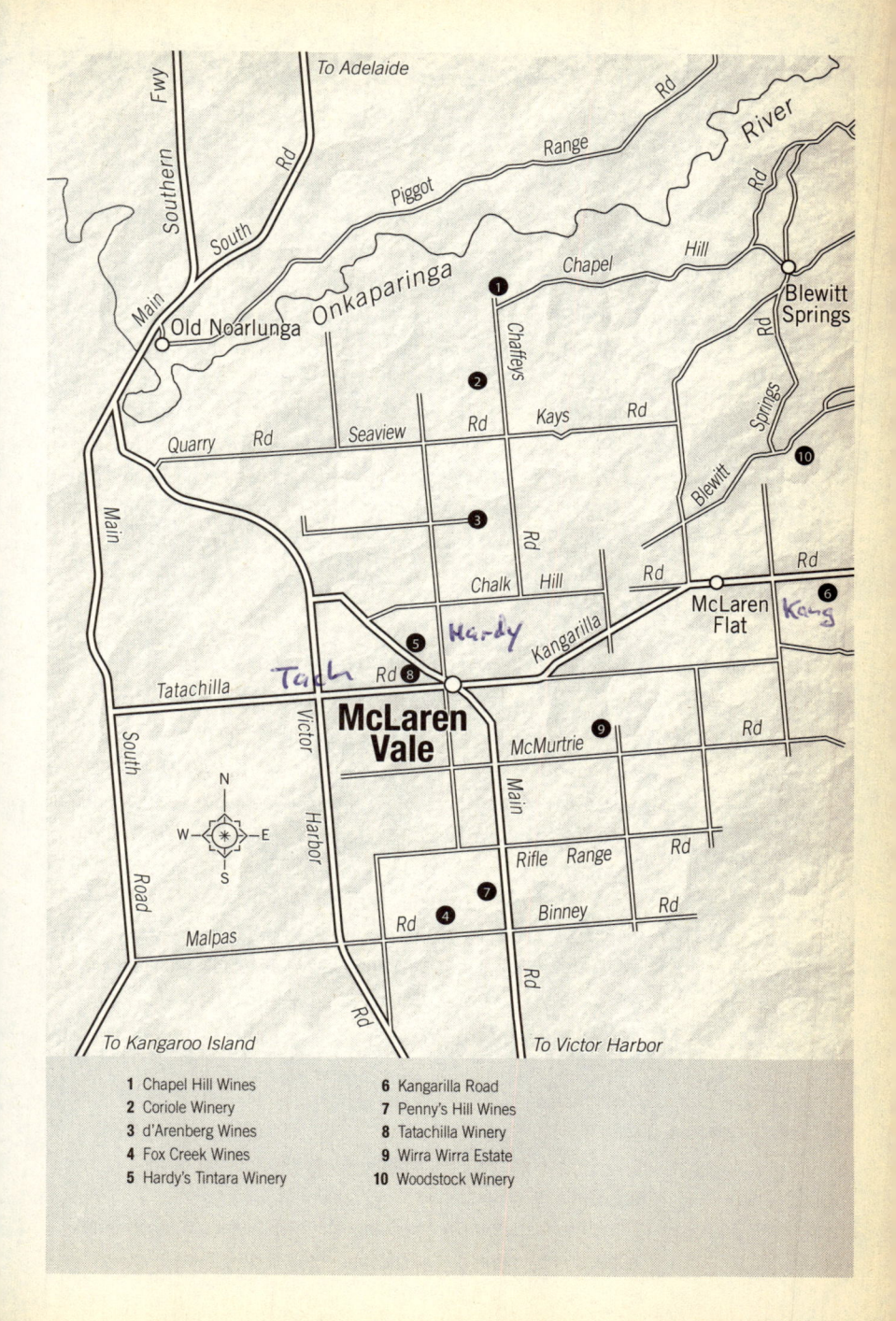

1 Chapel Hill Wines
2 Coriole Winery
3 d'Arenberg Wines
4 Fox Creek Wines
5 Hardy's Tintara Winery
6 Kangarilla Road
7 Penny's Hill Wines
8 Tatachilla Winery
9 Wirra Wirra Estate
10 Woodstock Winery

McLAREN VALE

Wineries

Chapel Hill

WM Pam Dunford, Michael Fragos, Angela Meaney
CD 12 noon–5 pm daily
P
G

Chapel Hill Road, McLaren Vale

T 08 8323 8429   **F** 08 8323 9245   **E** winery@chapelhillwine.com.au
W www.chapelhillwine.com.au

The wines here are good and reasonably priced. They include Unwooded and Reserve Chardonnay and Verdelho, and Shiraz, Cabernet Sauvignon and tawny port. The cellar door is located in the historic nineteenth-century stone church from which the winery takes its name. Perched on top of one of McLaren Vale's prettiest hills, it and the adjacent lawns enjoy an impressive panorama of the vineyards and the ocean. Buy some local produce from the cellar door and have a picnic with a view. The winery also has an attractive guesthouse (see Accommodation).

Coriole

WM Grant Harrison
CD 10 am–5 pm Mon–Fri, 11 am–5 pm weekends and public holidays

Chaffey's Rd, McLaren Vale

T 08 8323 8305   **F** 08 8323 9136

This innovative, small-scale winery has a growing reputation for quality. The reds are the go here and the range is interesting; it includes Shiraz (of course) and Cabernet Sauvignon but also Sangiovese, Merlot and, more recently, Nebbiolo and Barbera. Coriole also makes a Chenin Blanc, a Semillon and a Semillon Sauvignon Blanc blend. The tasting room is in an 1860s ironstone building set amid colourful gardens. The pleasant cafe serves lunchtime platters of Woodside cheeses (from the Adelaide Hills), local preserved meats, olives and pickled vegetables. Coriole even sells its own extra virgin cold-pressed olive oil. What more could you want?

d'Arenberg

WM Chester d'Arenberg Osborn
CD 10 am–5 pm daily
R

Osborn Rd, McLaren Vale

T 08 8323 8206   **F** 08 8323 8423   **E** winery@darenberg.com.au
W www.darenberg.com.au

The d'Arenberg Winery was established by the Milton family in the 1890s. The restored nineteenth-century homestead includes a cellar door and also houses the d'Arry's Verandah restaurant (see Food and Dining). The winery has a strong tradition of making robust wines and still produces excellent reds that typify the McLaren Vale style, as well as whites of high quality. Try the Dead Arm Shiraz if you can afford it, or the Laughing Magpie Shiraz Viognier blend.

Fox Creek Wines

Malpas Rd, Willunga

T 08 8556 2403 **F** 08 8556 2104 **E** sales@foxcreekwines.com
W www.foxcreekwines.com

Daniel Hills **WM**
10 am–5 pm daily **CD**

A modern winery founded by members of the medical profession, this one has enjoyed remarkable success, winning awards almost from day one, in 1984. It now markets varietal wines made with Shiraz, Cabernet Sauvignon and Merlot, as well as blends of Cabernet Sauvignon and Merlot (Duet), Shiraz and Cabernet Franc (JSM), Shiraz and Grenache, and sparkling Shiraz Cabernet Franc (Vixen). The white wines are Chardonnay, Sauvignon Blanc, Verdelho and Semillon Sauvignon Blanc. The reds, as you might expect, are big, flavoursome wines with plenty of tannin—ideal for cellaring.

Hardy's Tintara Winery

202 Main Rd, McLaren Vale

T 08 8323 9185 **F** 08 8329 4155
E mclarenvale_cellardoor@brlhardy.com.au
W www.hardys.com.au

Simon White, **WM**
Robert Mann (reds),
Philip Reschke
(whites)
10 am–4.40 pm **CD**
daily

In 1876, Thomas Hardy recognised the potential of the rich loamy soils of McLaren Vale and purchased the Tintara winery and vineyard. Two years later, the Mortlock Flour Mill was converted into a winery. Carefully restored, it is now the seat of Hardy's Tintara. The cellar door showcases all BRL Hardy wines. The Tintara range offers wines of character and complexity. Shiraz, including the famous Eileen Hardy Shiraz, Cabernet Sauvignon and Grenache make up the reds, Chardonnay and Sauvignon Blanc the whites; there is also a selection of fortified wines. An art gallery at the winery exhibits works by South Australian and other Australian artists.

Kangarilla Road Vineyard and Winery

WM Kevin O'Brien
CD 10 am–5 pm Mon–Fri, 11 am–5 pm weekends and public holidays

Kangarilla Rd, McLaren Vale

T 08 8383 0533   **F** 08 8383 0044   **E** kangarillaroad@bigpond.com

This small, family-owned winery is set in lovely countryside and is one of relatively few Australian wineries to grow Zinfandel (though the number is increasing). The resulting wine is a fresh, spicy light red—delicious when slightly chilled. Other varieties grown include Chardonnay, Viognier, Cabernet Sauvignon and Shiraz.

Penny's Hill Wines

WM Ben Riggs
CD 10 am–5 pm daily
C

Main Willunga Rd, McLaren Vale

T 08 8556 4460   **F** 08 8556 4462   **E** info@pennyshill.com.au
W www.pennyshill.com.au

Based in an imposing 1855 property called Ingleside, this is a newish (the first wines were produced in 1995), small-scale operation that has come a long way in a short time. The range includes Chardonnay, Semillon, Shiraz and Grenache, as well as a Botrytis Semillon, red blends and a port. The wines are available for tasting and sale, and visitors can lunch in the Red Dot cafe (see Food and Dining). There is also plenty of open space for kids to run around.

Tatachilla Winery

WM Michael Fragos, Justin McNamee
CD 10 am–5 pm Mon–Fri, 11 am–5 pm Sun and public holidays

151 Main Rd, McLaren Vale

T 08 8323 8656   **F** 08 8323 9096
E enquiries@tatachillawinery.com.au
W www.tatachillawinery.com.au

Tatachilla was established in 1901 and owned by Penfolds for much of its existence. It has changed hands several times in recent years, but has flourished since its acquisition by a local grower, Vic Zerella, and Keith Smith, formerly an executive with Kaiser Stuhl. In 2002, it became part of the Lion Nathan group. The winery makes a large range of wines from fruit sourced across South Australia, which offer top quality at reasonable prices. They include reds, whites and sparkling wines—unusually, they make a

Sparkling Malbec as well as a Pinot Noir NV. The Breakneck Creek budget range offers good value in varietals, including Chardonnay, Merlot, Cabernet Sauvignon and Shiraz. The excellent Foundation Shiraz is the flagship wine made exclusively from McLaren Vale fruit, though the Keystone Grenache Shiraz is regarded as a quintessential McLaren Vale style. The Partners range features the highly successful Merlot from the Clarendon vineyard. The whites include an excellent McLaren Vale Chardonnay, a dry, unwooded Growers Chenin Blanc Semillon Sauvignon Blanc, and a lightly oaked Chardonnay.

Wirra Wirra Estate

McMurtrie Rd, McLaren Vale
T 08 8323 8414   **F** 08 8323 8596   **E** info@wirra.com.au

Samantha Connew **WM**
10 am–5 pm daily **CD**
P
BBQ

The classic 1894 South Australian ironstone buildings that house this family-owned winery were extended in 2003 to provide an expanded cellar door facility. The whites have long been regarded as the best buy here, but nowadays the reds are equally good. The McLaren Vale Shiraz is popular, as are the Scrubby Rise blend of Shiraz, Cabernet Sauvignon and Petit Verdot and the Church Block blend of Cabernet Sauvignon, Shiraz and Merlot. Of the whites, the Chardonnay, Sauvignon Blanc, and the Semillon Sauvignon Blanc blend are the best options. Petanque balls can be borrowed if you feel like a little gentle exercise.

Woodstock Winery

Douglas Gully Rd, McLaren Vale
T 08 8383 0156   **F** 08 8383 0437
E woodstock@woodstockwine.com.au
W www.woodstockwine.com.au

Scott Collett **WM**
9 am–5 pm daily **CD**
R

Robust reds and stylish whites are made at this small, family-owned winery using Cabernet Sauvignon, Shiraz, Grenache, Chardonnay, Riesling and Semillon. Food platters are available every day and there is also a restaurant, the Coterie (see Food and Dining).

Wine tours and activities

Based in Adelaide, Integrity Tours and Charter operates a range of itineraries including winery tours in McLaren Vale that also take in wildlife centres and other places of interest nearby (**T** 08 8382 9755). Personalised tours of the wineries are also organised by McLaren Vale Tours, who will pick you up from local accommodation; small groups are a speciality (**T** 0414 784 666).

If, however, you think the only way to tour the wineries of McLaren Vale is by limo, Southern Spirit Tours are the people for you. By the hour or by the day, their chauffeured, seven-seater classic, an LTD V8, will carry you along the food and wine trail in roomy comfort (**T** 0407 223 361).

Food and Dining

The food here is good, plentiful and, on the whole, reasonably priced. High-quality local produce includes meat—veal, turkey and venison from local farms, seafood from the Gulf of St Vincent—olives, hazelnuts and almonds and fruit (checking out the roadside stalls in season is worthwhile).

Blessed Cheese at 150 Main St, McLaren Vale has a cafe (see below) but also a local-produce store and cheese shop. It specialises in what it describes as 'cheese and wine integration' courses, which involve matching the best regional, national and international cheeses to the wines of the McLaren Vale—a tough job but someone has to do it! Cheese and chocolate making classes are also offered (**T** 08 8323 7958).

McLaren Vale Olive Groves at Lot 34, Warners Rd, McLaren Vale, has become a local icon and is particularly renowned for its quality pickled olives. The olives are hand-picked and pickled in a traditional method without chemicals. The cellar door also sells a variety of gourmet foods, preserves and marinades as well as wine (**T** 08 8323 8792).

Mount Compass Venison is at 26 Main Road, Mount Compass, just past Willunga, and well worth a detour. It offers a range of fresh local venison, smallgoods, gourmet relishes, oils and fruit juices; you can also get a light lunch and good coffee (**T** 08 8556 8216   **E** compassvenison@bigpond.com **W** fleurieupeninsula.com.au/compassvenison).

Market 190, located right in the heart of McLaren Vale at 190 Main Road, McLaren Vale, provides quality gourmet foods made with the best local ingredients, including cheeses, oils, sauces, smallgoods, flowers and pastes (**T** 08 8323 8558   **F** 08 8323 7505   **E** wayne@market190.com.au   **W** www.market190.com.au).

Lunch options in McLaren Vale include some of the best winery cafes and restaurants in Australia, with most offering good value for money. In addition, there are several cafes that provide simple lunches, and picnic places are not hard to find.

Blessed Cheese, 150 Main St, McLaren Vale   **T** 08 8323 7958. Something of a local institution, this brightly painted cafe offers some of the best light meals, lunches and organic coffee in McLaren Vale. There are gourmet baguettes filled with local produce, as well as focaccias and cheese platters, and a range of cakes— wedding cakes are a speciality.

The Coterie, Woodstock Winery, Douglas Gully Rd, McLaren Vale   **T** 08 8383 0156 **F** 08 8383 0437   **O** 9 am–5 pm Mon–Sat, 12 pm–5 pm Sun and public holidays. Regional platters and 'shared plates', which include dips, smoked meats, pates, cheeses and sundried tomatoes, are available all day, and lunch specials are available from midday. The latter include hearty soups and main courses such as kangaroo and red wine pie, venison sausages on potato with Swiss brown mushrooms, and flathead and chips.

d'Arry's Verandah Restaurant, d'Arenberg Vineyard and Winery, Osborn Rd, McLaren Vale   **T** 08 8323 8710   **F** 08 8323 8423   **E** winery@darenberg.com.au **W** www.darenberg.com.au   **O** 12 pm–5 pm daily Oct–Easter, Wed–Sun only Easter–Sept. The restaurant overlooks McLaren Vale and the Willunga Escarpment, so the views are sublime. The food is of a consistently high standard and uses plenty of local produce. As well as local meat and game, Asian influenced dishes such as Normanville roast lamb, crispy-skinned grain-fed chicken, scallops with wakame salad, and baked snapper with Jerusalem artichokes all grace the menu. Several fabulous desserts are available every day.

Limeburner's Restaurant, Marienberg Winery, McLaren Vale   **T** 08 8323 8599 **O** From 12 noon for lunch and dinner daily. Limeburner's is a stylish restaurant serving modern Australian cuisine made with locally sourced produce. Lemon pepper kangaroo in an Asian salad, Mount Compass venison and Aldinga turkey have all appeared on the seasonally changing menu. There are also vegetarian pasta dishes, seafood and desserts to complement the extensive wines from Marienberg itself and from other McLaren Vale wineries, most of which are available by the glass. The terrace is opened up to the sun in fine weather. A lovely place to eat.

Red Dot Cafe, Penny's Hill Wines, Main Willunga Rd, McLaren Vale **T** 08 8556 4460 **F** 08 8556 4462 **E** info@pennyshill.com.au **W** www.pennyshill.com.au **O** 10 am–4.30 pm daily, 12 pm–3 pm for lunch. In the Gedney Room, Red Dot Cafe's tapas-style seasonal menu allows you to try a selection of dishes, many of which are made with local produce. Sample the dips with McLaren Vale olive oil and dukkah, steamed asparagus with soft poached egg and shaved Romano cheese, arancini—saffron risotto balls stuffed with bocconcini—or marinated grilled quail with preserved, lime-scented couscous. Desserts include a Fleurieu cheese plate with Kangaroo Island Brie.

Salopian Inn, cnr McMurtrie and Willunga Rds, McLaren Vale **T** 08 8323 8769 **O** From 12 noon Thurs–Tues for lunch, from 7 pm Fri–Sat for dinner. An iconic restaurant with a legendary wine list, the Salopian Inn offers a diverse modern menu that uses local produce whenever possible and provides good value. Wines are available by the glass, or you can choose a bottle from the extensive collection, literally by descending into the cellars of this amazing old property. Dishes include local yabbie and scallop mille-feuille, carpaccio of Onkaparinga Valley venison, Fleurieu pork with caramelised apple and walnuts, local oysters and Coorong beef. There are also vegetarian options, salads and scrumptious desserts.

Accommodation

Chapel Hill Winery Guest House, Chapel Hill Road, McLaren Vale **T** 08 8323 8429 **F** 08 8323 9245 **E** winery@chapelhillwine.com.au **W** www.chapelhillwine.com.au. This two-storey, airconditioned chalet guesthouse is set in the vineyards, a short walk from the winery and cellar door. It has fabulous views of the Onkaparinga River National Park and the Gulf of St Vincent, as well as luxurious accommodation with a fully equipped kitchen (with dishwasher and microwave), outdoor barbecue area, spacious living/entertaining areas with open fireplace, television, DVD/VCR and CD, two queen-sized bedrooms with ensuites, and two twin bedrooms with a large shared bathroom. Full breakfast provisions are included.

McLarens on the Lake Motel and Restaurant, Kangarilla Road, McLaren Vale **T** 08 8323 8911 **F** 08 8323 9010 **E** edward@mclarensonthelake.com.au. McLaren's offers luxurious accommodation in a picturesque setting. The lake (complete with resident ducks and geese), stately gums and surrounding lawns also make the motel an ideal venue for picnics, weddings and functions. A restaurant and a courtyard cafe complete the picture.

McLaren Ridge Log Cabins, Lot 2, Whitings Rd, McLaren Flat **T** 08 8383 0504 **E** mclaren@chariot.net.au **W** www.mclarenridge.com. The accommodation here consists of two unusual, luxuriously appointed, hexagonal cabins situated on a secluded vineyard property, with great views over the Southern Vales. Sleeping up to six people, the cabins are comfortable and well equipped: the kitchens include microwave ovens, the bedrooms are airconditioned, the living areas have a TV, video player and CD player, and there are outside tables and a barbecue.

Travel Information

How to get there
By road McLaren Vale is only 35 km from the centre of Adelaide, a mere half-hour drive. Take the A13 Main South Road via Morphett Vale towards Willunga.

Other attractions
The South Australian Whale Centre in Railway Terrace, Victor Harbor, houses fascinating presentations spread over three floors on the life of cetaceans and other creatures—including sea lions and penguins—and whale-watching (**T** 08 8552 5644 or 1900 931 223 **F** 08 8552 5142 **E** info@sawhalecentre.com **O** 11 am–4.30 pm). Onkaparinga National Park offers delightful scenery and invigorating walks for all levels of ability: the Echidna Trail is comparatively easy, but the Nature Trail is for fit and experienced bushwalkers only (**T** 08 8278 5477).

For kids
If you want a day packed full of fun and adventure, try Greenhills Adventure Park in Waggon Rd, Victor Harbor, where activities range from golf and go-karts to waterslides and archery. You can easily spend a whole day here—and the kids will think you're a legend (**T** 08 8552 5999 **F** 08 8552 5001 **E** sally@greenhills.com.au **W** www.greenhills.com.au).
For a more tranquil experience, visit Urimbirra Wildlife Experience on Adelaide Rd, Victor Harbor. Set on 16 landscaped hectares of the Hindmarsh Valley, it is home to more than 400 native species, including birds, mammals and reptiles (**T** 08 8554 6554 **E** urimbirra@fleurieupeninsula.com.au).

Events
June: Sea and Vines Festival (food and wine festival, with events at numerous wineries)

Information
McLaren Vale and Fleurieu Visitor Centre, Main Rd, McLaren Vale
T 08 8323 9944 **F** 08 8323 9949
E information@visitorcentre.com.au
W www.fleurieupeninsula.com.au

Tasmania

Northern Tasmania

Tasmanian wine was first produced in 1823 and gained international recognition when it won awards at the Paris Wine Show of 1848. However, due to a lack of skilled labour and a perception that there was a limited market for its products, the industry went into decline soon after and virtually ceased to exist for a century.

A revival began in the 1950s. In Northern Tasmania, Jean Miguet, a Frenchman, established a vineyard at Lalla in the Tamar Valley, which would become Providence Vineyard. More vine planting took place in the 1960s and in the early 1970s Dr Andrew Pirie started his pioneering work at Pipers Brook on the eastern side of the Tamar. His belief that the soil and climate were suited to growing a wide range of (particularly white) grapes was borne out by his subsequent success. Pipers Brook evolved into several thriving businesses that extended vine cultivation to other parts of the Tamar Valley and eventually took over a number of other businesses including Jansz and Heemskerk. Some wineries have become part of national or international wine companies, but the majority of vineyards in the region are still small and family-owned, with most measuring less than 5 ha.

The region is split into two main areas: the west bank of the Tamar Valley to the north of Launceston, where many vineyards almost reach the water's edge, and the Piper's Brook area to the east of the Tamar, which includes Lilydale and Lebrina and is higher and cooler.

This distribution means that a circuit tour can be planned in either direction. However,

Key

T	Telephone
F	Fax
E	Email
W	Website
WM	Winemaker
CD	Cellar door
P	Picnic facilities
PA	Play area for children
BBQ	Barbecue facilities
GT	Guided tours
C	Cafe
R	Restaurant
O	Opening hours
B&B	Bed and breakfast
H	Hotel/Inn
M	Motel
G	Guesthouse
SCA	Self-catering accommodation

heading north from Launceston along the A7 is recommended as the views over the river from several of the cellar doors are magnificent. The route is well signposted and takes you over the Batman Bridge to Bell Bay, Pipers River, Lalla and Lilydale.

What to buy

Northern Tasmania is justly famous for its cool-climate wines—principally white wines including Sauvignon Blanc and Chardonnay as well as the Alsace trio of Riesling, Pinot Gris and Gewurztraminer. Riesling in particular has been gaining in popularity and has scored some notable successes. Some of Northern Tasmania's Pinot Noirs are outstanding, and Cabernet Sauvigon and Petit Verdot are grown successfully in warmer areas. Sparkling wines represent around 20 per cent of production in Tasmania and are a speciality at a number of wineries, among them Clover Hill and Pipers Brook.

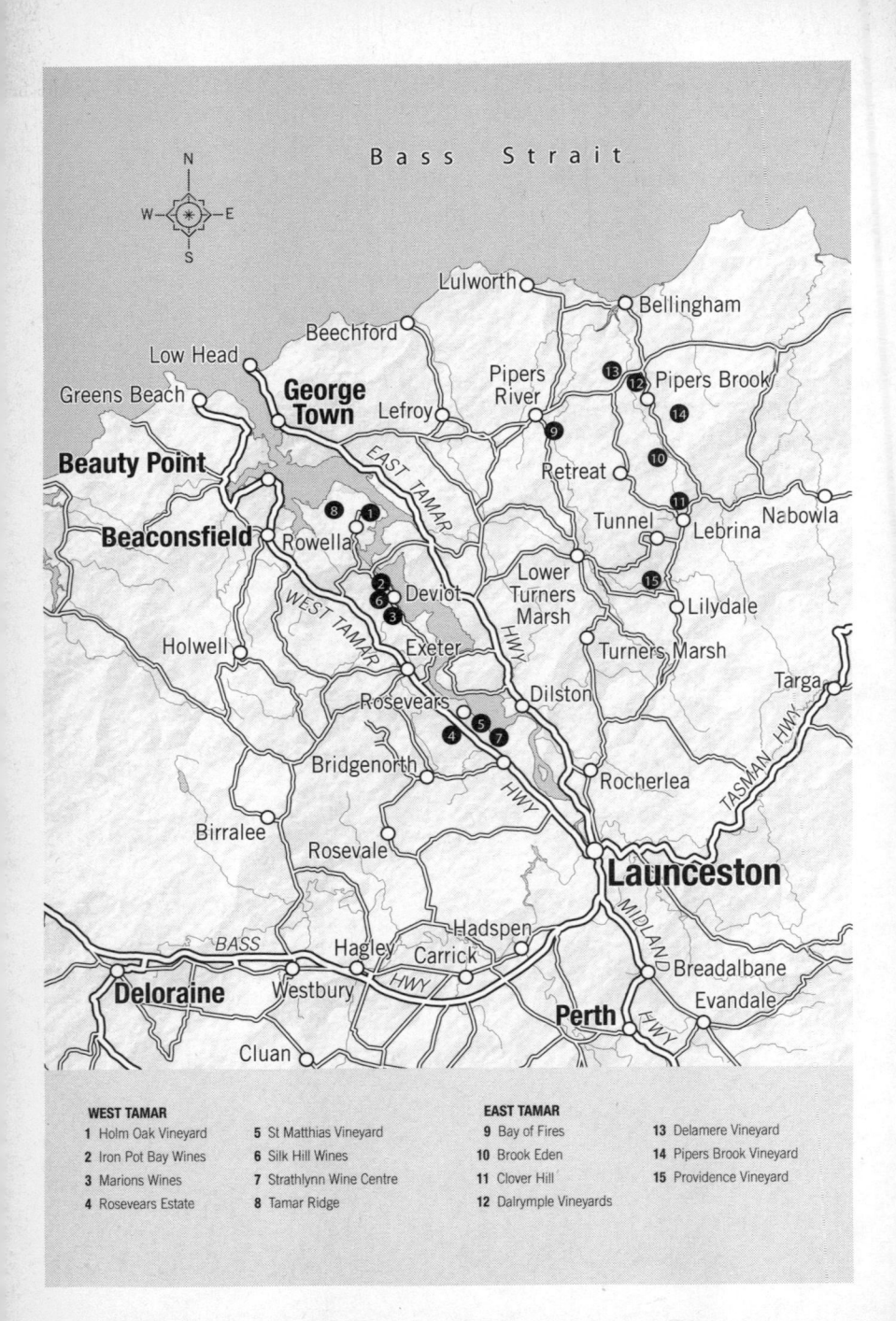

WEST TAMAR
1. Holm Oak Vineyard
2. Iron Pot Bay Wines
3. Marions Wines
4. Rosevears Estate
5. St Matthias Vineyard
6. Silk Hill Wines
7. Strathlynn Wine Centre
8. Tamar Ridge

EAST TAMAR
9. Bay of Fires
10. Brook Eden
11. Clover Hill
12. Dalrymple Vineyards
13. Delamere Vineyard
14. Pipers Brook Vineyard
15. Providence Vineyard

Wineries

West Tamar

Holm Oak Vineyard

11 West Bay Rd, Rowella

T 03 6394 7577 **E** holmoak@southcom.com

Full-bodied and flavoursome Riesling, Pinot Noir and Cabernet are the pick here, with Chardonnay and a rosé also available.

Nicholas Butler
10 am–5 pm daily
Oct–June, restricted hours during winter months

WM
CD

Iron Pot Bay Wines

766 Deviot Rd, Deviot

T 03 6394 7320 **F** 03 6394 7346 **E** retreat@bigpond.com.au
W www.ironpotbay.com.au

Only white wines are made from the grapes grown in this small maritime-influenced vineyard on the banks of the Tamar. The wines include Chardonnay, Pinot Grigio, Traminer, Semillon and Sauvignon Blanc, and offer distinctive and delicate flavours. Visitors can also taste a selection of Northern Tasmanian cheeses. The winery is located right by the Batman Bridge and the picnic area has lovely views over the river.

Dr Andrew Pirie
11 am–5 pm
Sep–May, Jun–Aug by appointment

WM
CD
P

Marions Vineyard

361 Foreshore Drive, Deviot

T 03 6394 7434 **F** 03 6394 7050 **E** marions@netspace.net.au

A small winery set in a beautiful riverside vineyard, with gardens and olive groves, Marions produces a diverse range of estate wines ranging from Chardonnay, Pinot Gris and Viognier to Cabernet Merlot, Cabernet Sauvignon, Pinot Noir and Zinfandel. It is claimed to be one of the best locations for ripening Cabernet in West Tamar. A casual Mediterranean-style restaurant is open daily in the season (Oct–May) and moderately priced chalet accommodation is available if it's just too hard to leave (though booking ahead is recommended). The winery also hosts a steady stream of conventions and weddings.

Mark Semmlers
10 am–5 pm daily

WM
CD
P
BBQ
R
SCA

Rosevears Estate

WM Dr Andrew Pirie
CD 10 am–5 pm daily
P
R
G
SCA

1A Waldhorn Drive, Rosevears

T 03 6330 1800 **F** 03 6330 1810 **E** rosevearsestate@bigpond.com
W www.rosevearsestate.com.au

Overlooking the Tamar River, this stylish modern winery (with restaurant) is well worth a visit. It produces a range of white and red wines, both still and sparkling. Try the Rosevears Estate Pinot Noir, Pinot Noir Rosé and Estate Riesling. There are pleasant picnic spots overlooking the river and accommodation is available in stylish chalets, whose log fires are a real bonus in winter. The owners also operate Iron Pot Bay Wines, located just down the road near the Batman Bridge, which is also open all year.

St Matthias Vineyard

WM Michael Glover
CD 10 am–5 pm daily
BBQ

113 Rosevears Drive, Rosevears

T 03 6330 1700 **F** 03 6330 1975

Owned by one of the pioneers of the modern Tasmanian wine industry, Moorilla Estate (see Southern Tasmania), this vineyard enjoys sweeping views over the Tamar River. Sample the prize-winning St Matthias Cabernet Merlot blend, but also the Riesling, Chardonnay and Pinot Noir. Gourmet barbecue lunches are available on Sundays during summer, accompanied by a jazz band.

Silk Hill Wines

WM Gavin Scott
CD By appointment

324 Motor Rd, Deviot

T 03 6394 7385 or 0400 418 163 **F** 03 6326 2350

Enthusiast Gavin Scott makes some of Tasmania's best Pinot Noir as well as a dry rosé in the French style, but both are available only in small volumes.

Strathlynn Wine Centre and Restaurant

WM René Bezemer
CD 10 am–5 pm daily

95 Rosevears Drive, Rosevears

T 03 6330 2388 **F** 03 6330 2599 **E** strathlynn@pipersbrook.com
W www.valleyofthesenses.com

This spectacularly located riverside vineyard has a fine restaurant (see Food and Dining) and acts as a tasting centre for the Strathlynn, Pipers Brook and Ninth Island estates. The wines are well made and for the most part well priced. The cellar door and gift shop sell the wines and a number of accessories, and often display some terrific local Tasmanian crafts.

Tamar Ridge

Auburn Rd, Kayena

T 03 6394 1111 **F** 03 6394 1126 **E** info@tamarridgewines.com.au
W www.tamarridgewines.com.au

Michael Fogarty **WM**
10 am–5 pm daily **CD**

Originally called Rochecombe, this winery was renamed and revived by Josef Chromy, a meat wholesaler with a passion for wine. Now owned by Gunns, the logging and agribusiness group, it is one of the largest vineyards in Tasmania and the company has ambitious plans for further expansion. The range of wines is extensive, with whites predominant, and of consistently high quality. The whites include Riesling, Chardonnay, Pinot Gris, Gewurztraminer, Sauvignon Blanc, a notable Blanc de Noir, a sparkling wine and a Botrytis Riesling Sauvignon Blanc blend. The reds are Cabernet Sauvignon, Pinot Noir and Merlot, the first of which is especially impressive.

East Tamar

Bay of Fires

40 Baxters Rd, Pipers River

T 03 6382 7622 **F** 03 6382 7225 **E** bayoffires@brlhardy.com.au
W www.brlhardy.com.au

Francine Austin **WM**
10 am–5 pm daily **CD**
P
PA

The small vineyard was originally planted by the Roche family, and for some years was owned by Pipers Brook; it is now part of the BRL Hardy Group. The range includes a sparkling wine (Arras), Bay of Fires Chardonnay, a Pinot Gris that is in high demand, Sauvignon Blanc, and Riesling. Also available are two Pinot Noirs and a Pinot Rosé. The grounds are pleasantly situated in a scenic spot close to the Pipers River, and the extensive lawns are ideal for picnics.

Brook Eden

167 Adams Rd, Lebrina

T 03 6395 6244 **E** jojobowen@bigpond.com

Mike Fogarty **WM**
(contract)
10 am–5 pm daily **CD**

Part of a cattle property, this is another small, family-owned vineyard. As well as the premium Riesling, Chardonnay and Pinot Noir, you should sample the delicious Ashgrove Farm handmade cheeses.

Clover Hill

WM Leigh Clarnette
CD 10 am–5 pm daily
Sept–June
P

60 Clover Hill Rd, Lebrina
T 03 6395 6114 **F** 03 6395 6257 **E** cloverhill@vision.net.au
W taltarni.com.au

Clover Hill was established by Taltarni in the mid-1980s as a specialist sparkling wine producer and has a sister winery at Lalla Gully a few kilometres to the south. The wine is terrific and the picnic facilities on a deck overlooking Bass Strait enjoy one of the best views in Tasmania. Think of something to celebrate here!

Dalrymple Vineyards

WM Bert Sundstrup
CD 10 am–5 pm daily

Pipers Brook Rd, Pipers Brook
T/F 03 6382 7222 **E** dalrymplewine@microtech.com.au
W www.dalrymplevineyards.com.au

High-quality wines (award-winning Sauvignon Blanc, wooded and unwooded Chardonnay and Pinot Noir) are available at reasonable prices at this small winery set in pretty countryside. The cellar door overlooks the vine-covered hillside—and an old red telephone box!

Delamere Vineyard

WM Richard Richardson
CD 10 am–5 pm daily

4238 Bridport Rd, Pipers Brook
T 03 6382 7222 **E** dalrymple@microtech.com.au

Take in the serene vineyard views over this family-owned estate from the cellar door and taste the award-winning still and sparkling wines, which include Chardonnay, Pinot Noir and Sauvignon Blanc. The Delamere Vineyard Reserve Pinot Noir is a standout.

Pipers Brook Vineyard

WM René Bezemer
CD 10 am–5 pm daily
GT 11 am, 3 pm
Oct–Apr
C
G

1216 Pipers Brook Rd, Pipers Brook
T 03 6382 7527 **F** 03 6334 9112 **E** cellardoor@pbv.com.au
W www.pbv.com.au

This winery was founded in 1974 by the pioneering Dr Andrew Pirie, but was taken over by the Belgian company Kreglinger, not long after which Dr Pirie departed. The striking, architect-designed building is set within rolling vineyards. The wines are highly regarded, especially the flagship Pinot Noir, Chardonnay and Riesling. The Pirie Cuvee sparkling is top quality and priced accordingly. The gift shop in the tasting area stocks a good range of accessories and cards. A second label, Ninth Island, has a reputation for providing excellent value for money. Its Pinot Noir and Pinot Grigio are good examples, as is the soft, rich Tamar Blend. Located a few kilometres to the south, the Ninth Island Vineyard has a children's playground and picnic area.

Providence Vineyards
236 Lalla Rd, Lalla
T 03 6395 1290 **F** 03 6395 2088 **E** info@providence-vineyards.com.au **W** www.providence-vineyards.com.au

Andrew Hood **WM**
(contract)
10 am–5 pm daily **CD**
P

One of Tasmania's older vineyards, established by Frenchman Jean Miguet in 1956, Providence is set in beautiful country outside Lalla. Chardonnay, Riesling and Pinot Noir (one of Tasmania's finest) predominate here, but the dessert Semillon is worthy of consideration and verjuice is also a speciality. You can taste a range of products from other wineries here, so if your time is limited you may want to make this your first stop. Providence also ships wine anywhere in Australia at moderate cost.

Wine tours and activities

Valleybrook Wine Tours in Launceston offers winery tours in air-conditioned comfort; tours and pick-ups can be arranged to suit your needs (**T** 03 6334 0586 or 0400 037 250 **E** info@valleybrook.com.au **W** www.valleybrook.com.au). The Bench Mark Tasmania Wine Gallery, at 135 Paterson St, Launceston, not only sells wine magazines and a wide range of Tasmanian, mainland and international wines, but also offers advice on touring the local wineries (**T** 03 6331 3977). Pindari Cellars, at 137 Wellington St, Launceston, is a superior kind of wine merchants, carrying almost 1,000 wines, many of them local favourites (**T** 03 6334 3244).

Food and Dining

Tasmania produces a huge range of gourmet foods, including seafood, smoked meats and cheeses, and this area is no exception. Restaurants range from modest to outstanding, with many serving fresh local produce whenever possible. At 2 Bridge St, Launceston, the Mill Providore and Gallery in Richies Mill sells a range of local gourmet produce (T 03 6331 0777). The Pyengana Dairy Company's cheese factory, at St Columba Falls Rd, 26 km out of St Helens, is well worth a visit (T 03 6373 6157). You can tour the factory to see cheese being made and buy freshly made produce at the cafe. The varieties range from traditional cheddar styles and washed rind cheeses to a truffled cheese—made with Tasmanian truffles, of course.

There is a Swiss flavour to a number of enterprises in Tasmania, the famous Grindelwald resort outside Launceston being but one example, so perhaps not surprisingly a number of specialist chocolate makers are thriving. They include the Swiss Chocolatier at 82 George St, Launceston (T 03 6334 3411), and d'Anvers Chocolates at 12 The Hub Arcade, Devonport (T 03 6424 3068).

The Exeter Markets take place at Exeter's Launceston Showground every second Sunday of the month.

West Tamar and Launceston

Fee & Me, cnr Charles and Frederick Sts, Launceston T 03 6331 3195 F 03 6331 1617 E info@feeandme.com.au W www.feeandme.com.au O 7 pm–late Tues–Sat. Fiona Hoskin and Peter Crowe's multi-award-winning restaurant has become a landmark in Launceston's dining scene. Seafood is featured as well as locally reared meat and poultry. Entrée-sized portions can be mixed and matched. A succinct wine list complements the menu; alternatively, you can order dishes matched with wines by the glass. Don't miss out—and make sure you book ahead.

Rosevears Waterfront Tavern Hotel, 215 Rosevears Dr, Rosevears T 03 6394 4074. A superbly sited pub with a welcoming dining room, Rosevears serves above-average fare, including seafoood, to guests and the hungry hordes.

Stillwater River Cafe, Richies Mill, Patterson St, Launceston T 03 6396 4153 F 03 6331 2325 E stillwater@microtech.com.au W www.stillwater.net.au

O 8.30 am–late daily. This stylish, casual cafe and restaurant on the waterfront serves daily specials using fresh local produce, especially seafood and game. The degustation menu is highly recommended. The courtyard area and river deck are ideal for summer dining and Cataract Gorge is close by if you need a bit of gentle exercise afterwards.

Strathlynn, Strathlynn Wine Centre, 95 Rosevears Rd, Rosevears **T** 03 6330 2388 **F** 03 6330 2599 **O** 12 noon–3 pm. Daniel Alps' restaurant showcases the best of Tasmanian produce in its modern Australian à la carte menu and seasonal specials—the venison, beef and seafood are all excellent. The deck and the restaurant have spectacular views up the Tamar.

East Tamar

Pipers Brook Winery Cafe, 1216 Pipers Brook Rd, Pipers Brook **T** 03 6382 7527 **F** 03 6334 9112. Lunches, morning and afternoon teas are available in this small but pleasant cafe, which has a sunny central courtyard. There are daily specials and you can buy wines by the glass or bottle.

Accommodation

West Tamar

Conmel Cottage, 125 Rosevears Drive, Rosevears **T/F** 03 6330 1466 **E** conmel.cottage@bigpond.net.au. This charming and comfortable modern cottage is set back from the road and overlooks vineyards and the river. It has a well-equipped kitchen and a beautifully kept herb garden that visitors are encouraged to use when cooking. Generous breakfast provisions are included in the tariff.

Tamar House, 85 Rosevears Dr, Rosevears **T** 03 6330 1744 **F** 03 6330 2035 **E** info@tamarhouse.com **W** www.tamarhouse.com.au. Set amid gardens and orchards on the banks of the river of the same name, just 15 minutes from Launceston, Tamar House has comfortable suites with bathrooms and cooking facilities.

Tamar River Retreat, 123 Kayena Rd, Kayena (16 km north-east of Exeter) **T/F** 03 6394 7030 **E** info@tamarriverretreat.com.au **W** www.tamarriverretreat.com.au. Enjoy the fabulous views, fish from the jetty or just take a ramble along the riverside. Simple, home-cooked evening meals are available. The accommodation is conveniently situated for visiting several local wineries.

East Tamar

Pipers Brook, 1216 Pipers Brook Rd, Pipers Brook **T** 03 6382 7527 **F** 03 6334 9112 **W** www.cottage@pbv.com.au. Cottage accommodation is available at this renowned estate (see Wineries).

Plovers Ridge Country Retreat, 132 Lalla Rd, Lilydale **T** 03 6395 1102. The retreat is situated on a 30-acre property on the edge of Lilydale (just up the road from Providence Vineyard) where the owners grow organic garlic. It has a self-contained unit and a self-contained guest room in one wing of the homestead, which enjoys great views over the Lilydale Valley. The facilities are good and meals can be provided if arranged in advance.

Travel Information

How to get there
By road The region is 3–4 hours from Hobart via the Midland Hwy and only a 20–30 minute drive north of Launceston.
By air Qantas, Jetstar and Virgin Blue all fly direct to Launceston from Melbourne (40 minutes); direct flights are also available in season from Sydney (1 hour 40 minutes). Rex Regional Express flies daily from Melbourne direct to Devonport and Burnie.
By sea The *Spirit of Tasmania I* and *II* car ferries sail from Melbourne to Devonport (departing at 9 pm and arriving at 7 am). The *Spirit of Tasmania III* sails for Devonport from Sydney three times a week (departing at 4 pm on Fri, 5 pm on Sun, 6 pm on Tues), taking around 20 hours to complete the journey; the ferry has cabin and hostel-style accommodation and a wide range of on-board activities and entertainment.

Other attractions
The Waterbird Haven Trust near Rosevears protects half a kilometre of Tamar River waterfront, home to a remarkable collection of native and exotic waterbirds; it also offers bed and breakfast accommodation (**T** 03 6394 4087).

Don't miss the Tasmanian Chairlift, a spectacular ride over the scenically splendid Cataract Gorge and Reserve on the Esk River (**T** 03 6331 5915). You should also explore the Cliff Grounds and enjoy a snack at the restaurant.

About 70 species of lavender flower amid enchanting gardens at Lavender House, Rowella, which also has a gift shop and tearoom (**T** 03 6394 7559). Further afield, the Bridestowe Estate Lavender Farm at Nabowla, near Scottsdale, occupies a stunning setting (**T** 03 6352 8182).

For kids
Penny Royal World in Paterson St, Launceston, has recreations of historic buildings, an underground barge ride and a tram ride, but the highlight is an old-fashioned lolly factory and shop (**T** 03 6331 6699). Kids and adults can test their putting skills at Krazy Putt, at 361 Gravelly Beach Rd, Gravelly Beach (**T** 03 6394 4243), and test their sense of direction at Glengarry Bush Maze, Jaydee Rd, Glengarry (**T/F** 03 6396 1250). Grubb Shaft Gold and Heritage Museum, at West St, Beaconsfield, has interactive displays, working models of mining machinery and barbecue and picnic facilities (**T** 03 6383 1473).

Thousands of delightful seahorses can be viewed on tours run by Seahorse World, which depart every half hour from Shed 1A, Inspection Head Wharf, Beauty Point (**T** 03 6383 4111). You can also take a close look at wild seals during glass-bottomed-boat tours around Tenth Island with Seal and Sea Seal Adventure Tours (**T** 0419357 or 0418 133 179) and watch fairy penguins wend their way home with Fairy Penguin Twilight Tours, Low Head Rd, Low Head (**T** 0418 361 860). Wear some warm clothes as the breezes can be very chilly.

Events
Jan: Tasmanian Wine Show, Launceston
Feb–Mar: Festival of the Senses, including Festivale, Launceston's 3-day food, wine and entertainment festival
Mar: Mercury Northern Vineyards Open Weekend

Information
Launceston Travel and Information Centre, Cornwall Sq, 12–16 St John St, Launceston **T** 03 6336 3133 or 1800 651 827

Southern Tasmania

Southern Tasmania's wine industry got off to a promising start, when in 1823 a wine made by Bartholomew Broughton from grapes grown at New Town in Hobart won a prize at the Paris Wine Show. But it then went into decline. A number of German emigrants fleeing religious persecution in Silesia planted vines near present day Swansea in the 1830s; the vines thrived and some still produce grapes, but production was on a very small scale. The very cool climate and the perceived lack of a market for wines meant that few were willing to test the waters again until the 1950s. In that period, Claudio Alcorso, an Italian textile manufacturer and art enthusiast, planted grapes in the Derwent Valley at what was to become Moorilla Estate, encouraging others to follow. Careful viticulture and canny experimentation with selected grape varieties in various soils produced rewarding results, and there was growing recognition that the wide fertile valleys north and south of Hobart, in particular, provided good opportunities to grow Pinot Noir, Pinot Gris, Riesling and Gewurztraminer, among others. Recently, there has been steady growth, with the quality of the wines improving dramatically, particularly in the last five years or so.

The region is divided into three main subregions, with somewhat different climates. The Huon Valley is extremely cool, though with a moderating maritime influence. The Coal and Derwent valleys have a more continental climate with winter frosts and higher summer temperatures. The East Coast enjoys warmer weather and better ripening conditions.

Key

T	Telephone
F	Fax
E	Email
W	Website
WM	Winemaker
CD	Cellar door
P	Picnic facilities
PA	Play area for children
BBQ	Barbecue facilities
GT	Guided tours
C	Cafe
R	Restaurant
O	Opening hours
B&B	Bed and breakfast
H	Hotel/Inn
M	Motel
G	Guesthouse
SCA	Self-catering accommodation

What to buy

Elegant whites with subtle flavours, distinctive sparkling wines and some delicious light reds are the best buys. Gewurztraminer, Riesling and Pinot Gris are sometimes cited as the white varieties most suited to the climatic conditions, but Sauvignon Blanc, Sylvaner, Chardonnay, Pinot Noir and even Cabernet Sauvignon also provide surprisingly good results. Coal Valley produces some lean and subtle Chardonnays and Rieslings, but there is Cabernet, Pinot Noir and Merlot here as well. The East Coast has produced good Cabernet Sauvignon (unusual in Tasmania) and some of the best Pinot Noirs in the country.

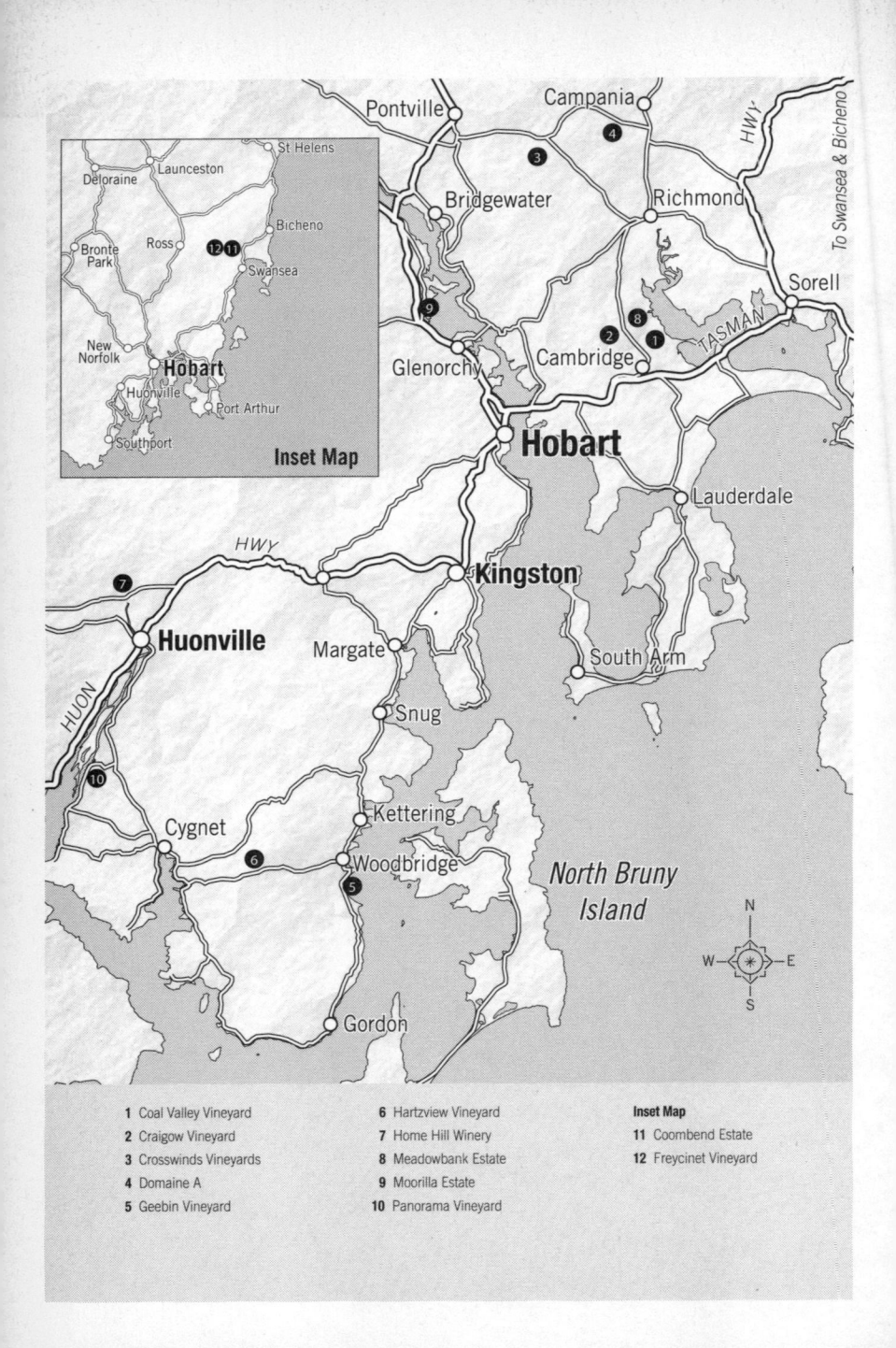

1 Coal Valley Vineyard	**6** Hartzview Vineyard	**Inset Map**
2 Craigow Vineyard	**7** Home Hill Winery	**11** Coombend Estate
3 Crosswinds Vineyards	**8** Meadowbank Estate	**12** Freycinet Vineyard
4 Domaine A	**9** Moorilla Estate	
5 Geebin Vineyard	**10** Panorama Vineyard	

164 AUSTRALIA'S BEST WINE TOURS

Wineries

Coal and Derwent Valleys

Coal Valley Vineyard

257 Richmond Rd, Cambridge
T 03 6248 5367   **F** 03 6248 4175   **E** coalvalley@bigpond.com.au
W www.coalvalley.com.au

Andrew Hood **WM**
(contract)
CD
R

The winery enjoys stunning views over the Coal River and Barilla Bay. The newly renovated restaurant is likely to be a winner, with its emphasis on fresh local produce. The wines are superb: Coal Valley Pinot Noir is a prizewinner and the Cabernet Merlot, Riesling and Chardonnay are also of a high standard.

Craigow Vineyard

528 Richmond Rd, Cambridge
T 03 6248 5379   **F** 03 6248 5482   **E** info@craigow.com.au
W www.craigow.com.au

Julian Alcorso **WM**
11 am–5 pm daily **CD**
between Christmas
and Easter,
11 am–4 pm
weekends only
in winter

This is a small operation but was one of the first to be established in the Coal Valley area, and the wines—mainly Riesling (including a botrytis), Gewurztraminer, Pinot Noir and a little Chardonnay—are very good indeed. The cellar door is in an old and very cute workman's cottage with lovely views over vineyards and valley. Cheese platters and coffee are available with tastings. The wines are sold at other wine centres and are also available by mail order.

Crosswinds Vineyard

10 Vineyard Dr, Tea Tree
T/F 03 6268 1091

Andrew Vasiljuk **WM**
10 am–5 pm daily **CD**
Oct–May,
10 am–5 pm
weekends only
June–Sept

This is a very small vineyard producing mainly Pinot Noir and Chardonnay (and Sparkling Chardonnay) as well as some Riesling and Cabernet Sauvignon. The production volume is tiny (700 cases), but the wines are good—the unwooded Chardonnay is crisp and light, and the Pinot Noir has won a string of awards.

Domaine A

WM Peter Althaus, Velten Tiemann
CD 10 am–5 pm Mon–Fri, weekends by appointment

105 Tea Tree Rd, Campania

T 03 6260 4174 **F** 03 6260 4390 **E** althaus@domaine-a.com.au
W www.domaine-a.com.au

A former IBM executive in Europe, Althaus makes award-winning Cabernet Sauvignon and Pinot Noir. As well, he grows Cabernet Franc and Petit Verdot, which are used in blends. Wines for immediate drinking are sold under the Stoney Vineyard label.

Meadowbank Estate

WM Andrew Hood (contract)
CD 10 am–5 pm daily
R

699 Richmond Rd, Cambridge

T 03 6248 4484 **E** office@meadowbankwines.com.au
W www.meadowbankwines.com.au

This award-winning new winery complex with restaurant, barrel room and entertainment facilities enjoys a splendid position overlooking vines and river. The wines range from excellent Sauvignon Blanc through unwooded and lightly oaked Chardonnays to Pinot Noir and Cabernet Sauvignon. The 2003 Pinot Gris is especially fine. The tasting area of the cellar door offers a sampling of six wines and a cheese plate for a modest price. Many musical and artistic events are held here throughout the year—try to time your visit to coincide with one.

Moorilla Estate

WM Michael Glover
CD 10 am–5 pm daily
P
BBQ
GT
R
G

655 Main Rd, Berriedale

T 03 6277 9900 **F** 03 6249 4093 **E** wine@moorilla.com.au
W www.moorilla.com.au

This iconic winery was founded by the Tasmanian wine pioneer Claudio Alcorso and occupies a delightful setting overlooking the Derwent River 15 minutes from Hobart. The dry Moorilla Estate Riesling is outstanding and the Chardonnay and Pinot Noir are also highly regarded. The winery has a restaurant (open for lunch every day) and modern chalet accommodation offering views of the river (rates vary seasonally; booking recommended). In addition, Alcorso's original house, designed by Sir Roy Grounds, is now a museum of antiquities and function centre. It has some remarkable artefacts, so make sure you take the time to visit it.

The winery regularly hosts concerts and other functions—check the schedule before you go. Major renovations are due to be completed in 2005.

Huon Valley

Geebin Vineyard

3729 Channel Hwy, Birchs Bay

T 03 6267 4750 **F** 03 6267 5090 **W** www.geebin.alltasmanian.com

Heavenly views across the D'Entrecastaux Channel await visitors to this tiny vineyard. The Riesling is terrific and the Chardonnay and Cabernet Sauvignon are good too. Guests at the vineyard's bed and breakfast (see Accommodation) can attend a special tasting of the wines before dinner.

Andrew Hood (contract)
10 am–5 pm daily

WM
CD
B&B

Hartzview Vineyard

70 Dillons Rd, Gardners Bay

T 03 6295 1623 **F** 03 6295 1723 **E** hartzviewwine@trump.net.au
W www.hartzview.com

Hartzview Pinot Noir is the go here although Chardonnay (wooded and unwooded) and a sparkling Sauvignon Blanc Semillon, Pinot Gris and Riesling are also made. The speciality is a range of intensely flavoured fruit wines and liqueurs made from fruit and using no preservatives. Hartzview also carries a range of wines from another 10 Huon Valley wineries—useful if your time is limited—and some delicious local cheeses and gourmet produce. As the name suggests, the winery has lovely views of the Hartz Mountains. The property is dotted with the old sheds formerly used by contract fruit pickers.

Robert Patterson
9 am–5 pm daily

WM
CD
P
BBQ
G
SCA

Home Hill Winery and Restaurant

38 Nairn St, Ranelagh

T 03 6264 1200 **F** 03 6264 1369 **E** homehill@bigpond.com
W www.homehillwines.com.au

A first-class boutique winery housed in a striking rammed-earth and glass building, Home Hill makes a range of wines including an unwooded Chardonnay, Pinot Noir, Sylvaner and sparkling cuvee

Jim Chatto,
Peter Dunbabin
10 am–5 pm daily
Daily for lunch,
Fri–Sat for dinner

WM
CD
R

as well as a late-harvest sticky. The restaurant serves fresh meals made with local ingredients along with fine local wines; it's popular, so book ahead.

Panorama Vineyard

WM Michael Vishacki
CD 10 am–5 pm Wed–Mon
P
BBQ
GT

1848 Cygnet Coast Rd, Cradoc
T 03 6266 6304 **F** 03 6266 4382
E panoramavineyard@hotmail.com
W www.taswinedirect/panorama

The drive here along the Cygnet coastal road (C 639) is one of the loveliest in this part of Tasmania, and the aptly named winery and small vineyard occupy a splendidly scenic setting. The long ripening period in this area assures great depth of flavour, which can be tasted in the mouth-watering (and prize-winning) Pinot Noir as well as the delicious Chardonnay and Sauvignon Blanc. Cabernet Sauvignon, a rosé, port and pear liqueur are also available. The garden has an impressive collection of roses, and picnic tables can be used by visitors to the cellar door. Highly recommended.

East Coast

Coombend Estate

WM Andrew Hood (contract)
CD 9 am–6 pm daily
P
SCA

Coombend Vineyard, Swansea
T 03 6257 8256 **F** 03 6257 8484 **E** coombendest@vision.net.au

Carved out of a large sheep property, this small, family-owned business produces high-quality wines as well as excellent olive oil. The setting is rolling coastal countryside with a scenic backdrop of wooded hills. The wines include a clean, flavoursome Sauvignon Blanc, Riesling, Cabernet Sauvignon and a rosé. Self-catering cottages are available (see Accommodation).

Freycinet Vineyard

WM Claudio Radenti
CD 10 am–4 pm daily in winter, 9 am–5 pm daily in summer
P
BBQ

15919 Tasman Hwy, Bicheno
T 03 6257 8574 **F** 03 6257 8454 **W** www.freycinetvineyard.com.au

Fabulously sited on the eastern slopes of the coastal range in a small, sheltered valley head, the vineyard produces excellent Pinot Noir, Chardonnay, Cabernet Sauvignon, Riesling and Merlot.

Wine tours and activities

The Tasmanian Wine Centre at 201 Collins St, Hobart, is an ideal place to get your bearings. The knowledgeable staff offer tastings and can arrange winery tours at short notice. They will also help you track down wines from vineyards that are not open to the public. The centre has a good website and an online ordering service (**T** 03 6234 9995 **F** 03 6234 9977 **E** taswines@tasmanian-wine.com.au **W** www.tasmanian-wine.com.au **O** 8 am–6 pm Mon–Fri, 9.30 am–5 pm Sat). The 9-11 Gasworks, at 2 Macquarie St, Hobart, has been voted Best Bottle Shop in Tasmania for a number of years and is considered by many to be the best in Australia. It stocks a wide range of products from small wineries and has a 'thirteen-to-the-dozen' policy, whereby customers pay for twelve bottles and receive a thirteenth free.

Food and Dining

Hobart's Salamanca Markets (**O** 8.30 am–3 pm Sat) have gained international fame for their food as a result of the Taste of Tasmania culinary festival, which takes place here annually and greets the arrival of the Sydney to Hobart Yacht Race. The markets' stalls, restaurants and cafes are an ideal place to view and sample the vast range of quality produce made all over Tasmania. These products may be available in many parts of Australia, but there's nothing like tasting a food at the point of origin. Specialities include seafood such as oysters, ocean trout and salmon, as well as a great diversity of cheeses and fruits. Many of these goods can be also be purchased at the Providore, Peppermint Bay resort, Channel Hwy, Woodbridge, south of Hobart on the Huon Peninsula **T** 03 6267 4088. Sample the sheep's cheeses, quinces, fragrant local olive oil, or house smoked salmon.

Coal and Derwent Valleys and Hobart

Barilla Bay Oysters, 1388 Tasman Hwy, Cambridge **T** 03 6248 5458 **F** 03 6248 5559 **E** barillabay@trump.net.au **W** www.barillabay.com.au **O** 7.30 am–5 pm Mon–Fri, 9 am–5 pm weekends. A brand new oyster bar, cafe and 'gourmet village' pay homage to the not-so-humble oyster. Farm tours (45 minutes) and tastings are available at modest cost (free for children under 10). You can also pick up a travel pack for your picnic or to take home.

Lebrina, 155 New Town Rd, Newtown, Hobart **T** 03 6228 7775 **O** From 6.30 pm for dinner Tues–Sat. This restaurant is fast gaining a dedicated following. Scott Minervini's food is modern European-influenced Australian cuisine of a high standard, incorporating a range of high-quality seasonal Tasmanian produce and put together with great skill. There are good soups, veal and duck dishes, local salmon, quail and a game pie. Desserts include crème brulée and Tasmanian fruit in season, and the cheese board is generous. The wide-ranging wine list includes wines from some less well-known Tasmanian vineyards. If in doubt take advice—you won't regret it.

Meadowbank Estate, 699 Richmond Rd, Cambridge **T** 03 6248 4484 **E** office@meadowbankwines.com.au **W** www.meadowbankwines.com.au **O** 10 am–5 pm daily. This stylish and light and airy restaurant overlooking the vineyards has won several tourism awards. Even if you can't stop for a leisurely lunch, you can still order a cheese plate, snacks or a coffee throughout the day.

Huon Valley

Home Hill Winery Restaurant, 38 Nairn St, Ranelagh **T** 03 6264 1200 **F** 03 6264 1069 **E** homehill@bigpond.com **W** www.homehillwines.com.au **O** 10 am–5 pm daily for snacks and lunch, from 6 pm Fri–Sat for dinner. The stylish brasserie restaurant at Home Hill serves à la carte meals and fine local wines. The menu changes seasonally and features local produce such as Huon Valley lamb and venison, Spring Bay scallops and tiger prawns. A soup of the day and specials are usually on offer, too. It's popular, so book ahead.

Accommodation

Coal and Derwent Valleys

Prospect House, 1384 Richmond Rd, Richmond **T** 03 6260 2207. This licensed bed and breakfast in a large Georgian house offers fresh produce and a stylish ambience. The rooms are comfortable and well equipped and there is also a restaurant.

Huon Valley

Geebin Vineyard and B&B, 3729 Channel Hwy, Birchs Bay **T** 03 6267 4750 **F** 03 6267 5090 **W** www.geebin.alltasmanian.com. The comfortable bed and breakfast accommodation at this beautifully sited vineyard (see Wineries) consists of two private suites with a pretty waterside garden. Meals and snacks are available.

Hartzview Vineyard, 70 Dillons Rd, Gardners Bay **T** 03 6295 1623 **F** 03 6295 1723 **E** hartzviewwine@trump.net.au. The vineyard's self-contained, three-bedroom cottage has breathtaking views of the surrounding vines, forests and mountains. Breakfast provisions, including freshly baked bread, are available but otherwise you'll need to take your own supplies as the location is blissfully remote.

Heron's Rise Vineyard, Saddle Road, Kettering **T** 03 6267 4339 **F** 03 6267 4245 **E** cwhite@vision.net.au **W** www.heronsrise.com.au. Situated on a small vineyard, these two comfortable, hand-built cottages are set back from the main road amid gardens of lavender and grevillea. They have fully equipped kitchens, comfy beds and open fireplaces for winter, and the large windows and open-plan design admit plenty of natural light.

East Coast

Coombend Estate, Coombend Vineyard, Swansea **T** 03 6257 8256 **F** 03 6257 8484 **E** coombendest@vision.net.au. The accommodation here consists of two beautifully presented cottages that are well equipped, homely, and welcoming. Both have log fires that can be lit in winter. The walks from the front door to nearby coastal viewpoints offer stunning views.

Travel Information

How to get there

By road For the Coal and Derwent valleys, head north from Hobart on the Tasman Hwy towards Sorell, then turn left towards Cambridge (B 31) and Richmond. From Richmond, you can either take the short route back via Risdon Vale or the long one via Bridgewater and the Brookner Hwy. For the Huon Valley, take the Huon Hwy (A6) south from Hobart to Kingston. You then need to decide whether to take the Channel Hwy to Margate and Snug, and continue from there round the coast towards Cygnet and the Huon Valley, or stay on the A6 to Huonville and then turn left to Woodstock and Cradoc.

By air Qantas, Virgin Blue and Jetstar have direct connections to Hobart from all the eastern state capitals. Rex Regional Express also offers direct flights from Melbourne.

By sea The *Spirit of Tasmania I* and *II* car ferries sail from Melbourne to Devonport (departing at 9 pm and arriving at 7 am). The *Spirit of Tasmania III* sails for Devonport from Sydney three times a week (departing at 4 pm on Fri, 5 pm on Sun, 6 pm on Tues), taking around 20 hours to complete the journey; the ferry has cabin and hostel-style accommodation and a wide range of on-board activities and entertainment.

Other attractions

The centre of Hobart has much to offer in the way of historic buildings—Tasmanians take their heritage values pretty seriously these days. There are stone buildings of distinction and enough reminders of early convict days to convince you that Hobart, the second-oldest settlement after Sydney, has one of the better preserved legacies of colonial rule. Parliament House in Murray St was built in 1835 and parts of the Tasmanian Art Gallery and Museum date back to 1805. The Georgian warehouses along Salamanca Place and the heritage precinct of Battery Point are also fine examples of early Australian colonial architecture.

The Tasmanian Maritime Museum in Argyle St has fascinating displays on ocean exploration and whaling, as well as a host of photographs, artefacts from sailing ships and exhibits on today's fast catamarans (**T** 03 6234 1427).

The Cascade Brewery at 140 Cascade Rd offers regular tours for the beer enthusiast (**T** 03 6221 8300). They take approximately two hours and run at 9 and 10 am and 1 and 1.30 pm Mon–Fri (or more often depending on demand). The Tasmanian Art Gallery and Museum at 40 Macquarie St has some excellent displays of contemporary and historical art, both colonial and Aboriginal. It also preserves the stuffed and mounted remains of (possibly) the last Tasmanian Tiger or thylacine (**T** 03 6211 4177 **O** 10 am–5 pm daily). Salamanca Arts Centre at 77 Salamanca Pl includes art galleries, theatres and craft outlets (**T** 03 6234 8414).

The Lark Distillery at 14 Davey St, Hobart, makes several distinctive liqueurs using fruit from many parts of Tasmania, including a Tasmanian Bush Liqueur made with pepperberries picked high in Tasmania's alpine areas. It also produces a sweet schnapps flavoured with Tasmanian apples, a single-malt whisky, and spirits (gin and vodka) infused with flavours such as pepperberry and cherry (**T** 03 6231 9088 **W** www.larkdistillery.com.au).

Hobart's natural assets are legion too. Drive to the top of Mount Wellington for sweeping views of city and water. The Derwent River also offers numerous opportunities for water-based activities or just gazing out over the waterway and surrounding country. A mere 70 km (80 minutes) away, you can experience a bit of what Tasmania is most famous for—its pristine forests. The Tahune Forest Airwalk allows you to view a forest of Huon pines at canopy level. If you haven't got a head for heights, you can take the Huon Pine Walk on the valley floor, which passes trees that are up to 300 years old—and it's free. The visitor centre has a cafe and observation deck.

For kids

No kid's visit to Tasmania would be complete without a tour of the Cadbury Chocolate Factory at Cadbury Rd, Claremont (bookings essential **T** 03 6249 0111). You can view diverse Aussie wildlife at Talune Wildlife Park in Gardners Bay, and you can even stay the night in self-contained on-site cabins (**T** 03 6295 1775). Bonorong Wildlife Park in Brighton, half an hour north of Hobart, also has numerous live specimens of native fauna, including Tasmanian Devils (**T** 03 6268 1184).

Events

Mar: Taste of the Huon (**T** 03 6224 1918), Southern Vineyards Open Weekend (**T** 03 6239 1741)
Nov: Royal Hobart Wine Show (**T** 03 6372 6812)
Dec–Jan: Taste of Tasmania (opposite Salamanca Place, **T** 03 6238 2100)

Information

Tasmanian Travel and Information Centre, 20 Davey St, Hobart
T 03 6230 8233   **F** 03 6224 0289
E tasbookings@tasvisinfo.com.au
W www.discovertasmania.com

Victoria

Bendigo

The Bendigo region's first wine grapes were planted as early as 1856, soon after the beginning of the gold rush that brought significant numbers of people to central Victoria, and by the 1870s its wines were being praised by wine show judges as far away as Europe. The variety of wines produced was broader than that of many other regions at the time, ranging from whites and light reds to sturdy reds.

By the 1890s, however, phylloxera had spread to Bendigo and many of the vines were destroyed. It was not until the late 1960s and early 1970s that the winegrowing industry was re-established, when pioneers such as Stuart Anderson of Balgownie Estate Vineyard began producing powerful reds. Anderson was followed by Ian Leamon of Chateau Leamon, Graeme Leith and Sue Mackinnon of Passing Clouds, and others. Through the 1980s and 1990s, the trickle turned into a stream and now some 25 vineyards have been established in the region.

The climate is generally warm, continental and well suited to the production of red wines, although parts of the southern area are somewhat higher and cooler. Rainfall is relatively evenly spread through the growing period, but low overall, making irrigation necessary. The undulating countryside provides a variety of aspects and soil conditions. Parts of the region are covered by established eucalypt forest, but there also good grazing lands, orchards and vineyards.

The two main winegrowing areas are the Loddon Valley, in the north-west, and the Granite Slopes area, to the south. Each can be toured in

Key

T	Telephone
F	Fax
E	Email
W	Website
WM	Winemaker
CD	Cellar door
P	Picnic facilities
PA	Play area for children
BBQ	Barbecue facilities
GT	Guided tours
C	Cafe
R	Restaurant
O	Opening hours
B&B	Bed and breakfast
H	Hotel/Inn
M	Motel
G	Guesthouse
SCA	Self-catering accommodation

a rough circuit, the first starting along the Calder Highway towards Bridgewater, Inglewood and Rheola, returning to Bendigo via Newbridge and Marong. The southern circuit detours off the Calder Highway to Mundurang, Faraday and Harcourt. It is good touring country, encompassing historic villages and small towns, such as Maldon, with its elegant nineteenth-century architecture, as well as the larger centres of Castlemaine and Bendigo. The latter especially has much to draw the tourist: many of the fine buildings built there during the gold rush are still in use today, including hotels, banks and commercial premises, all testifying to a period of vigorous growth.

What to buy

It is commonly accepted that Shiraz is the region's most rewarding drop, producing rich, full-bodied reds, but Cabernet Sauvignon is next in volume terms and is producing wines of great character. Merlot is also grown and some Pinot Noir. You can find good Chardonnay, Riesling and Sauvignon Blanc, but generally conditions are too hot for the growing of refined or elegant whites.

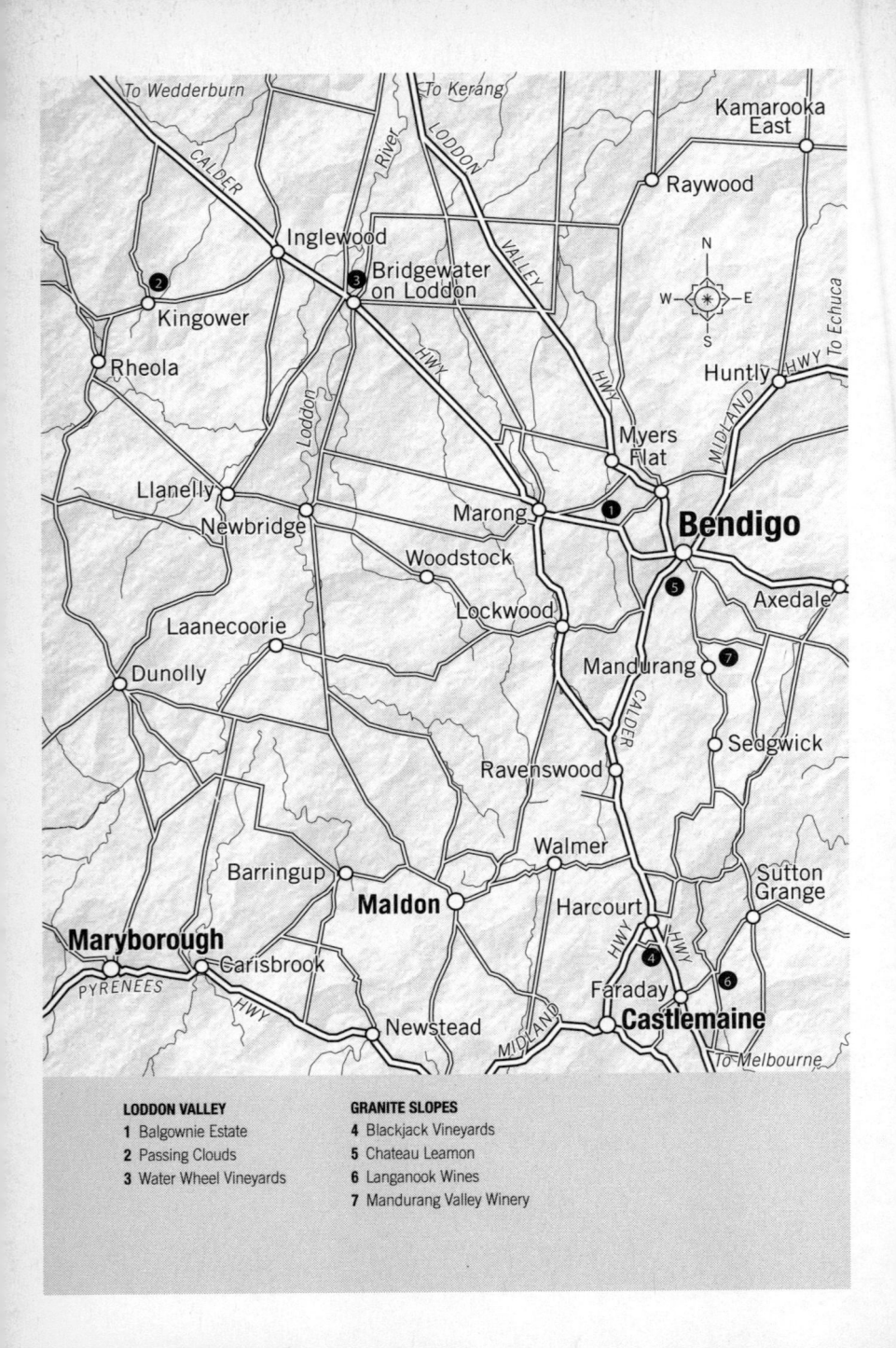

LODDON VALLEY
1 Balgownie Estate
2 Passing Clouds
3 Water Wheel Vineyards

GRANITE SLOPES
4 Blackjack Vineyards
5 Chateau Leamon
6 Langanook Wines
7 Mandurang Valley Winery

Wineries

Granite Slopes

Blackjack Vineyards
Calder Hwy, Harcourt
T/F 03 5474 2355

Nestled in the beautiful Harcourt Valley, this small vineyard offers a friendly welcome and a chance to taste some excellent full-bodied reds. The wines are have recently achieved wider recognition and the Shiraz, Cabernet and Merlot are much sought after, so check their availability before you visit.

Ian McKenzie, Ken Pollock
11 am–5 pm weekends and public holidays when stocks available, Mon–Fri by arrangement
WM CD

Chateau Leamon
Calder Hwy, Bendigo
T 03 5447 7995 **F** 03 5447 0855 **E** wine@netcon.net.au
W www.chateauleamon.com.au

The hillside vineyard at Chateau Leamon was established on the northern slopes of Big Hill in 1973. It produced its first wines in 1977 and soon gained awards and critical acclaim. Owner and winemaker Ian Leamon has since maintained a consistently high standard of winemaking. The range includes full-flavoured Shiraz, Cabernet Merlot, Riesling and Semillon, as well as a Reserve Cabernet Sauvignon and a Merlot Cabernet Franc. All are lovely, complex wines that will improve in the cellar for several years.

Ian Leamon
10 am–5 pm
Wed–Mon
WM CD

Langanook Wines
91 McKittricks Rd, Sutton Grange
T 03 5474 8250 **E** mhunter@netcon.net.au

Situated in secluded Sutton Grange, on the slopes of Mount Alexander, the winery and cellar door are constructed of local granite and rely exclusively on solar power. The good-value wines include a Cabernet Sauvignon Merlot Cabernet Franc blend, a Reserve Cabernet blend, a peppery Syrah (Shiraz to you and me), and a lightly oaked Chardonnay Viognier blend. The vineyard is at an altitude of 450 m and consequently the climate is cooler than elsewhere in the region, resulting in a slow ripening period that produces intense flavours.

Matt Hunter
11 am–5 pm weekends and public holidays, Mon–Fri by appointment
WM CD

Mandurang Valley Winery

WM Wes Vine
CD 11 am–5 pm weekends, public and school holidays; Mon–Fri by appointment
P
BBQ

77 Fadersons Lane, Mandurang
T 03 5439 5367 **F** 03 5439 3850
E mvwines@mandurangvalleywines.com.au
W www.mandurangvalleywines.com.au

Mandurang Valley prides itself on making high-quality wines that are 'home grown, hand picked, and estate vintaged and bottled'. The results, including Riesling, Sauvignon Blanc, Chardonnay, Pinot Noir, Cabernet Sauvignon and Shiraz, are also stylish and moderately priced. Food is available in the form of light, Italian-style seasonal platters of antipasto or cheeses for lunch and homemade cakes (seasonal quince, apple and pear) for afternoon teas.

Loddon Valley

Balgownie Estate

WM Tobias Ansted
CD 11 am–5 pm daily
R
SCA

Hermitage Road, Maiden Gully
T 03 5449 6222 **F** 03 5449 6506
E cellardoor@balgownieestate.com.au
W www.balgownieestate.com.au

The two main wines here are Shiraz and Cabernet Sauvignon, both of which seem to yield distinctive local styles, with mint and eucalypt notes and some pepper, particularly in the Shiraz. Two other wines, Pinot Noir and Chardonnay, come from small vineyard parcels, and are produced in very limited quantities; they are also of high quality. The cellar door incorporates the Bendigo Wine Museum. Moderately priced luxury accommodation is available in the form of two self-contained units that overlook the vines, a short walk from the cellar door.

Passing Clouds

WM Graeme Leith and Sue Mackinnon
CD 12 noon–5 pm weekends, but call ahead

Kurting Rd, Kingower
T 03 5438 8257 **F** 03 5438 8246 **W** www.passingclouds.com.au

One of the first vineyards to be established in the area, this small winery has a reputation for producing robust local Shiraz, also included in a Shiraz Cabernet blend called Graeme's Blend and a

Merlot Grenache Shiraz blend called Angel Blend. In addition, Passing Clouds makes a good Pinot Noir with fruit sourced partly from the Yarra Valley.

Water Wheel Vineyards

Raywood Rd, Bridgewater-on-Loddon
T 03 5437 3060 **F** 03 5437 3082 **E** winery@waterwheelwine.com
W www.bendigowine.com.au

Situated on the banks of the Loddon River in the shadow of the historic water-powered Water Wheel flour mill, the picturesque cellar door is situated in a cosy building surrounded by thriving vines. The wines range from zesty Sauvignon Blanc and buttery Chardonnay to some of the best reds in the region—a wonderful Shiraz, a smooth Cabernet Sauvignon and a rich Shiraz Cabernet Malbec blend.

Bill Trevaskis, **WM**
Peter Cumming
11 am–5 pm daily **CD**
Oct–Apr; 11 am–
5 pm Mon–Fri,
1 pm–4 pm
weekends and
public holidays
May–Sept

P
BBQ

Wine tours and activities

Bendigo Winery Tours, based at 83 Cahills Rd, Bendigo can arrange packages including accommodation and food as well as winery tours (**T/F** 03 5439 3635 **E** info@bendigowinerytours.com.au **W** www.bendigowinerytours.com.au).

Food and Dining

Bendigo is set in lovely country and has recently begun to make the most of its natural produce. Restaurants now regularly feature fine local fare and in season the range is substantial. There are roadside stalls, orchards and olive groves as well as produce markets and a wide variety of shops. The Bendigo Farmers' Markets are held on the second Saturday of each month at The Showgrounds, 42–47 Holmes Rd (**T** 03 5444 4646 **O** 8 am–1 pm). For fresh fruit, vegetables and meats try the Bendigo Produce Barn, 170 Eaglehawk Rd, Bendigo (**T/F** 03 5444 5000). The Green Olive at 11 Bath Lane, Bendigo, has all kinds of Mediterranean foods, good coffee and cheeses (**T** 03 5442 2676).

Balgownie Estate, Hermitage Road, Maiden Gully **T** 03 5449 6222 **F** 03 5449 6506 **E** cellardoor@balgownieestate.com.au **W** www.balgownieestate.com.au **O** Daily for lunch. The restaurant offers simple but satisfying casual dining. The foods are chosen to complement and enhance the flavours of the wines.

Bazzani, Howards Pl, Bendigo **T** 03 5441 3777 **F** 03 5443 9995 **E** office@bazzani-bendigo.com **W** www.bazzani-bendigo.com. **O** 12 pm–3 pm Mon–Sat, 12 pm–6 pm Sun. A long-established favourite with a comfortable main restaurant, Bazzani also incorporates a European terrazza-style courtyard with umbrellas for open-air dining, which lends the place a European air. The extensive à la carte menu uses regional produce and is supplemented by pasta and risotto specials.

Fortunes Restaurant, All Seasons Quality Resort, 171–183 McIvor Rd, Bendigo **T** 03 5443 8166 **F** 03 5441 5221 **E** info@allseasonsbendigo.com.au **W** www.allseasonsbendigo.com.au. The balanced à la carte menu features international dishes, and changes seasonally. Local meat and vegetables are featured, and specials include pastas, risotto, three kinds of Caesar salad, and fish.

Jojoes, 4 High St, Bendigo **T** 03 5441 4471 **F** 03 5441 4510 **E** jojoes@jojoes.com.au **W** www.jojoes.com.au **O** 12 noon–late daily. This stylish cafe has an extensive à la carte menu featuring gourmet pizzas and a range of pasta dishes, which is supplemented by seasonal specials incorporating local produce. The wide-ranging wine list includes several local wines and some are available by the glass. Open-air dining is an option.

Whirrakee Restaurant and Wine Bar, 17 View Point, Bendigo **T** 03 5441 5557. **O** Wed–Fri for lunch, from 6 pm Tues–Sat for dinner. Whirrakee has a modern menu, friendly service and boasts a good range of Bendigo's local wines, many carefully aged, to accompany the great food. Local meats, vegetables, cheeses and fruits are used for dishes that range from Asian-influenced noodles to Greek pies and salads. Servings are generous and the Brutus salad, which replaces bacon with prosciutto and uses garlic breadsticks instead of croutons, is a new take on the tired Caesar.

Accommodation

All Seasons Quality Resort, 171–183 McIvor Rd, Bendigo **T** 03 5443 8166 **F** 03 5441 5221 **E** info@allseasonsbendigo.com.au **W** www.allseasonsbendigo.com.au. One of the best in Bendigo and central Victoria, this hotel offers country-style hospitality, a restaurant, pool and $3^1/_2$ hectares of landscaped grounds to explore.

Byronsvale B&B, 51 Andrews Road, Maiden Gully, Bendigo **T** 03 5447 2790 **F** 03 5447 3094 **E** byronsb&b@hitech.net.au Handy for vineyards (close to Balgownie) and local restaurants, yet secluded, Byronsvale offers three fully self-contained suites in an old stone building. Breakfast provisions are included. Byronsvale also has its own vineyard.

Lynne Vale Estate, 83 Cahills Road, Mandurang **T/F** 03 5439 3635 or 0411 873 788 **E** lynnevale@netcon.net.au **W** www.bendigowinerytours.com. Also a winery, Lynne Vale offers three ensuite rooms with queen beds in homestead-style accommodation.

Travel Information

How to get there
By road Bendigo is approximately a 1.5-hour drive from Melbourne via the Calder Hwy.
By train You can still travel to Bendigo by V-line rail (**T** 13 61 96 **W** www.viclink.com.au).

Other attractions
As well as some stunning gold-rush architecture, Bendigo has one of Australia's premier tourist attractions. The Central Deborah Gold Mine at 76 Violet St provides a superb introduction to the city and its rich mining history. Once a real mine and still used for training purposes, it contains quartz reefs flecked with gold and can be reached from Bendigo via a historic tram line (**T** 03 5443 8722 **W** www.central-deborah.com).

For kids
The Discovery Science and Technology Centre at 7 Railway Pl, Bendigo, houses a range of exhibits that are added to every three months. They include hands-on, fun features such as an

'astro-trainer' for aspiring astronauts, a water-filtering plant, and a 7-m-high gravity slide (**T** 03 5444 4400 **F** 03 5444 4566 **E** fun@discovery.asn.au **W** www.discovery.asn.au **O** 10am–4pm daily, extended during school holidays).

The oldest working pottery in the country, Bendigo Pottery at Epsom, 6.5 km north of Bendigo, has a fascinating array of pottery and artworks, and, for a small fee, kids can have a go at making pots. The pottery also incorporates the Living Wings and Things Butterfly House, a collection of bird, butterfly and reptile displays (**T** 03 5448 4404 **F** 03 5448 4873 **E** bpottery@bendigo.net.au **W** www.bendigopottery.com.au).

Events
Mar: Bendigo Winemakers Festival (annual)
Sept: Bendigo Shiraz dinner (annual)
Oct, second Sat: Bendigo Heritage Uncorked
Dec: Bendigo Wine and Food Expo

Information
Bendigo Visitor Information Centre, 51–67 Pall Mall, Bendigo
T 1800 813 153 or 03 5444 4433
F 03 5444 4447 **W** www.bendigotourism.com
Bendigo Winegrowers Association
T 1300 656 650 **F** 03 5435 2548
W www.bendigowine.org.au

Geelong

The history of vine-growing and wine production in the Geelong area began more than 150 years ago, when a Swiss migrant named David Pettavel planted grapes near the township. The vines thrived until the 1870s, by which time around 400 ha had been planted and there were more than 100 vineyards. However, by the late 1870s a combination of politics, the 1890s recession and phylloxera—which had been imported to the port of Geelong from France—had destroyed the vineyards.

It was not until the 1960s and 1970s that the vineyards were re-established. The revival was led by a small band of winemakers including Daryl and Nini Sefton at the Idyll Vineyards in the Moorabool Valley (now part of Jindalee) and Tom Maltby at Mount Anakie and later, the Prince Albert winery at Waurn Ponds and Bannockburn. In the 1980s and 1990s, Geelong saw a significant expansion in the area under vine and in the number of wineries.

The region encompasses a number of areas with different microclimates that influence the growing of grapes and hence the flavour of the wines. The Bellarine Peninsula, for example, has a maritime climate, whereas the hills and valleys of the Anakie, Barwon and Moorabool Valley areas have a warmer, continental climate.

The majority of Geelong wineries are family owned and operated and you will find that the owner is usually the winemaker or at least has a hand in the process. Although Geelong has not received the recognition of the two more glamorous wine regions close to Melbourne,

Key

T	Telephone
F	Fax
E	Email
W	Website
WM	Winemaker
CD	Cellar door
P	Picnic facilities
PA	Play area for children
BBQ	Barbecue facilities
GT	Guided tours
C	Cafe
R	Restaurant
O	Opening hours
B&B	Bed and breakfast
H	Hotel/Inn
M	Motel
G	Guesthouse
SCA	Self-catering accommodation

Yarra Valley and the Mornington Peninsula, it produces some extremely good wines and offers the tourist some delightful experiences. The area has some beautiful countryside, and gazing at the Melbourne skyline over Port Phillip Bay or the You Yangs from the Bellarine Peninsula can be a magical experience.

The options for touring include heading north-west of Geelong along the Moorabool and Barwon river valleys, taking in Bannockburn and Lethbridge, or heading to the south of Waurn Ponds and then to the east of Geelong along the Bellarine Peninsula via Drysdale towards Portarlington.

What to buy

The largely cool maritime climate of Geelong and the Bellarine Peninsula is particularly well suited to the production of Chardonnay and Pinot Noir, and several styles of both are available. In recent years, Pinot Gris, Riesling, Sauvignon Blanc, Cabernet Sauvignon and even Shiraz have also done well here.

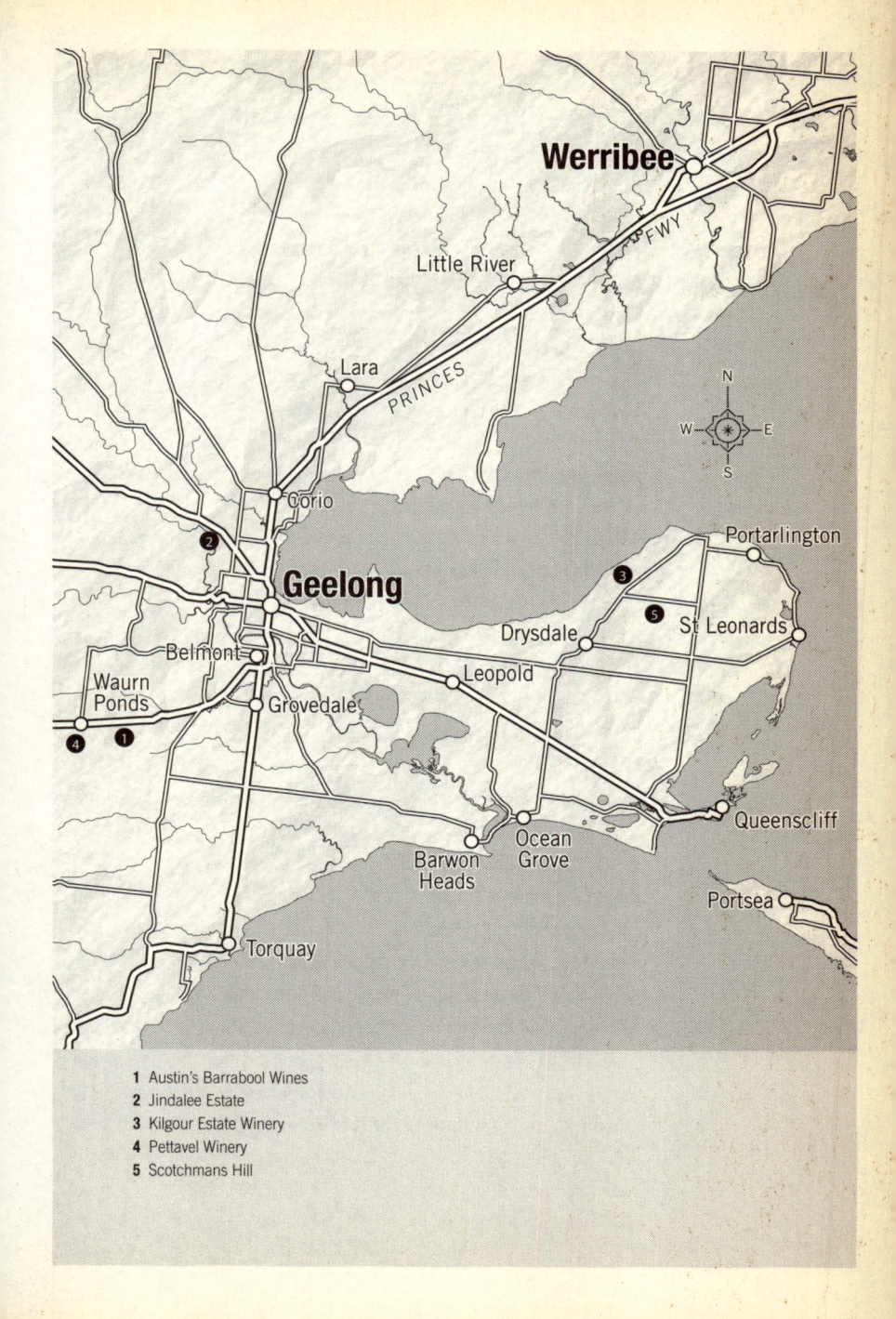

1 Austin's Barrabool Wines
2 Jindalee Estate
3 Kilgour Estate Winery
4 Pettavel Winery
5 Scotchmans Hill

GEELONG 187

Wineries

Austin's Barrabool Wines

WM Scott Ireland (contract), Pamela Austin
CD By appointment

870 Steiglitz Rd, Sutherlands Creek
T 03 5281 1799 or 0417 520 063 **F** 03 5281 1673
E abwines@abwines.com.au

Family-owned, this small winery produces excellent Chardonnay (Ellyse) and Pinot Noir, as well as Sauvignon Blanc, Riesling, Shiraz, Cabernet Sauvignon and Merlot. It is open only by appointment, but the wines are worth the effort.

Jindalee Estate

WM Andrew Byers, Chris Sargeant
CD 10 am–5 pm daily

256 Ballan Road, Moorabool
T 03 5276 1280 **F** 03 5276 1537 **E** sales@jindaleewines.com.au
W www.jindaleewines.com.au

Jindalee was formerly known as the Idyll Vineyard, and the vines here are the oldest in the region and among the oldest in Victoria. The Fettler's Rest range is made with grapes from the family-owned estate—the name celebrates a railway track that passes through the property and is still in use today—and includes Chardonnay, Gewurztraminer and a strong, earthy Pinot Noir. The winery also makes a range using grapes grown near Mildura, called Jindalee.

Kilgour Estate Winery

WM Karen Coulstone (contract)
CD 10.30 am–6 pm daily
BBQ
C Wed–Sun for lunch

85 McAdams Lane, Bellarine
T/F 03 5251 2223 **W** www.winegeelong.com.au

Kilgour's small vineyard produces fresh fruit-driven wines, including Chardonnay and Pinot Noir as well as Pinot Gris and Cabernet Sauvignon. The wines are good and the views from the winery are spectacular. A cafe serves lunches, its menu changing frequently depending on what's in season. Barbecues are also provided.

Pettavel Winery

65 Pettavel Rd, Waurn Ponds

T 03 5266 1120 **F** 03 5266 1140 **E** pettavel@pettavel.com
W www.pettavel.com

Peter Flewellyn **WM**
10 am–5.30 pm **CD**
daily
R

Named in recognition of pioneer winemaker David Pettavel, who arrived from Switzerland in 1842 and planted some of the region's first vines, this new winery has much to offer. The winery buildings were built from Tasmanian sandstone, recycled timbers and vineyard stones, incorporate a good restaurant (see Food and Dining), and are surrounded by landscaped gardens. They also offer a fine view over Shiraz vines to the original Pettavel homestead. The wines include the Evening Star range, which takes in Chardonnay, Riesling, a Sauvignon Blanc Semillon blend and a Cabernet Merlot. The Platina series includes a Merlot Petit Verdot blend, a Pinot Noir and a Cabernet Sauvignon/Cabernet Franc blend. Skilful winemaking at reasonable prices.

Scotchmans Hill

190 Scotchmans Road, Drysdale

T 03 5251 3176 **F** 03 5253 1743 **E** info@scotchmanshill.com.au
W www.scotchmanshill.com.au

Robin Brockett **WM**
10.30–4.30 pm **CD**
daily

One of the first wineries to be established during the 1960s revival, this is now the biggest in the Geelong area and a must for all wine tourists. The cellar door and gardens enjoy terrific views. Some of the generally marvellous wines are from single vineyards, such as the Norfolk and Sutton vineyards. The Scotchmans Hill Sauvignon Blanc, Chardonnay and Pinot Noir are all highly regarded. The range also includes Riesling, a Cabernet Sauvignon Merlot and a Shiraz. The Swan Bay label, intended for early-drinking wines, includes Chardonnay and Pinot Noir as well as a Sauvignon Blanc Semillon. In the same ownership is Spray Farm Estate vineyard, a few kilometres down the road at 2275 Portarlington Rd, Bellarine. The views from here, to the You Yangs and across Port Phillip Bay to Melbourne, are spectacular. Spray Farm hosts a festival concert and other summer events, and its function centre, in the National Trust-listed historic homestead, is becoming very popular for weddings.

Wine tours and activities

Gallivantours can arrange flexible half- or full-day tours of the local wineries (**T** 03 5244 0908 or 0438 244 240 **F** 03 5244 2429 **E** gallivantours@bigpond.com **W** wwwgallivantours.com.au).

Food and Dining

Some seriously good food is available in the Geelong area, and seafood is one of the main attractions, as you would expect from a town positioned right on Port Phillip Bay. Cultured mussels are widely available and if you head down the road to Portarlington on the Bellarine Peninsula you can buy them direct from the farms at Portarlington Pier. Irrewarra Sourdough Bakery Cafe in James St, Geelong, which also has branches elsewhere in the area, sells a range of good breads, as does La Madre bakery in Bell Park. There are several places where you can pick your own fruit during the harvest, including Irewarra Strawberries at 30 Ballarat Rd, Colac (**T** 0409 556 952), and Tuckerberry Hill, Drysdale (**T** 03 5251 3468). The Geelong Farmers' Markets are held every second Saturday in Little Malop St, Geelong; the stalls sell a wide range of fresh fruit and vegetables, breads, marinated olives, sun-dried tomatoes, pickles and preserves, as well as good coffee and snacks.

Le Parisien, 15 Eastern Beach Rd, Geelong **T** 03 5229 3110 **O** 11 am–late daily. The menu is strongly French influenced—it starts with onion soup and is in French as well as English—and there is a focus on crepes and seafood, but other dishes including poultry, lamb's kidneys and salads (including a spicy Basque) are available.

Pettavel Winery, 65 Pettavel Rd, Waurn Ponds **T** 03 5266 1120 **F** 03 5266 1140 **E** pettavel@pettavel.com **W** www.pettavel.com **O** Daily for lunch, dinner from 6.30 pm Fri in summer and last Fri of month at other times. The restaurant celebrates fresh local food and flavours, including seafood. The imaginative menu changes frequently and offers some of the best food to be found in an Australian winery—

grilled fish, roast pigeon, veal with potato rosti, spiced rabbit with baby beetroot, and desserts to die for!

Sailor's Rest, 3 Moorabool St (cnr Eastern Beach Rd), Geelong T 03 5224 2241 O 9 am–late daily Oct–Apr, 11 am–late daily May–Sept. An old favourite, this cafe, bar and restaurant is busy and buzzy and has a casual alfresco balcony dining area with views over the bay. The à la carte menu features open sandwiches, wraps, dips, pastas, and specials as well as seafood, including salt-and-pepper calamari, and chargrills. An extensive wine list includes many wines available by the glass.

2 Faces, 8 Malop Street, Geelong T 03 5229 4546 F 03 5224 1533 E 2faces@datafast.net.au W www.geelonginfo.com/2faces O From 6 pm Tue–Sat. This stylish licensed restaurant in a heritage 1857 stucco building offers great modern Australian food reflecting Asian and Mediterranean influences. A regularly updated six-course grazing menu, à la carte and specials are available.

Accommodation

Four Points by Sheraton, 10–14 Eastern Beach Rd, Geelong T 03 5223 1377 F 03 5223 3417 W www.fourpoints.com.au. Luxurious and well-located, on the revitalised Geelong waterfront, Four Points also has fine views across Corio Bay. A range of room styles is on offer and there are bars and a restaurant.

Lilydale House B&B, 100 Dog Rocks Rd, Batesford T 03 5276 1302 F 03 5276 1026 E belcher@bigpond.com W www.innhouse.com.au/lilydale. This comfortable, well-appointed accommodation occupies a beautiful rural setting. Children by arrangement.

Staughton Vale Vineyard, Winery and Restaurant, 20 Staughton Vale Rd, Anakie T 03 5284 1477 F 03 5284 1229 E staughtonvalewines@bigpond.com. This recently completed bed and breakfast at a beautifully located vineyard has two motel-style units with spa and shower, as well as a self-contained one-bedroom cottage.

Views' End Bed & Breakfast, 261–9 Scotchmans Rd, Bellarine **T** 03 5253 1695 **E** viewsend@bigpond.com **W** www.viewsend.tourvic.com.au. Views' End has a good location, great views and beautiful gardens that are part of the Open Garden Scheme. There is a separate guest entrance and the rooms have king, queen or twin beds. Fully cooked breakfasts and other meals can be arranged.

Travel Information

How to get there
By road Geelong is a 50-minute drive south-west of Melbourne along the M1 Princes Fwy.
By train There is a frequent V-line train service from Melbourne's Spencer St Station to Geelong (**T** 13 61 96 or 03 9619 1111).

Other attractions
The National Wool Museum, 26–32 Moorabool St, Geelong, is the city's major tourist attraction, offering fascinating insights into the pastoral industry and its importance to the city and the nation as a whole. Located in an impressive 1872 bluestone building, originally an historic wool store, it houses a fabulous collection of documents and photographs. Visitors can also listen to shearers' songs and tales, and watch working machinery including baling machines, a carpet-weaving loom and delivery trucks. Well worth a visit (**T** 03 5222 2900 **F** 03 5222 1118).

Heading south from Geelong leads to the Great Ocean Road, an area of spectacular natural beauty with plenty of good food and accommodation and breathtaking coastal scenery.

For kids
Along the city's waterfront, 100 painted poles depict the history of the area—great for photographs! Also on the waterfront are parklands, the beach itself and a children's pool at Eastern Beach. The Ford Discovery Centre, cnr Gheringap and Brougham Sts, Geelong, charts the history of the Ford Motor Company in Australia and worldwide, and the future of the automobile. It has many interactive displays, some showing how cars are made and tested.

Events
Jan: Scandia Geelong, multicultural food and wine festival; Summer Music Festival, Scotchmans Hill (**T** 03 5251 3176)
Feb: Pako Festa, food and music festival
Aug: Taste of the Grape, Geelong Waterfront

Information
Geelong Visitor Information Centre, National Wool Museum, 26 Moorabool St, Geelong **T** 1800 620 888 or 03 5222 2900 **F** 03 5223 2069
Geelong & Great Ocean Road Visitor Information Centre, cnr Princes Hwy and St Georges Rd, Corio **T** 1800 620 888 or 03 5275 5797 **F** 03 5223 2069
Geeelong Wine Association
W www.winegeelong.com.au

Grampians

The Grampians region has a long history of winemaking and is known primarily as the birthplace of Australia's sparkling wine industry. As in other areas of Australia, particularly New South Wales and Victoria, the gold rushes of the mid-nineteenth century saw an influx of population and the widespread planting of vines—some of the vines still used in this part of Victoria are more than 130 years old. Among those who arrived in the late 1850s were a Frenchwoman, Anne-Marie Blampied, her husband Jean-Pierre Trouette, and her brother Emile. They established St Peter's Vineyard, and it is believed that they were the first to introduce to Australia the bottle-fermentation process, or *méthode champenoise*, used to make sparkling wines.

In the years that followed the Great Western area became the focus of sparkling-wine production under the auspices of Hans Irvine, who purchased a vineyard from the estate of Joseph Best in 1887 and brought to Australia another Frenchman, Charles Pierlot, to make the wines according to the French method. In the late 1800s, there were up to 90 grape growers in the Grampians area, with more than 3000 ha under vines, making both sparkling and still wines. In 1918, Irvine's vineyard was purchased by Benno Seppelt (it is now part of Seppelt's Great Western Estate), who did much to increase the popularity of sparkling wines during the early part of the twentieth century.

The subsequent decline of the wine industry as a result of World War I and the Depression saw many of the vineyards returned

Key

T	Telephone
F	Fax
E	Email
W	Website
WM	Winemaker
CD	Cellar door
P	Picnic facilities
PA	Play area for children
BBQ	Barbecue facilities
GT	Guided tours
C	Cafe
R	Restaurant
O	Opening hours
B&B	Bed and breakfast
H	Hotel/Inn
M	Motel
G	Guesthouse
SCA	Self-catering accommodation

to grazing land. A few survivors, such as Best's and Seppelt, kept winemaking alive in the area, but it was not until the late 1960s that production was re-established on a significant scale, with the replanting of vines on grazing land.

The soils around Great Western are mainly infertile gravel and granite sand over clay, and the climate is cool—ideal conditions for producing light-bodied, astringent wines of high acidity. The majority of the vineyards are planted on river flats and undulating country, but some lie on steeper slopes. Most of the wineries are to be found scattered along the Great Western Highway, with concentrations around Great Western and Ararat, and Halls Gap, the gateway to the Grampians National Park.

What to buy

Sparkling wines are a regional speciality and several grape varieties are grown specifically for use in these wines, including Pinot Noir, Pinot Meunier, Chardonnay and Ondenc, though this last variety is rare now. Chardonnay, Riesling and Pinot Gris are also used for crisp, white still wines. The Grampians is one of the major areas for Shiraz production, and the best of the resulting wines offer great intensity and flavour. Some Cabernet Sauvignon is also grown.

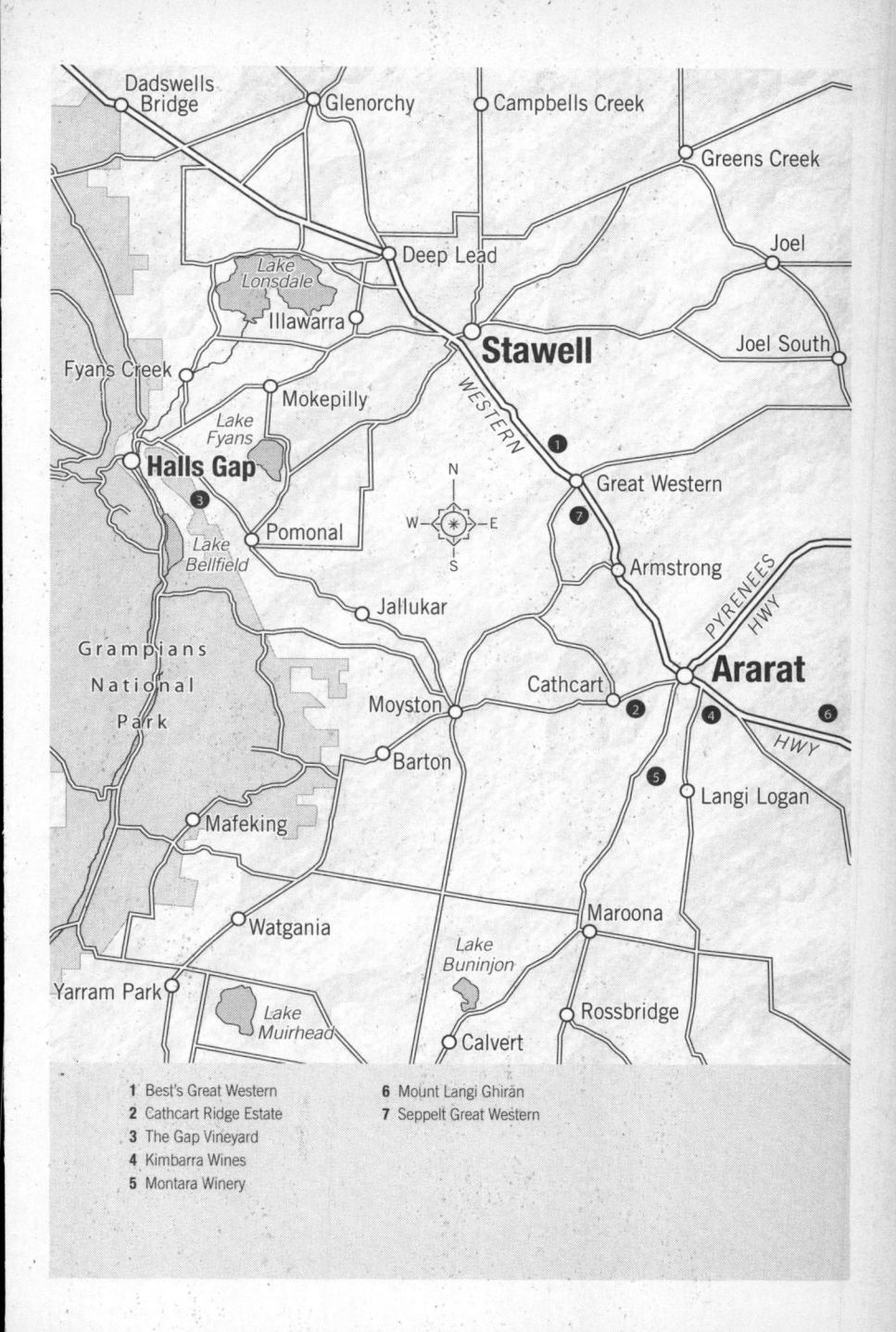

1 Best's Great Western
2 Cathcart Ridge Estate
3 The Gap Vineyard
4 Kimbarra Wines
5 Montara Winery
6 Mount Langi Ghiran
7 Seppelt Great Western

Wineries

Best's Great Western

WM Viv Thomson
CD 10 am–5 pm
Mon–Sat, 11 am–4 pm Sun
P
GT

111 Bests Rd, Concongella, Great Western

T 03 5356 2250 **F** 03 5356 2430 **E** info@bestswines.com
W www.bestswines.com

Established in 1866, the historic Best's Congella vineyard is a must for wine tourers. Visit the friendly cellar door and take the self-guided cellar walk. The wines include Shiraz, Cabernet Sauvignon and Pinot Meunier, as well as whites including Riesling and Chardonnay. The Thomson Family Shiraz or Bin 0 Shiraz are top of the range, but the Victoria Shiraz is pretty good too. Top wines.

Cathcart Ridge Estate

WM David Farnhill
CD 10 am–5 pm daily
BBQ
SCA

Halls Gap–Moyston Rd, Ararat

T 03 5352 1997 **F** 03 5352 1558 **E** finewine@netconnect.com.au
W www.cathcartwines.com.au

This small, family-owned winery makes Shiraz, Merlot, Cabernet Sauvignon and Chardonnay as well as a Tawny Port. It also has accommodation, located close to the rustic cellar door. In recent years, experiments with a number of Italian grape varieties, including Dolcetto, Sangiovese and Pinot Grigio, have been undertaken here.

The Gap Vineyard

WM Trevor Mast
CD 10 am–5 pm daily
P
PA

Pomonal Road, Halls Gap

T 03 5356 4252 **F** 03 5356 4545 **E** masts@netconnect.net.au

Owned by the Mount Langi Ghiran Winery, this vineyard is set in bushland with spectacular views of the craggy Mount William peaks. It offers a range of wines that includes a Shiraz Grenache blend, Chardonnay, Riesling, Cabernet Sauvignon and a Late Harvest Riesling and port. All the wines are well made and offer good value for money.

Kimbarra Wines

422 Barkly St, Ararat

T 03 5352 2238 **F** 03 5352 1950
E kimbarrawines@netconnect.com.au
W www.kimbarrawines.com.au

Though a small operation, Kimbarra produces excellent Riesling, Shiraz, Cabernet Sauvignon and, in some years, a Shiraz Cabernet blend and a Late Picked Riesling. Ian McKenzie, a former winemaker at Seppelt Great Western, keeps the standards high.

Peter Leeke, **WM**
Ian McKenzie
9 am–4.45 pm **CD**
Mon–Fri
(closed 12.30 pm–
1.30 pm and on
weekends)

Montara Winery

76 Chalambar Road, Ararat

T 03 5352 3868 **F** 03 5352 4968 **E** montara@connect.com.au
W www.montara.com.au

Enjoy spectacular views while tasting wines that are 100 per cent estate grown and bottled. The range includes Riesling and Chardonnay, as well as Pinot Noir, Shiraz, Merlot and Cabernet Sauvignon, and a vintage port. The setting—picturesque vines beneath a mountain backdrop—complements the wines superbly. The winery hosts an annual Scarecrow Festival as part of the Grampians Gourmet Festival in May.

Mike McRae **WM**
10 am–5 pm **CD**
Mon–Sat,
12 pm–4 pm Sun
P

Mount Langi Ghiran

80 Vine Road, Buangor

T 03 5354 3207 **F** 03 5354 3277 **E** langi@connect.com.au
W www.langi.com

This was one of the first vineyards to be resurrected in the early 1960s, when Italian migrants the Fratin brothers began to plant Shiraz grapes in lieu of their first choice of Merlot, which was then unavailable. The wines here are extremely good, especially the reds, and Shiraz remains a speciality. The Cabernet Sauvignon and Merlot are also of a high standard, and the Billi Billi Creek blend of Shiraz and Cabernet Sauvignon is ideal for early drinking. The Yellow Tailed Cockatoo range of whites includes a Riesling and a classy Pinot Gris. The refurbished winery and cellar door have great views.

Trevor Mast **WM**
9 am–5 pm **CD**
Mon–Fri,
12 pm–5 pm
Sat–Sun
P
BBQ

Seppelt Great Western

WM Arthur O'Connor
CD 10 am–5 pm daily
P
BBQ
GT

Moyston Rd, Great Western
T 03 5361 2239 **F** 03 5361 2200 **E** judy.murray@southcorp
W www.seppelt.com.au

The birthplace of the Australian sparkling wine industry, Seppelt Great Western is now part of the giant Southcorp group. The full range of sparkling wines can be tasted, including the Original Sparkling Shiraz, but there is also a wide selection of good-value still wines, notably Chardonnay and Pinot Noir, Pinot Gris and Merlot. Make sure you also visit the heritage-listed 'Drives', 3 km of tunnels originally built by miners and used since 1868 for storing and maturing wines.

Wine tours and activities

Based in Ararat, Grampians/Pyrenees Tours arranges winery tours for small groups of up to 12 people. The tours can include lunch or gourmet platters, and pick-ups can be arranged. The company also offers tours of other parts of the region (**T** 03 5352 5075 or 0417 559 370 **F** 03 5352 4835 **E** tours@grampianspyreneestours.com.au **W** www.grampianspyreneestours.com.au).

Food and Dining

There is a growing awareness that the Grampians has the potential to supply a wealth of great foods, and a number of local producers are leading the way. Grampians and Mount Zero Olives, in Mount Zero Rd, Laharum, is a family-owned business committed to sustainable agriculture. It sells olive oils, preserves such as beetroot relish, and other regional produce at a shop and cafe in an atmospheric old weatherboard schoolhouse with a set of magnificent old Italian olive-crushing stones in the courtyard (**T** 03 5383 8280). Red Rock Olives, cnr Tunnel and Halls Gap Rds, Pomonal, also produces a range of delicious olive oils, table olives and tapenades (**T** 0401 700 868). The appropriately named Green Eggs in Great

Western supplies top-quality fresh eggs from free-range birds (**T** 03 5356 2221). At Pomonal Berry Farm, on the Halls Gap–Pomonal Rd, Pomonal, a range of jams and jellies is made from organically grown berries (**T** 03 5356 2221).

The Kookaburra Restaurant, Main Rd, Halls Gap **T** 03 5356 4633 **O** From 6 pm Tue–Sun for dinner, 12 pm–3 pm Sat–Sun for lunch. This combined cafe-bar-restaurant has an enviable location with fine views of the surrounding mountains, and serves terrific food, including its own venison and fresh local produce.

Royal Mail Hotel, Dunkeld **T** 03 5577 2241 **F** 03 5577 2577 **O** 7 am–9 am for breakfast, 12 noon–2 pm for lunch, 6 pm–10 pm for dinner, daily. Sample dishes made with regional produce in the refurbished restaurant of this country hotel. The wine list is terrific.

The Vines Cafe and Bar, 74 Barkly St, Ararat **T** 03 5352 1744 **O** 9 am–5 pm daily, dinner till 11 pm Sat–Sun. This award-winning cafe-bar-restaurant has a commitment to using regional produce whenever possible—with great results. Book ahead.

Accommodation

Halls Gap Colonial Motor Inn, Grampians Rd, Halls Gap **T** 03 5356 4344 **F** 03 5356 4442 **E** bw90853bestwestern.com **W** www.hallsgapcolonial.bestwestern.com.au. Situated in the heart of Halls Gap, the inn offers comfortable accommodation and a licensed restaurant.

Marwood Retreat, Flat Rock Rd, Halls Gap **T** 03 5356 4231 **F** 03 5356 4513 **E** marwood@netconnect.com.au **W** www.visitvictoria.com/marwood. A five-star, award-winning, executive retreat, Marwood is situated in the Grampians National Park, close to Grampians and Pyrenees wineries. You can choose between

Tuscan-style units and 'water-pavilions', and take breakfast and dinner in the restaurant. The luxury comes at a price, but special packages are available, particularly midweek.

Mountain Grand Guest House/Boutique Hotel, Main Rd, Halls Gap **T** 03 53564232 **E** info@mountaingrand.com.au **W** www.mountaingrand.co.au. Set in pleasant surroundings, Mountain Grand offers older-style accommodation, dining facilities, afternoon teas and picnic lunches.

Travel Information

How to get there
By road The Grampians region is approximately 3 hours' drive from Melbourne. Follow the Western Hwy through Ballarat and Ararat.

Other attractions
The Grampians is mountaineering and bushwalking country, and there are many walks of varying degrees of difficulty, catering for every level of skill and fitness. Mount Arapiles attracts climbers from all over Australia and the climbs are spectacular. The Grampians National Park, Victoria's largest national park, has short, relatively easy tracks as well as those requiring overnight camping (**T** 03 5356 4381 **W** www.parkweb.vic.gov.au).

A peculiar local institution is the 'Stawell Gift', a 'foot race' held every year. Its fascinating history can be explored at the Stawell Gift Hall of Fame in Lower Main St, Stawell, which displays videos, trophies and photographs of this extraordinary event.

For kids
Halls Gap Wildlife Park and Zoo, Halls Gap, is home to native and exotic animals, ranging from wallabies to monkeys; during school holidays there are special ranger-led activities including night bushwalks to spotlight animals in their habitat (**T** 03 5356 4668).

Events
Jan: Great Western Picnic Races
Easter Weekend: Stawell Gift, Stawell
Apr–May: Grampians Grape Escape (**W** www.grampiansgrapeescape.com.au)
May: Grampians Gourmet Festival, Halls Gap (**T** 1800 657 158)

Information
Ararat Visitor Information Centre, 91 High St, Ararat **T** 1800 657 158 or 03 5355 0281 **F** 03 5355 0280 **W** www.visitararat.com.au
Grampians & Halls Gap Visitor Information Centre, Grampians Rd, Halls Gap **T** 1800 065 599 or 03 5356 4616 **F** 03 5356 4570 **E** hallsgap.info@ngshire.vic.gov.au **W** www.visitgrampians.com.au

Mornington Peninsula

The winegrowing history of the Mornington Peninsula dates back to the 1860s, when a few acres of vines were planted near Dromana. By the early twentieth century these were no longer being harvested due to a lack of interest in light table wines and a government that favoured dairy farming and milk production over winemaking. A revival occurred only in the early 1970s with the establishment of a number of boutique wineries.

Today, the Mornington Peninsula has more than 160 vineyards, including 35 with cellar doors that have flourished over the past three decades. These wineries are popular destinations for day trips from Melbourne, and the tourist services here are among the best of any Australian wine region. Accommodation options, for example, are myriad, and there is a fine range of restaurants. The area's many other attractions include picturesque, undulating countryside, spectacular bay views and sweeping beaches, including the sheltered sands of the bay and the more exposed 'back' (oceanside) surf beaches. There are also 15 top-class golf courses, theatres, art galleries, markets (including one at Mornington Racecourse), pick-your-own orchards, and boat trips into the bay.

From a winemaking point of view, the main distinguishing feature of the Mornington Peninsula is the strong influence of the maritime climate on the vines—only the Margaret River region of Western Australia is similar. Frost is not a problem, but rain and wind can delay ripening of the grapes. In addition, the subregions of

Key

T	Telephone
F	Fax
E	Email
W	Website
WM	Winemaker
CD	Cellar door
P	Picnic facilities
PA	Play area for children
BBQ	Barbecue facilities
GT	Guided tours
C	Cafe
R	Restaurant
O	Opening hours
B&B	Bed and breakfast
H	Hotel/Inn
M	Motel
G	Guesthouse
SCA	Self-catering accommodation

Dromana, Main Ridge, Red Hill, Merricks and Moorooduc Downs vary considerably in microclimate and soil. Great skill and dedication are therefore required of both growers and winemakers, and the choice of grape variety is crucial for success. Despite this—or perhaps because of it—the wines can be superb.

What to buy

The Mornington Peninsula is renowned for its Pinot Noir, so much so that the area is promoting a biannual Pinot festival. But there is a lot of good Chardonnay and Pinot Gris (Pinot Grigio) as well as Shiraz, Cabernet Sauvignon and Dolcetto. More recently, Gamay and Merlot have also made an appearance.

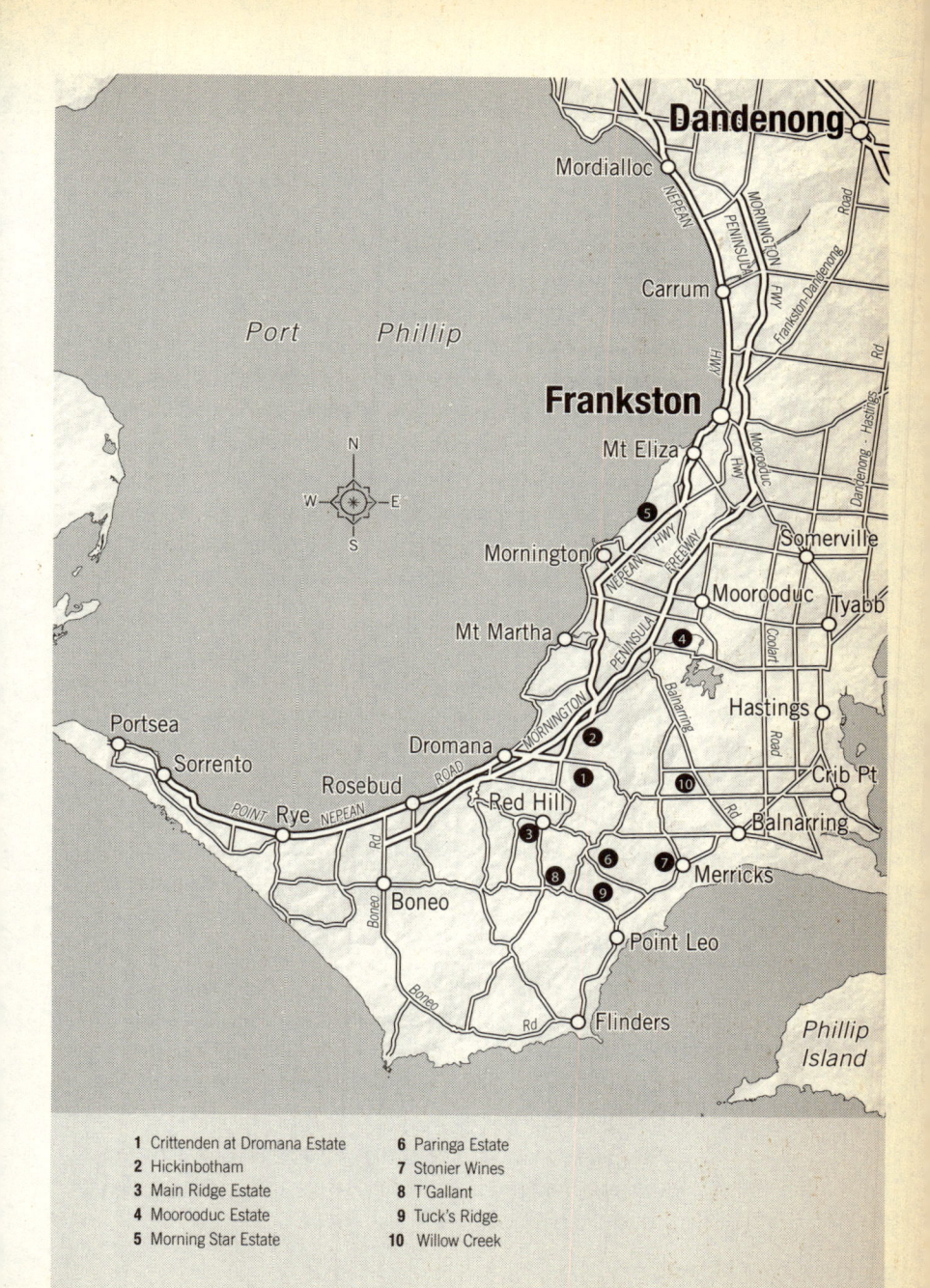

1 Crittenden at Dromana Estate
2 Hickinbotham
3 Main Ridge Estate
4 Moorooduc Estate
5 Morning Star Estate
6 Paringa Estate
7 Stonier Wines
8 T'Gallant
9 Tuck's Ridge
10 Willow Creek

Wineries

Crittenden at Dromana Estate

WM Garry Crittenden, Judy Gifford Watson
CD 11 am–4 pm daily, 11 am–6 pm in summer
P
PA
BBQ
C
R

25 Harrisons Rd, Dromana
T 03 5987 3800 **F** 03 5981 0714

This is the new set-up for Garry Crittenden, formerly the winemaker at nearby Dromana Estate. The range of wines reflects his mastery of winemaking principles as well as his exploration of Italian varietals such as Sangiovese, Barbera, Nebbiolo, Arneis and Dolcetto. The vineyard and lake views make the whole experience of tasting wines and eating delicious food in the adjacent restaurant (see Food and Dining) a relaxing and satisfying one. There is also a children's playground with swings and a trampoline.

Hickinbotham

WM Andrew Hickinbotham
CD 11 am–5 pm Mon–Fri, 11 am–6 pm Sat–Sun
P
PA
BBQ
C

194 Nepean Hwy, Dromana
T 03 5981 0355 **F** 03 5987 0672 **E** hickwine@hotkey.net.au
W www.hickinbothamwinemakers.com.au

The Hickinbotham name is well known in Victorian winemaking circles—Andrew's father Ian founded Mount Anakie in the Geelong region and his grandfather Alan was a viticultural scientist at Roseworthy. A refreshingly informal atmosphere prevails at the cellar door and the wines on offer provide an interesting combination of grapes and styles. They range from a blend of Unwooded Chardonnay and the little-known (in Australia) Aligote white grape to Pinot Noir, Cabernet Merlot, Shiraz Cabernet Grenache and Strawberry Kiss, a sparkling wine made from strawberries. Hickinbotham also makes a sweetish white from the little-known Taminga grape. Music is a feature at weekends, with live performances by jazz trios or blues bands (usually Sun but also Sat in summer), and there is a cafe that serves light meals. A relaxing and rewarding place to visit.

Main Ridge Estate

80 William Rd, Red Hill
T 03 5989 2686 **F** 03 5931 0000 **E** mrestate@mre.com.au
W www.mre.com.au

Main Ridge was one of the first small-scale boutique wineries on the peninsula. The atmosphere is friendly and low key, and the wines are excellent. Nat White and his wife Rosalie were early leaders of the Pinot Noir revolution; they also grow small quantities of Chardonnay grapes, which make an excellent wine.

Nat White **WM**
12 noon–4 pm **CD**
Mon–Fri,
12 noon–5 pm
weekends

Moorooduc Estate

501 Derril Rd, Moorooduc
T 03 5971 8506 **F** 03 5971 8580 **W** www.moorooducestate.com.au

This stylish and highly successful winery, cellar door and restaurant complex is one of the best on the peninsula. Luxurious accommodation is also available. The wines are split into three ranges according to grape source and winemaking style. The delicious Estate Chardonnay and silky Pinot Noir are supported by Cabernet Sauvignon and Shiraz.

Dr Richard McIntyre **WM**
11 am–5 pm **CD**
weekends
Weekends for lunch, **R**
Fri and Sat
for dinner
SCA

Morning Star Estate

1 Sunnyside Rd, Mount Eliza
T 03 9787 7760 **F** 03 9787 7160 **E** email@morningstarestate.com.au
W www.morningstarestate.com.au

This boutique complex comprises accommodation, a restaurant (see Food and Dining) and a conference centre with superb facilities, all set in a grand old building surrounded by beautiful gardens that sweep down to the sea. It has some of the area's most spectacular views, which take in its own vineyards. The wines range from Pinot Gris and Pinot Noir to Chardonnay, Shiraz and Cabernet Sauvignon. Only small quantities are made but the cellar door also sells wines from many other Mornington Peninsula wineries. Seafood barbecues are a feature of weekend lunchtimes and the atmosphere is relaxed and casual.

Sandro Mosele **WM**
10 am–5 pm daily **CD**
Bookings **H**
03 9788 6611

Paringa Estate

WM Lindsay McCall
CD 11 am–5 pm daily
C Wed–Sun for lunch, Fri–Sat for dinner, other times in summer; bookings 03 5931 0136

44 Paringa Rd, Red Hill South
T 03 5989 2669   **F** 03 5931 0135   **E** info@paringaestate.com.au
W www.paringaestate.com.au
Try the reds here, especially the Shiraz and Pinot Noir; good whites are on offer, too, notably Chardonnay and Pinot Gris. Family-owned, this is a charming set-up with a cafe and immaculately kept roses at the end of the vine rows.

Stonier Wines

WM Tod Dexter, Geraldine McFaul
CD 12 noon–5 pm daily, 11 am–5 pm in summer

362 Frankston–Flinders Rd (cnr Thompson's Lane), Merricks
T 03 5989 8300   **F** 03 5989 8709   **E** stoniers@stoniers.com.au
W www.stoniers.com.au
This small-scale but highly successful producer of Chardonnay and Pinot Noir occupies a Daryl Jackson-designed winery. Two ranges are on offer, standard and reserve—go for the Reserve Pinot if you can afford it. Stoniers started out as a 'suck it and see' operation producing fresh wines for immediate consumption (Pinot Noir is that sort of wine), but some of the wines promise to develop well for a few years.

T'Gallant

WM Kathleen Quealy, Kevin McCarthy
CD 10 am–5 pm daily
R

1385 Mornington–Flinders Rd, Main Ridge
T 03 5989 6565   **F** 03 5989 6577   **W** www.tgallant.com.au
Spectacular views are on offer here, as well as good wines and a fine restaurant, La Baracca (see Food and Dining). T'Gallant is especially well known for its Pinot Noir and the Pinot Grigio is worth a try, too.

Tuck's Ridge

WM Phillip Kittle, Daniel Greene
CD 12 noon–5 pm daily

37 Shoreham Rd, Red Hill South
T 03 5989 8660   **F** 03 5989 8579   **E** tucks@satlink.com.au
W www.tucksridge.com.au
This successful operation occupies a stunning setting and has shown commitment and imagination in developing its wines from estate-grown grapes. Although Pinot Noir has been the focus of recent efforts, Chardonnay, Riesling and Merlot have also proved

successful in both the Tuck's Ridge and modestly priced Callanans Road ranges. In summer, the winery holds a number of special events, such as hosting local bands and a wine harvest 'grape-stomping' day in March, which have a relaxed atmosphere—bring along a rug or a deckchair. Reasonably priced fine food is available along with the wines. Even dogs are welcome, as long as their owners clean up after them!

Willow Creek

166 Balnarring Rd, Merricks North

T 03 5989 7448 **F** 03 5987 7584 **E** admin@willow-creek.com.au
W www.willow-creek.com.au

Phil Kerney **WM**
10 am–5 pm daily **CD**
R

Willow Creek's award-winning wines are top quality, particularly the Tulum Pinot Noir and the Tulum Chardonnay. The Unoaked Chardonnay and Cab Sav are also very fine. The winery has a good restaurant, Salix (see Food and Dining).

Food and Dining

The Mornington Peninsula has a burgeoning food and wine scene that rivals the best in the country. This is a fruit-growing area and the long list of fruit available in season includes peaches, nectarines, cherries, blueberries, strawberries and quince. A farm-gate list is available from local tourist information offices, and some farms and orchards let you pick your own (PYO) berries and vegetables in season (although some have a firm no-pick policy). Two places where you can PYO are Baker's Fresh Vegies at Rosebud (**T** 03 59886340) and Lowanville Farm at Red Hill (**T** 03 5931 0040). Another is Sunny Ridge Strawberry Farm at Main Ridge, which also has a cafe serving cream teas and homemade ice-cream as well as fruit and fruit wines (**T** 03 5989 6273).

A relatively recent addition to the peninsula, Trevor and Jan Brandon's Red Hill Cheese factory offers tastings and sales of goat's and cow's milk cheeses at

81 Arthurs Rd, Red Hill (T 03 5989 2035 O 12 noon–5 pm). They are a perfect accompaniment to some of the local wines. Fresh free-range farm eggs are available all year from Summerhill Farm at Main Ridge (T 03 5989 6077).

Red Hill Markets, held at Red Hill Recreation Ground (7 am–1 pm, first Sat of month, Sept–May) is one of the best regional markets and has fresh country produce, bakery and gourmet products and craft works, as well as buskers and entertainers. A relative newcomer to the Mornington food scene is locally produced olive oil from Victorian Olive Groves, which is increasingly being recognised for its quality (T 0418 392 157).

Critters Cafe and Wine Bar, Crittenden at Dromana Estate, 25 Harrisons Rd, Dromana T 03 5987 3800 F 03 5981 0714 O 12 noon–3 pm daily for lunch. Run by Garry Crittenden's wife Margaret, this winery restaurant offers light, Mediterranean-style lunches made with fresh ingredients, and a menu that changes regularly. There's an open deck with tables shaded by white umbrellas.

Jill's, Moorooduc Estate, Moorooduc T 03 5971 8506 W www.moorooducestate.com.au O Weekends for lunch, Fri–Sat for dinner. Served in a stylish room, the food here emphasises fresh local produce, notably cheeses.

La Baracca, T'Gallant Winery, 1385 Mornington–Flinders Rd, Main Ridge T 03 5989 6565 F 03 5989 6577 W www.tgallant.com.au O 12 noon–3 pm daily, from 7 pm Sat. Popularly known as 'The Shed', this is a welcoming trattoria that serves delicious, Italian-inspired fare at reasonable prices. The wood-fired pizzas, served at weekends, are excellent.

Morning Star Estate, 1 Sunnyside Rd, Mount Eliza T 03 9787 7760 F 03 9787 7160 E email@morningstarestate.com.au W www.morningstarestate.com.au O 10 am–5 pm for breakfast, lunch and tea; 6 pm–11 pm Fri–Sat for dinner. The restaurant offers stylish dining in an old schoolhouse built in 1936, with great views from both. Gourmet barbecues take place 11 am–5 pm Sat–Sun.

Paringa Estate Winery Restaurant, 44 Paringa Rd, Red Hill South T 03 5931 0136 F 03 5931 0135 E info@paringaestate.com.au W www.paringaestate.com.au O 12 noon–3 pm Wed–Sun (every day in summer) for lunch, from 6 pm Fri–Sat (Wed–Sun in summer) for dinner. This bright, airy cafe overlooks the vines from an elevated position and has a deck for sunny days. The à la carte menu (with specials) offers light, tasty, modern European food.

The Peak Restaurant, Arthurs Seat Rd, Dromana T 03 5981 4444 O 12 noon–3 pm Wed–Sun, 6.30 pm–10 pm Wed–Sat. This is worth a visit for the French food and local wines, as well as the superb views.

Salix Restaurant, Willow Creek Wines, Merricks North T 03 5989 7640 O Daily for lunch, Fri–Sat for dinner (booking recommended). The restaurant offers a modern international menu based on seasonal local produce. A pleasant ambience and good views over vines and valley complement the fine food.

Accommodation

The Black Rabbit B&B, Hillcrest Rd, Shoreham T 03 5989 8500 E blkrabbit@surf.net.au W www.weekendretreats.com.au/blackrabbit. Two comfortable limestone cottages offer rural and water views; a welcome feature is the tennis court for guests' use. Barbecues are provided and there are lovely walks in the gardens and adjacent forest. The only snag is that the accommodation is not suitable for children.

Cipriani's Flinders Country Inn, 165 Wood Street, Flinders T 03 5989 0933 F 03 5989 0059 E cipriani@nex.net.au W www.babs.com.au/cipriani. Accommodation here ranges from single rooms to doubles suites and self-contained units. There is a restaurant and the hotel has pleasant gardens. The inn is superbly located, near West Head, overlooking the Western Passage of Western Port and Philip Island.

Lindenderry Country House Hotel and Vineyard, 142 Arthurs Seat Rd, Red Hill T 03 5989 2933 F 03 5989 2936 E info@lindenderry.com.au W www.lindenderry.com.au. If you feel like a bit of luxury, then this is a great option. There are courtyard rooms and others with vineyard views and balconies. The facilities include an indoor swimming pool, the Linden Tree restaurant, comfortable lounge areas, and conference facilities.

Muranna Herb Farm and Cottages, 52 Tubbarubba Rd, Merricks North **T** 03 5989 7499 **F** 03 5989 7498 or 0428 654 630 **E** info@muranna.com.au **W** www.muranna.com.au. Children, families and pets are welcome by arrangement at these two comfortable cottages located in a tranquil rural setting. Facilities include a tennis court and croquet lawn and there are lovely walks. You can also buy the herbs that are so beautifully laid out in the garden beds.

Red Hill Retreat, 81 William Rd, Red Hill **T** 03 5989 2035 **F** 03 5989 2827 **E** enquiry@redhillretreat.com.au. Situated amid flowers and orchards, a mere stone's throw from the Main Ridge winery, the retreat's three self-contained guest suites are comfortably furnished and have good facilities (including business facilities if needed).

Wine tours and activities

Led by the knowledgeable Rob and Cheryl Wallace, Wallaces' Mornington Peninsula Winery Tours conduct winery tours for up to ten people in airconditioned vehicles (PO Box 1129, Carlton **T** 03 9347 3039 **F** 03 9347 5197 **E** robcct@bigpond.com).

Travel Information

How to get there

By road The drive from Melbourne to the Mornington Peninsula is a little over 80 km down the Nepean Hwy and takes about an hour.

Other attractions

The sparkling seaside views along the Mornington Peninsula coast are hard to beat and among the most beautiful vistas close to a capital city anywhere in Australia. The town of Mornington has become a haven for artists, and its streets are dotted with galleries and antique shops as well as fine-food outlets. Schnapper Point has an imposing granite obelisk commemorating the explorer Matthew Flinders, whose exploration of this coastline helped determine that Port Phillip Bay was a good site for settlement.

Arthurs Seat Reserve has great views and the re-opened Chairlift Ride offers a truly spectacular panorama of Bass Strait (11 am–5 pm daily Sept–May, but check times **T** 03 5987 2565). The reserve has barbecues and picnic tables as well as other amenities. Cape Schanck Lightstation and Museum at the southernmost tip of the peninsula also has breathtaking views and barbecue and picnic facilities. You can take a guided tour of the lighthouse or follow the steep but sturdy staircase and boardwalk that takes you down to the coastline and Pulpit Rock.

Splendid ocean beaches can be found near Portsea, including Cheviot Beach where then prime minister Harold Holt is thought to have drowned in 1967 (his body was never found). Sorrento is a pretty town whose intriguing mix of shops and cafes invites exploration.

For kids
More than just a maze, Ashcombe Maze in Shoreham Rd, Shoreham also has water gardens and rose gardens, and in summer offers a range of kids' activities, including the Great Gnome Hunt; check for details (**T** 03 5989 8387 **W** www.ashcombemaze.com.au).

Kids bored with wine touring will find solace at Ace Hi Ranch at Cape Schanck. It has a wildlife park and animal nurseries as well as horse and pony rides along the beach, and, for something different that is bound to attract interest, rides in Saracen and Centurion tanks! Trampolines and a giant swing are also available (**T** 03 5988 6262).

Arthurs Seat Maze, on Purves Rd, Arthurs Seat, is one of the oldest in Australia (**T** 03 5981 8449

www.arthursseatmaze.com.au). The Blowhole in Cape Nepean National Park is worth seeing on wild days—but keep your distance.

Mornington has a splendid pier and offers shops, cafes and a safe beach for kids to play on. Mornington Park at the end of Main St has a playground and a replica of the sailing ship HMS *Investigator*. The Mornington Railway Preservation Society has a collection of wonderfully preserved steam engines and carriages at Moorooduc Station. You can ride on the trains between Moorooduc, Tanti and Mornington (Sun in spring and summer, check times **T** 03 5975 3474).

Events
Jan: Pinot Noir Celebration, Dromana Strawberry Festival
Mar: Red Hill Annual Show, Red Hill Long Lunch and Sorrento Long Lunch
June: Winter Wine Weekend
Dec: Summer Wine Weekend

Information
Peninsula Visitor Information Centre, 395B Point Nepean Rd, Dromana
T 1800 804 009 or 03 5987 3078
W www.visitmorningtonpeninsula.org
Mornington Peninsula Vignerons Association **T** 03 5989 9377
F 03 5989 2387 **E** mpva@mpva.com.au
W www.mpva.com.au

Rutherglen

The Rutherglen wine industry originated during the local gold rush, which brought people and wealth to the area, creating a ready market for wines being made by local farmers. The first to plant vines had been German settlers in the 1850s, but it was ex-miners such as George Morris, John Campbell and the Sutherland Smith family who subsequently planted larger areas of vines in the 1860s and 1870s, thereby creating a proper industry and establishing some of the family associations that exist to this day.

These early growers discovered that conditions were ideal for producing the rich reds and fortified wines then becoming popular with the British working class. Exports were facilitated by the advent of the railway link with Melbourne in 1879. For a while, Rutherglen's wine industry flourished, but by the turn of the century it was in trouble, partly due to phylloxera. Thanks to some early experiments with phylloxera-resistant vines, the damage was minimised and the industry limped on through the first half of the twentieth century, sustained by the market for fortified wines. Following the table wine revolution of the 1960s and 1970s, wine production in the region expanded significantly.

Rutherglen's climate is characterised by adequate rainfall during the growing season, and warm to hot summer temperatures. During the ripening season, long, warm days and cool evenings help raise the sugar content of the grapes. The altitude varies between 150 and 250 m, with few uplands of any significance.

Key

T	Telephone
F	Fax
E	Email
W	Website
WM	Winemaker
CD	Cellar door
P	Picnic facilities
PA	Play area for children
BBQ	Barbecue facilities
GT	Guided tours
C	Cafe
R	Restaurant
O	Opening hours
B&B	Bed and breakfast
H	Hotel/Inn
M	Motel
G	Guesthouse
SCA	Self-catering accommodation

The area boasts a growing list of wineries, restaurants and producers of gourmet foods including cheeses, mustards, pickles, olives and some of the best farm produce in Australia. In addition, the area has a strong tradition of country hospitality, making it one of the most welcoming wine-touring regions in Australia.

Within an hour's drive of Rutherglen is the Milawa Gourmet Region and the emerging King Valley wine region, with some of the highest altitude vineyards in the country. It also boasts a vibrant Italian community and associated Mediterranean influences and culture.

What to buy

Rutherglen is famous for its robust reds, including Shiraz, Cabernet, Merlot and the increasingly popular Durif grape, and produces some excellent flavoursome whites. But it is best known for its Tokays, Muscats and other fortified wines, which are among the best in the world.

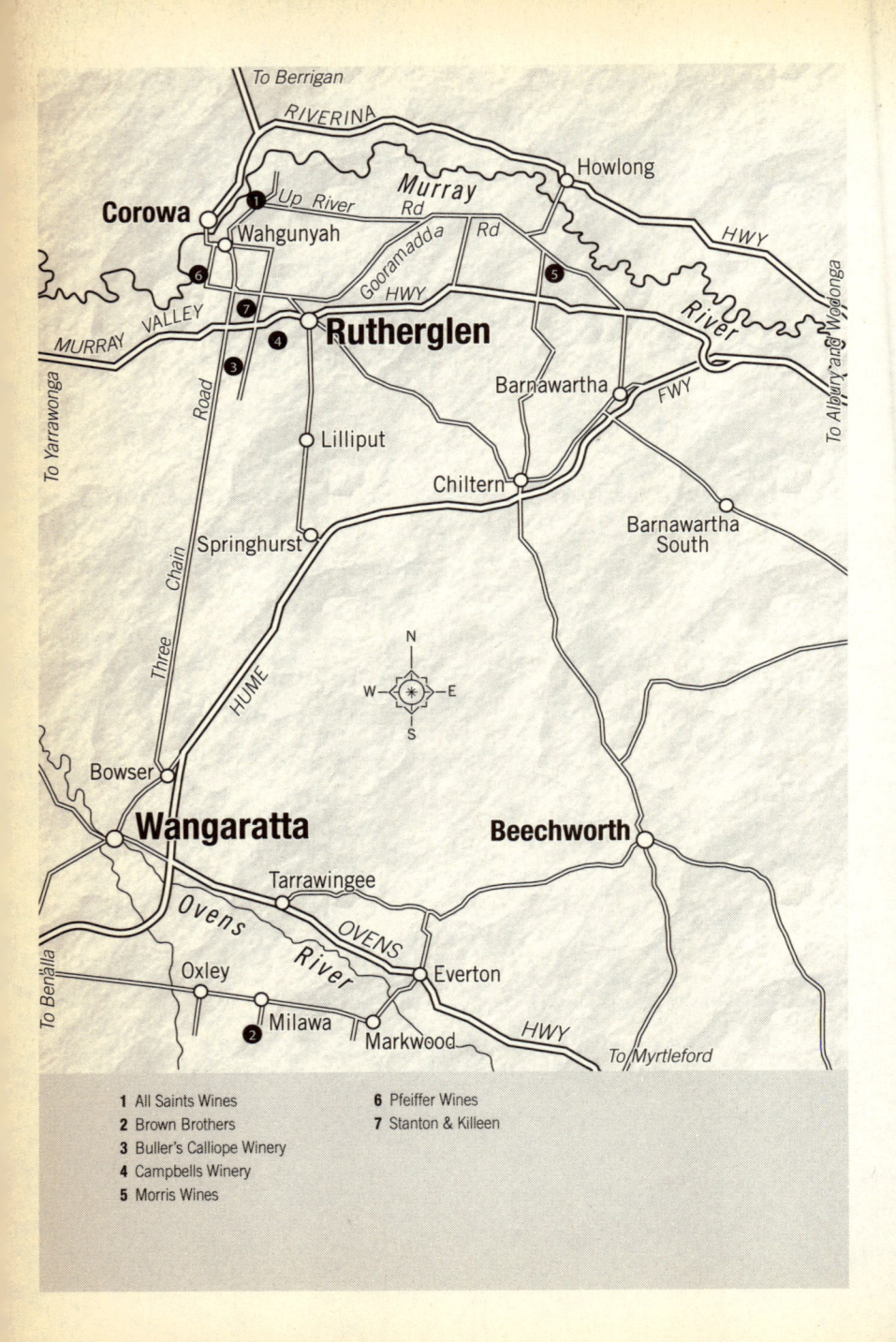

1 All Saints Wines
2 Brown Brothers
3 Buller's Calliope Winery
4 Campbells Winery
5 Morris Wines
6 Pfeiffer Wines
7 Stanton & Killeen

214 AUSTRALIA'S BEST WINE TOURS

Wineries

All Saints

All Saints Rd, Wahgunyah

T 02 6033 1922 **W** www.allsaintswine.com.au

One of Victoria's oldest wineries, dating back 120 years, All Saints is popular, and deservedly so, for it has excellent wines as well as its fine Terrace Restaurant, which overlooks the vineyards. Rich, full of flavour and high in alcohol, the wines reflect local styles. The Tokays and Muscats are of particularly high quality.

Dane Crane **WM**
9 am–5 pm **CD**
Mon–Sat,
10 am–5.30 pm
Sun
C
Daily for lunch, **R**
Sat for dinner
(bookings essential)

Brown Brothers Milawa Vineyard

Meadow Creek Rd, Milawa

T 03 5720 5547 **F** 03 5720 5511 **W** www.brownbrothers.com.au

With a history dating back to 1859, when George Harry Brown bought a property at Hurdle Creek, the Brown Brothers wine business is one of the great success stories of north-east Victoria. The company offers a wide range of varietal wines—more than 100 grape varieties have been grown in their vineyards. A number of styles and vintages are available only at the cellar door (and from a few specialist bottle shops), including Sangiovese, Tempranillo, Graciano, Cienna, Roussanne and Ruby Cabernet. Generally, the wines offer good quality at realistic prices right through the range, from the Everton blends of white and red through the lighter Barbera and Merlot to the bigger flavours of Shiraz and Cabernet Sauvignon. Fortified, dessert and sparkling wines are also available as well as Aged Riesling and Aged Chardonnay. You can eat lunch, matched with local wines, at the Epicurean Centre (open 11 am–3 pm). Brown Brothers holds an annual Easter Festival (Easter Sat–Mon), a fun-filled family affair featuring a farmers' market with gourmet produce, face painting, Easter-egg hunts and music.

Terry Barnett, **WM**
Wendy Cameron
9am–5 pm daily **CD**
P
C

Bullers

WM Andrew Buller
CD 9 am–5 pm Mon–Sat, 10 am–5 pm Sun

Calliope Vineyards and Winery, Three Chain Rd, Rutherglen
T 02 6032 9660 **F** 02 6032 8005 **E** rutherglen@buller.com.au
W www.buller.com.au

The emphasis here, at one of Rutherglen's best-known family-operated wineries, is on big reds and, especially, Muscats and Tokays. Shiraz and a Shiraz Mondeuse blend are prominent among the reds, along with a fruity but clean and fresh Sails Cabernet Rosé and a powerful Durif. The Fine Old Muscat and Fine Old Tokay are top-class fortifieds. Chardonnay and Marsanne are also part of the range. As well as the shaded and welcoming cellar door area, the winery has a spectacular bird park and gardens.

Campbells Winery

WM Colin Campbell
CD 9 am–5 pm Mon–Sat, 10 am–5 pm Sun
P
PA
BBQ

Murray Valley Hwy, Rutherglen
T 02 6032 9458 **E** wine@campbellswines.com.au
W www.campbellswines.com.au

Among the keys to the successful creation of world-class fortified wines are the practice of aging the wines in barrels and the blending of wines from different vintages to achieve a variety of styles. Having been in the same family since 1870, Campbells has more than a century's worth of different vintages to choose from, and the cellars that store their huge barrels are terrifically atmospheric. The extensive range of wines offers premium quality and is characteristic of the region. The fortifieds, particularly the liqueur Tokays, are renowned internationally, but the winery is perhaps most famous for its Bobbie Burns Shiraz. Regional food platters are available at the cellar door.

Morris Wines

WM David Morris
CD 9 am–5 pm Mon–Fri, 10 am–5 pm Sun

Mia Mia Vineyards, Rutherglen
T 02 6026 7303 **F** 02 6026 7445
W www.orlandowyndhamgroup.com

This historic, formerly family-owned winery is now part of the Orlando Wyndham group. The wines are rich, full flavoured and complex. They include Cabernet Sauvignon, Shiraz and the increasingly popular Durif, as well as Blue Imperial, a soft, fruity wine made from the little-known Cinsaut grape. Morris also makes a full-bodied Chardonnay and a Sparkling red blend of Shiraz and Durif. The tradition of producing fortified wines also lives on here, and the premium Liqueur Tokay is a prize-winner.

Pfeiffer Wines

167 Distillery Rd, Wahgunyah
T 02 6033 2805 E cellardoor@pfeifferwines.com.au
W www.pfeiffer.com.au

Chris Pfeiffer **WM**
9 am–5 pm **CD**
Mon–Sat,
10 am–5 pm Sun

PA
BBQ

This is another family enterprise that enjoys well-deserved support for its impressive variety of wines, ranging from a clean, citrus Riesling to well-made Pinot Noir, Shiraz and Cabernet Sauvignon. Make sure you also try the delicious, dry rosé made from Gamay (the Beaujolais grape), and the very good Tokay. The winery is set in bushland on the banks of Sunday Creek, and breakfasts and lunches held on the nearby Sunday Creek Bridge are very special occasions (put your name on their mailing list for notice of events like these). Picnic hampers, including vegetarian options, are available with 24 hours' notice, and there are shaded picnic areas. Dinners can also be arranged. Highly recommended.

Stanton & Killeen

Jacks Rd, Rutherglen
T 02 6032 9457 E sk_wines@netc.net.au
W www.stantonandkillenwines.com.au

Chris Killeen **WM**
9 am–5 pm Sat, **CD**
10 am–5 pm Sun

At this long-established family winery the focus is on big reds (Shiraz, Cabernets, Durif and Merlot) and ports, Muscats and Tokays. There are not too many frills here, just skilled winemaking and value-for-money wines, including some of the best in the area, notably the vintage ports.

Wine tours and activities

Several winery tours are available, but one of the most original is the Rutherglen stagecoach tour that starts from the Poacher's Paradise Hotel (where accommodation is also available), 120 Main St, Rutherglen (**T** 02 6032 7373). Alternatively, try one of the gourmet food and wine tours run by Shaun Maiden, who also operates 4WD and camping tours (**T** 03 5727 3382 **W** www.shaunswinerytours.com). Carlyle Winery Tours offers half- or full-day tours in a Rolls Royce Silver Shadow (**T** 02 6032 8544 **W** www.carlylehouse.com.au). Grapevine Getaway Winery Tours organise personalised tours and can arrange lunch stops (**T** 02 6032 8577 **W** www.grapevinegetaways.com.au).

Food and Dining

The area around Rutherglen offers fine produce as well as fine wines. Delicious local specialities include trout, cherries and olives. The Milawa Cheese Company on Factory Rd, Milawa, makes a range of award-winning cheeses and offers a ploughman's lunch at its historic factory, as well as dinner (Thurs–Sat). Try the goat camembert or ashed chèvre if you like goat's cheese—or even if you don't, as these are good enough to convert many people; the Milawa Blue is also a favourite (**T** 03 5727 3589 **F** 03 5727 3590 **W** www.milawacheese.com.au). Don't miss Milawa Mustards (**T** 03 5727 3202) for a good range of mustards, jams, dressings and condiments.

Gooramadda Olives at 1715 River Road, Gooramadda, is open weekends and public holidays and has olives and olive products for sale (**T** 02 6026 5658). Hotson's Cherries, at 143 Old Cemetery Road, Chiltern, offer punnets of cherries in season, fresh from the farm gate (**T** 03 5726 1358). Rokewood Orchards on Old Olympic Way, Table Top, specialises in growing stone fruit such as cherries, plums, peaches and nectarines; the produce is available for purchase on site (**T** 02 6026 2389 **O** Nov–Mar). Hume Weir Trout Farm on the Riverina Hwy, Lake Hume, sells fresh rainbow trout in a variety of smoked styles or as pate, and has a cafe stocked with fresh produce daily (**T** 02 6026 4334).

Beaumonts, 84 Main St, Rutherglen T 02 6032 7428 O 11 am–11 pm Wed–Sat, 3 pm–11 pm Tues, 9 am–5 pm Sun. Stylish regional food is served in this courtyard cafe. It is licensed and BYO (corkage charge applies).

Cafe Shamrock, 121B Main St, Rutherglen T 02 6032 8439 O From 6 pm daily. An eclectic mix of restaurant, wine bar and courtyard cafe, this establishment also sells local produce and wines. A house wine list accompanies the à la carte menu, but it's also BYO.

Food on Wood, Snow Rd, Milawa T 03 5727 3850 O Cafe and wine bar open for breakfast and lunch daily and for dinner Thurs–Sat 8 am–late; Mon–Wed 8 am–4 pm and Sun 8 am–5.30 pm. Generous servings of à la carte dishes and daily blackboard specials feature local produce, and local wines by the bottle or glass are served at reasonable prices. Be patient if they're busy.

King River Cafe, Snow Rd, Oxley T 03 5727 3461 F 03 5727 3733 E bon@netc.net.au W www.kingvalleycafe.com.au O 10 am–late Wed–Sun, 10 am–3 pm Mon. The meals here feature homemade produce ranging from chilli jam and cumquat marmalade to beetroot and fennel chutney. Many of the products are also available for sale. Adjoining the cafe, King Valley Cellars carries a wide range of local wines.

Le Cafe, Tuileries, 13–35 Drummond St, Rutherglen T 02 6032 9033 F 02 6032 8296 E info@tuileries.com.au W www.tuileriesrutherglen.com.au O From 6.30 pm daily for dinner, from 8 am Wed–Sun for breakfast and lunch. This upmarket restaurant puts on many of the local wine industry's best dinners and the food is of a very high quality. You can stay here, too (see Accommodation).

Rendezvous Restaurant, 68 Main St, Rutherglen T 02 6032 9114 O 6.30–late Thurs–Tues. Mediterranean food and a good selection of local wines are served in a cosy restaurant and courtyard. It's BYO too.

Rutherglen Wine Experience, 57 Main St, Rutherglen T 02 6032 9944 O 10 am–4 pm daily. 'The Experience' is the centre of wine touring in Rutherglen and its BYO cafe is a pleasant experience, too, offering light Mediterranean-inspired food either indoors or in an attractive courtyard.

Accommodation

Holroyd B&B, 28 Church St, Rutherglen **T** 02 6032 8218 **W** www.holroyd.visitrutherglen.com.au. This bed and breakfast has comfortable, well-furnished rooms, some with a theme—the tariff for the 'Tokay Room' includes a complimentary decanter of Tokay. Well-kept gardens are a bonus.

Lindenwarrah Country House Hotel, Milawa–Bobbinwarrah Rd, Milawa **T** 03 5720 5777 **E** info@lindenwarrah.com.au. Luxury accommodation with pool, restaurant with rooms overlooking vines, almost opposite Brown Brothers cellar door and close to the crossroads at Milawa, what else could you want? Well, you can also hire bikes here (for the RailTrail). The Merlot restaurant overlooks their own Merlot vines.

Milawa Lodge Motel, Snow Rd, Milawa **T** 03 5727 3326 **F** 03 5727 3799. Set in pleasant gardens, the motel is well located for walking to a number of Milawa's attractions, including the Brown Brothers winery, Milawa Cheese Factory, bakery, olive shop and mustard factory. Facilities include pool, spa, barbecues and Coopers Restaurant, which is licensed but also BYO.

Tuileries, 13–35 Drummond St, Rutherglen **T** 02 6032 9033 **F** 02 6032 8296 **E** info@tuileries.com.au **W** www.tuileriesrutherglen.com.au. Accommodation here is in luxurious suites with views over the vineyards. Guests can use a pool and tennis court, and there is an excellent restaurant, Le Cafe (see Food and Dining).

Woongarra Motel, cnr Main and Drummond Sts, Rutherglen **T** 02 6032 9588 **F** 02 6032 9951 **E** stay@motelwoongarra.com.au **W** www.motelwoongarra.com.au. As well as comfortable rooms with Internet access, the motel has a licensed cafe and in-ground pool. Non-smoking rooms are available.

Travel Information

How to get there
By road Rutherglen is just off the Hume Hwy, approximately 585 km (6 hours drive) from Sydney and approximately 274 km (3 hours drive) from Melbourne.

Other attractions
One of the main wine tourist experiences here is following the Muscat Trail, which takes in the Great Muscat Houses of Rutherglen (All Saints, Buller, Morris, Stanton & Killeen, Pfeiffer, Chambers and Campbells). To follow the trail, you can hire a bike from the Rutherglen Wine Experience Centre (see below); if you don't fancy cycling, you can join an organised tour from the centre. You can also take a stroll around Lake King, a scenic area to the west of Rutherglen's town centre between the golf course and the caravan park; it has a population of geese and ducks, and there are turtles in the lake.

Reached via Mia Mia Rd (allow at least 30 minutes to climb to the top), Mount Ochtertyre is a hill with scenic views. It was from this summit that the energetic explorer and surveyor Major Thomas Mitchell planned his crossing of the Murray River.

Further away, the towns of Beechworth and Yackandandah are well worth exploring for their heritage streetscapes and buildings, eateries and wineries. If you have half a day to spare, drive to the top of the granite 'island in the sky' of Mt Buffalo. On a clear day you can see a panorama of the Australian Alps.

For kids
Bullers Calliope Winery Bird Park, on Three Chain Rd, Rutherglen, has a large collection of rare and endangered species, including the Turquoisine Parrot (**T** 02 6032 9660). There is a local swimming centre, but if you prefer a natural pool try paddling at Lake Moodemere (5 km west of the town). There's also a childen's playground area at Apex Park, or you can feed the turtles and ducks at Lake King.

In nearby Wangaratta you can hire bikes and head for the hills on the RailTrail, a cycle way created from a disused railway line.

Events
Mar: Tastes of Rutherglen (features wine dinners, live entertainment, hot-air ballooning and wine touring
T 1800 622 87 or 1300 787 929)
June: Winery Walkabout (special events and tastings at a number of wineries)
Aug–Sept: Rutherglen Wine Show

Information
Rutherglen Wine Experience and Visitor Information Centre, 57 Main St, Rutherglen **T** 02 6033 6300 or 1800 622 871 **F** 02 6033 6311
W www.visitrutherglen.com.au or www.winemakers.com.au

Yarra Valley

Grape growing started in the Yarra Valley as early as the 1840s and enjoyed a period of great success in the 1880s and 1890s when Yarra wines won international recognition. However, a combination of a preference among the general public for fortified wines and a government keen to promote temperance and the consumption of milk resulted in dairying becoming the main economic activity in the valley, and not until the 1960s did the winemaking industry revive.

The new generation of grape growers and winemakers included Reg Egan of Wantirna Estate and, as was the case in other areas, members of the medical profession, including Dr John Middleton at Mount Mary and Dr Peter McMahon at Seville. Numerous independent vineyards were set up here at this time, including Coldstream Hills, the brainchild of James Halliday, a former lawyer whose passion for wine eventually overtook his interest in the law.

The Yarra Valley has attracted some of the world's largest wine companies as well as some of the most talented and passionate Australian winemakers, which tells you that something very special is happening here. The combination of a cool climate, varying altitudes and diverse soils (predominantly grey loam) make the Yarra a very good place to grow premium grapes—particularly those intended for the production of sparkling wines—and the long ripening period produces wines of intense varietal flavour and elegance.

The wineries are distributed throughout the valley with many clustered around the Maroondah and Melba Highways between

Key

T	Telephone
F	Fax
E	Email
W	Website
WM	Winemaker
CD	Cellar door
P	Picnic facilities
PA	Play area for children
BBQ	Barbecue facilities
GT	Guided tours
C	Cafe
R	Restaurant
O	Opening hours
B&B	Bed and breakfast
H	Hotel/Inn
M	Motel
G	Guesthouse
SCA	Self-catering accommodation

Lilydale, Healesville and Yarra Glen. For the wine tourist, the Yarra Valley is one of the best places to discover Victorian wines and wineries as the range of wines is especially wide and the tourism infrastructure is among the best in Australia. The region also has great food, some of the country's most beautiful vineyards, splendid countryside and historic villages.

What to buy
The wineries of the Yarra Valley make much good Chardonnay and pioneered the planting of Pinot Noir. However, they also make terrific Shiraz, Cabernet Sauvignon and a range of sparkling wines from Semillon, Sauvignon Blanc and Riesling. Experiments are also in hand with Pinot Gris, Marsanne and other varieties. Generally, the wines have immediate appeal when consumed young but will usually age well in the cellar. Variety and good value are to be found in abundance.

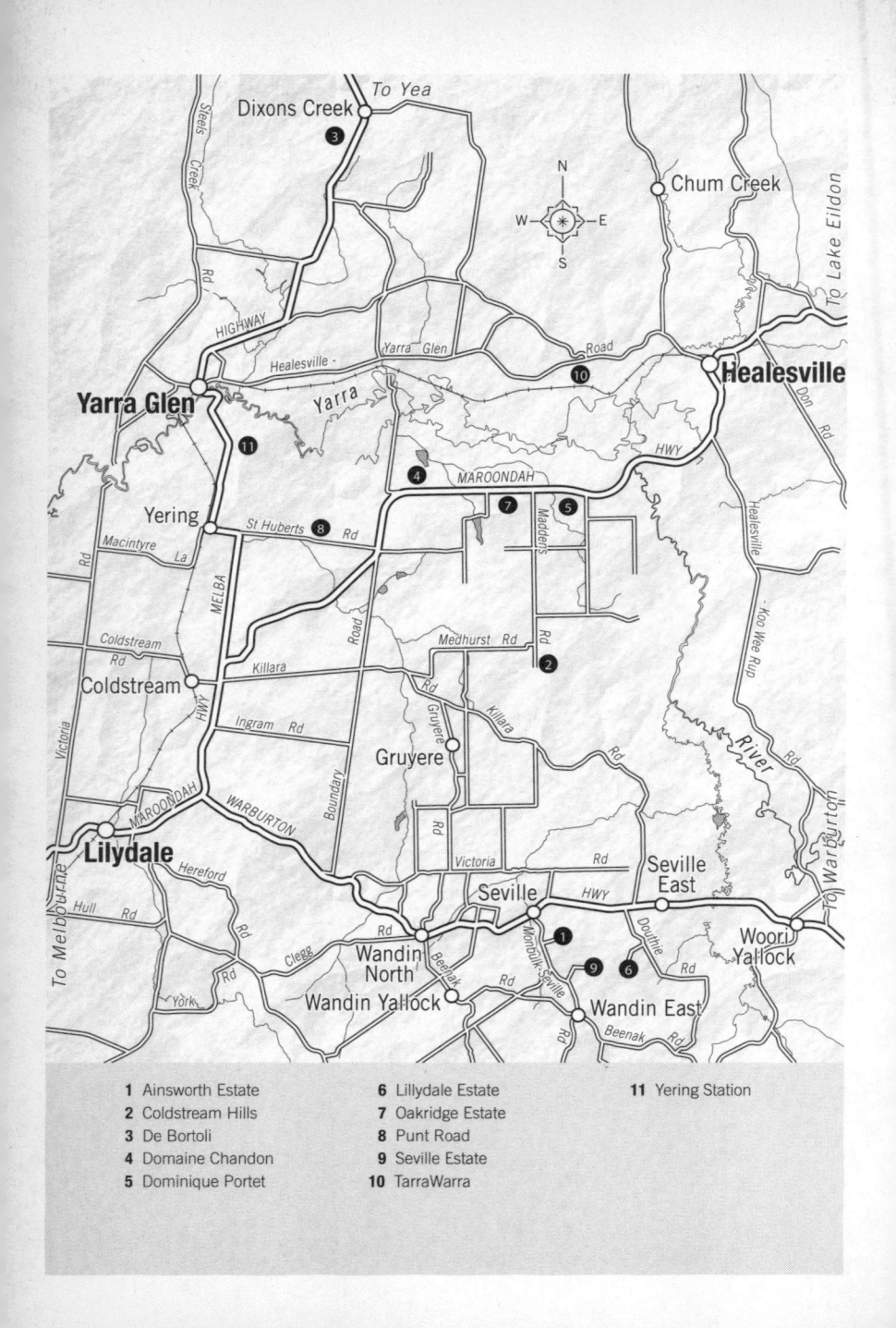

1 Ainsworth Estate
2 Coldstream Hills
3 De Bortoli
4 Domaine Chandon
5 Dominique Portet
6 Lillydale Estate
7 Oakridge Estate
8 Punt Road
9 Seville Estate
10 TarraWarra
11 Yering Station

Wineries

Ainsworth Estate

110 Ducks Lane, Seville

T 03 5964 4711 **F** 03 5964 4311 **E** sales@ainsworth-estate.com.au

A self-proclaimed 'boutique vineyard and winery', Ainsworth Estate is set in pretty country near Seville. As well as a modern cellar door, it has luxury apartments (see Accommodation) and a restaurant, making it an attractive destination for wine tourists looking for a relaxing break. The winery specialises in Pinot Noir, Chardonnay and Shiraz from estate-grown fruit, and Cabernet Sauvignon and other varieties sourced locally. Cheese platters and meals are available all day, and you can relax on the deck overlooking the vineyard.

Denis Craig — **WM CD R SCA**
10.30 am–5 pm Thu–Mon
From 11.30 am for lunch, from 6 pm for dinner

Coldstream Hills

31 Maddens Lane, Coldstream

T 03 5964 9410 **F** 03 5964 9389
E Coldstream.Hills@southcorp.com.au
W www.coldstreamhills.com.au

The vineyard that was established by James Halliday is now part of the Southcorp empire. However, it retains a small winery feel, and the wines continue to be made with care and achieve impressive show results. The Pinot Noir, sparkling Pinot Chardonnay, Chardonnay and Merlot are top quality. The setting is also superb, the cellar door looks out over the vineyards and trees of the Yarra Valley towards Mount St Leonard.

Andrew Fleming — **WM CD**
10 am–5 pm daily

De Bortoli

Pinnacle Lane, Dixons Creek

T 03 5965 2271 **F** 03 5965 2442 **E** sales2@debortoli.com.au

One of the most popular Yarra wineries and one of the largest family-owned wine companies in Australia, De Bortoli offers good wines at sensible prices across an impressive product range. They include selections from holdings in the Hunter Valley

Steve Webber — **WM CD P PA BBQ R**
10 am–5 pm daily

(Chardonnay), Yarra Valley (Pinot Noir) and Griffith (the remarkable Noble One). The Yarra Valley Shiraz shows white pepper characters and is consistently good.

Domaine Chandon

WM Tony Jordan, Neville Rowe, John Harris, James Gosper
CD 10 am–4.30 pm daily
GT
C

'Green Point', Maroondah Hwy, Coldstream
T 03 9739 1110 **F** 03 9739 1095 **E** info@domainechandon.com.au
W www.domainechandon.com.au

One of the most famous of the Victorian wineries, Domaine Chandon deserves its enviable reputation for good wines, good food and a marvellous setting. With views over the vines, the tasting room—along with everything else here—is classy, displaying an interesting blend of French and Australian style. You can buy tasting glasses of the wines with a complimentary platter of bread and locally made chutneys, or you can buy special platters of cheeses and antipasto dishes. The extensive list of sparkling wines is well worth exploring and the Green Point range of still wines offers particularly good value.

Dominique Portet

WM Dominique Portet
CD 10 am–5 pm daily
C

870 Maroondah Hwy, Coldstream
T 03 5967 5760 **F** 03 5962 3405

Dominique Portet produces a limited range of wines, but they are of a very high standard. The white is a snappy Sauvignon Blanc and the dry Rosé is a reminder of the lighter styles of southern France. Also available are Merlot, Shiraz and Cabernet Sauvignon and blends—the Heathcote Cabernet Shiraz 2001 is outstanding. French-style baguette sandwiches and food platters for two are available in the cafe.

Lillydale Estate

WM Jim Brayne, Max McWilliam
CD 11 am–5 pm Mon–Sun
R

45 Davross Court, Seville
T 03 5964 2016 **F** 03 5964 3009 **E** liloffice@mcwilliams.com.au
W www.mcwilliams.com.au

The majority of McWilliams Lillydale wines are made with fruit from the Lillydale vineyards, which were among the first to be re-established in 1976; the remainder are sourced from some of the Yarra's other best sites. These wines, along with some limited-release, cellar-door specials and the rest of the McWilliams' range of red, white and fortified wines, are all available for tasting at the cellar door; many can also be sampled in the restaurant (see Food and Dining). The local wines include the Lillydale Estate Sauvignon Blanc, Chardonnay, Gewurztraminer, Pinot Noir, Shiraz and a really good Cabernet Merlot.

Oakridge Estate

864 Maroondah Hwy, Coldstream
T 03 9739 1920   **F** 03 9739 1923   **E** info@oakridgeestate.com.au
W www.oakridgeestate.com.au

David Bicknell **WM**
10 am–5 pm daily **CD**
C

Tastings and sales take place at Oakridge's stylish visitor centre, which has a friendly atmosphere and spectacular valley views. The wines range from Chardonnay and Sauvignon Blanc through Pinot Noir, Cabernet Merlot and Cabernet Sauvignon to a rosé and Sparkling Chardonnay Pinot. A small number are available only at the cellar door. The winery cafe serves light lunches and snacks that use local produce whenever possible.

Punt Road

10 St Huberts Rd, Coldstream
T 03 9739 0666   **F** 03 9739 0633   **W** www.puntroadwines.com.au

Kate Goodman **WM**
10 am–5 pm daily **CD**
P
BBQ
By appointment **GT**

Punt Road makes a good range of wines at reasonable prices and the quality is generally very high. Sauvignon Blanc and Pinot Gris stand out as good value in the whites, but there is also a Semillon. The reds include Shiraz, Merlot and Cabernet Sauvignon.

Seville Estate

65 Linwood Rd, Seville
T 03 5964 2622   **F** 03 5964 2633   **E** wine@sevilleestate.com.au
W www.sevilleestate.com.au

Iain Riggs, **WM**
Dylan McMahon
By appointment **CD**
only, or join their
club for notification
of monthly events

Founded in the early 1970s, this is one of the Yarra's most influential vineyards and the wines, presented in Estate and Reserve ranges, can be among the valley's best. The spicy Shiraz is the flagship wine, but do not ignore the Chardonnay, Pinot Noir or Cabernet Sauvignon. The Reserve wines are not cheap, but good value. Overall, the quality is consistently high.

TarraWarra Estate

WM Clare Halloran
CD 11 am–5 pm daily

Healesville Rd, Yarra Glen

T 03 5962 3311 **F** 03 5962 3887 **E** enq@tarrawarra.com.au
W www.tarrawarra.com.au

The combination of striking architecture, a spectacular setting, a welcoming cellar door cum cafe and wine bar, and an art gallery devoted to modern Australian art make TarraWarra an unusual and attractive wine-touring destination. The wines come in two ranges, TarraWarra—try the complex Chardonnay—and Tin Cows, the latter encompassing more fruit-driven, ready-to-drink versions of Chardonnay, Pinot Noir, Shiraz and Merlot. TarraWarra also makes Kosher wines under the Kidron label.

Yering Station

WM Darren Rathbone, Tom Carson
CD 10 am–5 pm Mon–Fri, 10 am–6 pm weekends and public holidays
PA

38 Melba Hwy, Yarra Glen

T 03 9730 0100 **F** 03 9739 0135 **E** info@yering.com
W www.yering.com

In 1838, William Ryrie is said to have planted the first grape vines in Victoria at Yering Station, and in 1850 Paul de Castella was instrumental in converting the largely pastoral cattle property into vineyards and a winery. Today, this historic property boasts impressive new buildings, including a restaurant, cellar door and wine bar complex, and fine views to the surrounding hills. The range of wines includes excellent sparkling wines (as you'd expect from the French co-owner Devaux) and solid value in still wines under the Barak's Bridge and Yarra Edge labels. White wines predominate, but there are fine Pinot Noir, Shiraz, Cabernet Sauvignon and Merlot, too. A well-stocked produce shop is another plus for the visitor and a monthly farmers' market is held here in The Barn (10 am–3 pm third Sun of month).

Wine tours and activities

Yarra Valley Winery Tours at Healesville run regular winery tours, but they can vary itineraries depending on passenger needs and budgets (**T** 03 5962 3870 **F** 03 5962 3862 **E** info@yarravalleywinerytours.com.au **W** www.yarravalleywinerytours.com.au).

Food and Dining

The Yarra Valley produces a wide variety of terrific produce, ranging from cheeses and dairy products to game meat, fish and fresh vegetables. There are many orchards where you can pick your own fruit in season, farm-gate stalls selling fruit and veggies, and cafes and restaurants serving local produce. Top-quality retailers include the Yarra Valley Pasta Shop at Healesville (T 03 5962 1888) and Yarra Valley Game Meats, also at Healesville, which sells vacuum-packed aged and seasoned meats including venison, kangarooo, and quail as well as farmed rabbit (T 035962 5173). Cunliffe & Waters at Coldstream sell chutneys, relishes and a wide range of jams and marmalades (T 03 9739 0966). Montrose Meats, at 922 Mount Dandenong Tourist Rd, Montrose, specialises in top-quality meat as well as prepared products such as home-cured hams and smoked smallgoods (T 03 9728 2016). If you haven't tried freshwater Atlantic salmon caviar, you owe it to yourself to do so at Yarra Valley Salmon Caviar at Thornton (T 03 5773 2466). You can taste amazing cheeses at the Yarra Valley Dairy Company in McKeikans Rd, Yering, which also has a cellar door selling regional wines and a range of fresh fruit and preserved foods including products from Australian Harvest, Ann Creber and Jam Lady jams (T 03 9739 0023   O 10 am–4 pm Thurs–Mon).

Yarra Valley Platters can be purchased in many parts of the valley. The brainchild of the Yarra Valley Regional Food Group (T 03 9513 0677), they vary in content from place to place depending on season and outlet, but can include breads, meats, cheeses, preserves, dips and salads; they offer good value and support local producers.

The Yarra Valley Regional Food Group also produces a guide called Hidden Delights, which lists food producers, farm-gate 'taste and buy' opportunities, as well as shops, cafes and pick-your-own orchards. The guide is regularly updated and is indispensable for touring the region. In addition, local tourist offices publish a guide to the Yarra Valley Regional Food Trail, which lists all local specialist growers and producers (W www.yarravalleyfood.com.au)—watch out for the special signs as you drive around the region. Finally, a farmers' market is held monthly at The Barn, Yering Station Vineyard at Yarra Glen (10 am–3 pm third Sun of every month).

Cunninghams Inn, Warburton Hwy, Yarra Junction **T** 03 5967 1080 **O** 11 am–11 pm daily. Excellent local pub food is served in this historic inn with a pleasant beer garden and open fires in winter. The menu features a good list of local wines.

De Bortoli Winery restaurant, Pinnacle Lane, Dixons Creek, **T** 03 5965 2271 **F** 03 5965 2442 **E** sales2@debortoli.com.au **O** From 12 noon daily for lunch, from 6.30 pm Sat for dinner. This award-winning winery restaurant serves northern Italian food and maintains high standards, despite the large number of visitors. The menu, which changes seasonally and has daily specials, features pastas, risottos, game and seafood. Wines are available by the bottle or glass, and are carefully matched to the food. The special five-course Sunday lunch menu is very popular—book in advance. The restaurant has superb views over the vineyards and ranges beyond.

Fergusson's of Yarra Glen, Wills Rd, Yarra Glen **T** 03 5965 2237 **O** 12 pm–3 pm daily for lunch, Sat for dinner. Fresh local produce is used to create innovative dishes at reasonable prices.

Lillydale Vineyards Restaurant, Lillydale Vineyards, 45 Davross Court, Seville **T** 03 5964 2016 **F** 03 5964 3009 **E** liloffice@mcwilliams.com.au **W** www.mcwilliams.com.au **O** 11 am–5 pm daily (lunch 12 noon–3 pm). This 80-seat restaurant features an indoor barbecue facility where you can cook your own main course (meat or seafood), so you are sure it's cooked to your satisfaction. There is also an à la carte menu of entrees, desserts and salads to accompany your choice. The restaurant has lovely views over the Toolebewong Ranges.

Rochford's Eyton Restaurant, cnr Maroondah Hwy and Hill Rd, Coldstream **T** 03 5962 2119 **E** info@rochfordwines.com **O** 12 noon–3 pm daily. Try the two-course luncheon special at this smart and highly successful operation. There is a cafe as well as a restaurant serving modern, fresh seasonal food in a huge glassed-in area with great views. The outdoor terrace with umbrellas overlooks a lake and vineyard.

Accommodation

Ainsworth Estate, 110 Ducks Lane, Seville **T** 03 5964 4711 **F** 03 5964 4311 **E** sales@ainsworth-estate.com.au. These striking, modern apartments overlook the vines and are close to the cellar door of this boutique development. Airconditioned, the three units feature mezzanine sleeping areas and stylish finishes, and have good kitchen areas, outdoor decking and ensuite bathrooms. Book ahead.

Amethyst Lodge Bed & Breakfast, 139 Wills Rd, Yarra Glen **T** 03 5965 2559 **W** www.amethystlodge.com.au. The accommodation here is at the deluxe and super deluxe levels. Dinner is available if requested in advance.

Healesville Hotel, 256 Maroondah Hwy, Healesville **T** 03 5962 4002. As well as boutique accommodation, the hotel offers an award-winning restaurant with an impressive list of local wines, and a produce store. Packages including accommodation and access to the sanctuary (see Travel Information, Other attractions) are available at certain times of year.

Kiltynane Estate B&B, 510 Yarra Glen–Healsville Road, Tarrawarra (via Yarra Glen) **T** 03 5962 1897 **F** 03 5962 1897 **W** www.kiltynane.com.au. Inspired by French provincial style and set amid vineyards, these comfortable self-contained cottages have airconditioning and open fires. The location is convenient for many of the region's best wineries and restaurants.

Marion Park Gardens B&B, 189 Woods Point Rd, Warburton **T** 03 5966 5579 **E** info@marionparkgardens **W** www.marionparkgardens.com.au. A peaceful, secluded bed and breakfast surrounded by trees and gardens, Marion Park Gardens has nicely furnished rooms with airconditioning, a full breakfast service and a guests' entrance.

Valley Farm Vineyard, Valley Farm Rd, Healesville **T** 03 5962 5723 or 0438 002 101 **F** 03 5962 4718 **E** info@valleyfarm.com.au **W** www.valleyfarm.com.au. This self-contained accommodation in two cheerily decorated suites is cosy and comfortable and has lovely mountain views. An outdoor spa is provided for the use of guests.

Travel Information

How to get there
By road The Yarra Valley is just over an hour's drive from Melbourne. Take the Maroondah Hwy from Melbourne to Ringwood, and then follow the signs to Lilydale and Coldstream.

Other attractions
French influences are strong and widespread in the valley, even in the realm of sporting activities. Hot-air ballooning, known locally as 'Montgolfier ballooning', is popular and there is a good range of operators, including Go Wild Ballooning (**T** 03 9890 6339), Peregrine Ballooning (**T** 03 9730 2422) and Global Ballooning (**T** 1800 627 661). Take your pick!

For kids
The Healesville Sanctuary has more than 200 species of native birds and mammals and is well worth exploring (**T** 03 5962 4022 **W** www.zoo.org.au). The best fun available in the nearby Dandenong Ranges is Puffing Billy, a famous steam train that travels from Belgrave to Emerald, passing lush vegetation and cute villages that time has (almost) passed by (**T** 03 9754 6800). Not to be missed.

Events
Jan: Jazz in the Vines, TarraWarra Winery
Feb: Grape Grazing Festival (annual festival of musical events, food-matching and wine-tasting at various wineries **T** 03 5965 2100 **W** www.grapegrazing.com.au).
Mar: Longest Lunch (part of the Melbourne Food and Wine Festival)
Aug: Victorian Wine Week

Information
Yarra Valley Visitor Information Centre, The Old Courthouse, Harker St, Healesville (**T** 03 5962 2600
F 03 5962 2040
E info@yarravalleytourism.asn.au
W www.visitvictoria.com

Western Australia

Great Southern

In viticultural terms the Great Southern region remained relatively undeveloped until quite recently. Experimental plantings began in the late 1950s and early 1960s and showed great promise. By the 1970s, a number of wineries had begun operating and many more growers—mostly local farmers looking to diversify from poorly performing sheep stations—began planting vines. The success of early growers such as Alkoomi, Goundrey and Plantagenet encouraged others to join the industry, even if only on a part-time basis. More recently, the area has attracted some larger investors as well as many more small growers and winemakers.

By area, Great Southern is one of the largest wine regions in Australia, and it is divided into four subregions: Albany, Frankland River, Mount Barker and Porongurup. Climate and soils vary considerably, with some vineyards enjoying a long growing season and a moderating maritime influence whereas others, mainly inland, experience hotter, drier weather.

Mount Barker is the focus of the region, and other winegrowing regions radiate out from there—to the north along the Albany Highway, to the west along the Muir Highway and to the south and along the coast at Albany and Denmark. Although the majority of wineries are to be found in the triangle formed by Albany, Mount Barker and Denmark, some of the largest areas in development are around Frankland River and in Porongurup.

Key

T	Telephone
F	Fax
E	Email
W	Website
WM	Winemaker
CD	Cellar door
P	Picnic facilities
PA	Play area for children
BBQ	Barbecue facilities
GT	Guided tours
C	Cafe
R	Restaurant
O	Opening hours
B&B	Bed and breakfast
H	Hotel/Inn
M	Motel
G	Guesthouse
SCA	Self-catering accommodation

ALBANY
1 Montgomery's Hill
2 Wignalls Wines

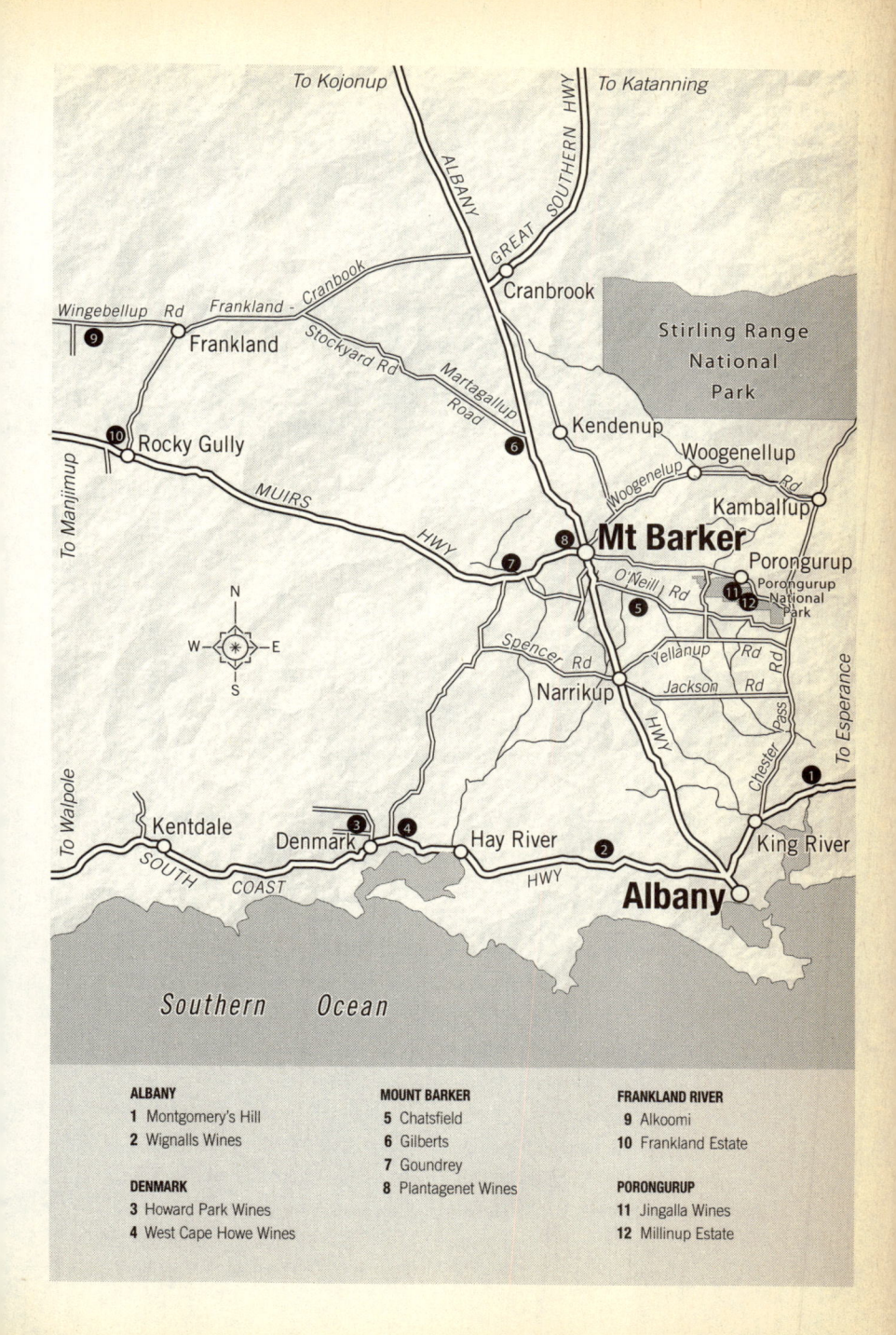

DENMARK
3 Howard Park Wines
4 West Cape Howe Wines

MOUNT BARKER
5 Chatsfield
6 Gilberts
7 Goundrey
8 Plantagenet Wines

FRANKLAND RIVER
9 Alkoomi
10 Frankland Estate

PORONGURUP
11 Jingalla Wines
12 Millinup Estate

What to buy

Cool-climate wines can be of exceptional quality here. The area is noted more for its whites than for its reds, and Riesling, Chardonnay and Sauvignon Blanc are generally the best options. But recently Cabernet Sauvignon, Shiraz and Merlot have yielded wines of high quality that offer intense fruit flavours and a distinctive regional style.

Wineries

Albany

Montgomery's Hill

WM Diane Miller (contract)
CD 11 am–5 pm daily
P
BBQ

Hassell Hwy, Kalgan River
T 08 9844 3715 **F** 08 9844 1104
E winesales@montgomeryshill.com.au
W www.montgomeryshill.com.au

This family-run vineyard produces a small range of both red and white wines from grapes grown on the property's north-facing slopes. Both Wooded and Unwooded Chardonnay are made as well as Sauvignon Blanc and the Kalgan Sunset blend of Sauvignon Blanc and Chardonnay for early consumption. There is a rich Cabernet Sauvignon, a Cabernet Sauvignon Cabernet Franc blend and the Kalgan Sunset Cabernet Franc Merlot. The cellar door is a charming rammed-earth structure, and cheese platters are available during tasting. One option when travelling to Montgomery's Hill for a tasting is to catch the *Kalgan Queen*, a small riverboat that departs from Emu Point in Albany at 9 am (booking strongly advised). The half-day tour will take you upriver for the tasting, giving you the chance to see some of the local wildlife on the way, and take you back again (**T** 08 9844 1949 or 0428 464 115 **E** captain@albanyaustralia.com).

Wignalls Wines

Chester Pass Rd (part of Hwy 1), Albany
T 08 9841 2848 **F** 08 9842 9003 **E** info@wignallswines.com.au
W www.wignallswines.com.au

Rob Wignall **WM**
12 noon–4 pm **CD**
daily (longer hours in summer)
BBQ

Wignalls was one of the first wineries to be established in this subregion. Its range includes two whites—Sauvignon Blanc and an award-winning Chardonnay—and a number of reds, including Cabernet Sauvignon and Pinot Noir, the latter an unusual choice for the region but a remarkably successful one. The cellar door has an attractive stone door and occupies a lovely setting amid trees.

Frankland River

Alkoomi

Wingebellup Rd, Frankland
T 08 9855 2229 **F** 08 9855 2284 **E** info@alkoomiwines.com.au
W www.alkoomiwines.com.au

Michael Staniford **WM**
10.30 am–5 pm **CD**
daily
SCA

Merv and Judy Lange and family have run this winery for more than 30 years, and today Alkoomi is the largest family-owned wine producer in Western Australia. The Langes planted their first vines in 1971—Riesling, Cabernet Sauvignon, Shiraz and Malbec—and produced their first wines in 1976. The red wines enjoyed early success and Alkoomi has continued to produce elegant Cabernet Sauvignon and Shiraz, and Cabernet blends. The quality of their Riesling has helped establish the reputation of Frankland River as one of the best areas for this variety in Australia, and the Sauvignon Blanc is also regarded as one of the country's best. The full range is divided between two labels, Alkoomi and Southlands, and also includes Merlot, Malbec, Cabernet Franc, Petit Verdot, Sangiovese, Semillon, Chardonnay and Viognier. The winery also offers accommodation in two chalets that each sleep up to seven people. Alkoomi also has a retail outlet in Albany, at 225 Lower Stirling Tce (**o** 10.30 am–5 pm daily).

Frankland Estate

WM Judy Cullam, Barrie Smith
CD 10 am–4 pm Mon–Fri, weekends and public holidays by appointment

Frankland Rd, Frankland
T 08 9855 1544 **F** 08 9855 1549

A major producer of wines in Frankland River since the early 1990s, this estate focuses on Riesling and Chardonnay, Cabernet and Shiraz. However, the flagbearer is Olmo's Reward. Named in honour of the Californian viticulturalist Dr Harold Olmo, who was the first to recognise the subregion's potential, it is a complex blend of Merlot and Cabernet Franc, with support from Cabernet Sauvignon, Malbec and Petit Verdot. The Isolation Ridge varietals (Chardonnay, Riesling, Shiraz and Cabernet Sauvignon) are all grown on the Estate. The Rocky Gully range is intended for easy drinking and includes a Riesling, Cabernets, and a Shiraz. There are also two distinctive single-vineyard Rieslings: Cooladerah and Poison Hill.

Mount Barker

Chatsfield

WM Diane Miller (contract)
CD By appointment

O'Neil Rd, Mount Barker
T/F 08 9851 1704 **E** chats@chatsfield.com.au
W www.chatsfield.com.au

Dr Ken Lynch and his wife Joyce have been growing very good grapes here on the western side of the Porongurup Range since they purchased the property in 1989—from which some excellent cool-climate wines have been made. Mount Barker Cabernet Franc, Chardonnay, Gewurztraminer, Riesling and Shiraz are all made here, with Shiraz perhaps being the star turn, although the Riesling certainly has a following.

Gilberts

WM Plantagenet Wines (Richard Robson)
CD 10 am–5 pm daily
R

RMB 438 Albany Hwy, Kendenup, Mount Barker
T 08 9851 4028 **F** 08 9851 4021 **E** gilberts@rainbow.agn.net.au

Set in a restored farm cottage, the cellar door and restaurant (see Food and Dining) are set back from the highway and surrounded by apple orchards and vineyards. The wines, seven in all, range from the Wooded Chardonnay and full-bodied Riesling through the

Alira Semillon Riesling blend to the Three Devils Shiraz Cabernet blend (from young and old vines), and Shiraz. The Reserve Shiraz, made purely from old vines, is a powerful wine and great value for money. A port is also available, at the cellar door only.

Goundrey Wines

Langton, Muirs Hwy, Mount Barker
T 08 9366 3900   **F** 08 9321 6281   **E** info@goundreywines.com.au
W www.goundreywines.com.au

David Martin **WM**
10 am–4.30 pm **CD**
daily
P
BBQ

Established in the early 1970s, Goundrey is now one of the largest wine-producing companies in Western Australia, and is owned by Canada's Vincorp. The wines, particularly the whites, can be very good and the stylish cellar door, which has huge glass windows, is set in pleasant gardens. There are several ranges, from the premium Reserve range to the second label, Fox River, which includes a Semillon Verdelho, Chardonnay, Shiraz Cabernet and Pinot Noir. The Homestead range includes a Classic White (Semillon Sauvignon Blanc blend), a Chenin Blanc and an Unwooded Chardonnnay. Goundrey also produces good reds in the Reserve range, including Shiraz and Cabernet Sauvignon from Mount Barker and a Pinot Noir sourced from Mount Barker and Pemberton.

Plantagenet Wines

Albany Hwy, Mount Barker
T 08 9851 2150   **F** 08 9851 1839   **E** sales@plantagenetwines.com
W www.plantagenetwines.com.au

Richard Robson **WM**
9 am–5 pm daily **CD**

The first of the Great Southern wineries, Plantagenet started in a very modest way in a former apple store, but has now been producing good and sometimes great wines for 30 years and become a much-revered local institution. The range is broad and encompasses several brands. The wines include Riesling, Chardonnay, Pinot Noir, Shiraz, Cabernet Sauvignon, Sauvignon Blanc and various blends. Some of the best are the Omrah Shiraz and Sauvignon Blanc, and the Mount Barker Chardonnay, Pinot Noir and Shiraz. The budget Hazard Hill Shiraz Grenache is great value.

Denmark

Howard Park Wines

WM Michael Kerrigan
CD 10 am–4 pm daily

Scotsdale Rd, Denmark
T 08 9848 2345 **F** 08 9848 2064 **E** denmark@hpw.com.au
W www.howardparkwines.com.au

This winery lies in the historic Parkhead property amid spectacular native forests of karri and marri trees that are home to abundant wildlife, and has a stylish, modern cellar door. The focus here is on producing small quantities of wines with distinct regional character. The Howard Park, Scotsdale and MadFish ranges are widely recognised as offering some of Western Australia's best-value wines. In particular, the Howard Park Riesling and Cabernet Sauvignon Merlot blend, the Scotsdale Pinot Noir, and the Madfish Chardonnay, Premium White and Premium Red should not be missed.

West Cape Howe Wines

WM Gavin Barry
CD 10 am–5 pm daily
P
BBQ

Lot 42 South Coast Hwy, Denmark
T 08 9848 2959 **F** 08 9848 2903 **E** wchowe@denmarkwa.net.au
W www.wchowe.com.au

From its modest beginnings as a contract winemaking operation, West Cape Howe Wines has rapidly gained an enviable reputation as a producer of premium Riesling, Oaked Chardonnay, Cabernet Sauvignon and Viognier. The core range also includes a bestselling Unwooded Chardonnay, a Semillon Sauvignon Blanc, a Shiraz, and a deservedly popular Cabernet Merlot.

Porongurup

Jingalla Wines

WM Diane Miller
CD 10.30 am–5 pm daily
P
PA
BBQ
SCA

Lot 9 Bolganup Dam Rd, Porongurup
T/F 08 9853 1023 **E** jingallawines@wn.com.au
W www.jingallawines.com.au

This small winery was started in 1979 by Nita and Geoff Clarke (Barry and Shelley Coad now help manage the winery) and has produced some very fine wines over the years. The range includes five successful whites—Riesling, Verdelho, Great Southern White (Semillon Chardonnay blend), Botrytis Riesling Verdelho, Late Harvest (Semillon Sauvignon Blanc blend)—and some pretty good reds too—Great Southern Red (Cabernet Sauvignon Shiraz), Shiraz Reserve, Cabernet Rouge (Cabernet Sauvignon and Riesling), and Cabernet Merlot. The cellar door has fabulous views of the Porongurup Range and lovely gardens, but you need to bring your own supplies. The winery also has a self-contained cottage on the vineyard (sleeping four), which is available for rent—check the availability in advance of a visit.

Millinup Estate

RMB 1280 Porongurup Rd, Porongurup
T/F 08 9853 1105 **W** www.millinupestate.ii.net

Diane Miller (whites), Mike Garland (reds) **WM**
B&B
SCA

This tiny vineyard has its own cricket pitch and one of the most scenic locations in this or any other region. The wines include the crisp Old Cottage Riesling and Twin Peaks Riesling, a Cabernet Sauvignon and a Cabernet Merlot blend. Bed and breakfast accommodation is available in the farmhouse and there are two self-catering cottages on the estate: Pioneer Cottage, which is rustic on the outside, but comfortable and welcoming inside (sleeping up to six); and Hillside Cottage, which is located near to the cellar door and has a double bed and sofa bed as well as breathtaking views of the Stirling Range.

Wine tours and activities

Tours of the wineries can be booked through Albany Escape Tours (**T** 08 9844 1945 or 0428 441 945 **W** www.albanyis.com.au/~escape), which also offers a range of scenic tours in the Great Southern region, Albany Scenic Tours (**T** 08 9844 1551), and Albany Limousines (**T** 08 9844 1797).

Food and Dining

Since its inception in 2002, the Great Southern Farmers' Market in Aberdeen St, Albany, has gone from strength to strength. Every Saturday morning (8 am–12 pm), locals and visitors arrive early to buy fresh food direct from the people that produce it. On sale, as well as fruit and vegetables, are fish, marron, venison, organic meats and eggs, sauces, honey, cheeses and yoghurt.

In season at Torbay Asparagus at Midway, South Coast Hwy, you can find not just asparagus (Sept–Dec) but also boysenberries, raspberries, silvanberries (Dec–Jan) and sweet corn (Dec–May). At Eden Gate Blueberry Farm on Eden Rd, Youngs Siding, 15 km east of Denmark, you can pick your own blueberries in season (Dec–April); if you don't want to pick, you can still buy from the farm-gate shop, which sells blueberries and a range of blueberry products, including jams, jellies, vinegars and wines (**T/F** 08 9845 2003). Albany is known for its seafood, including oysters and crabs, and another local speciality is farmed saltwater rainbow trout, which can be purchased at Colley's Seafood in Stirling St (**T** 08 9841 4257). The restaurants in Albany and Denmark all feature seafood dishes, and the quality is superb.

Pick up a Great Southern Food and Wine Touring guide from tourist information centres, and for more information on food see **W** www.greatsoutherntaste.wa.com.

Albany

Earl of Spencer, cnr Earl and Spencer Sts, Albany **T** 08 9841 1322 **W** www.earlofspencer.com.au **O** 12 noon–midnight Mon–Sat, 2 pm–9 pm Sun. This genuine old pub is open for lunch and dinner and serves pub food ranging from snacks to heartier fare. The salads are good and there is an impressive list of wines. The pub has a no-smoking policy.

The Naked Bean Cafe, 14 Peels Place, Albany **T** 08 9841 1815 **O** 8 am–5 pm Mon–Fri, 8 am–1 pm Sat. This casual cafe dishes up breakfasts, brunch and lunch, made with local produce whenever possible, and good lighter-style home-roasted coffee.

Ristorante Leonardos, 166 Stirling Tce, Albany **T/F** 08 9841 1732 **O** 6.30 pm–late Mon–Sat. Highly recommended, this intimate restaurant serves northern Italian-influenced food. It's advisable to book.

Mount Barker

Gilberts Wines Restaurant, RMB 438 Albany Hwy, Kendenup, Mount Barker **T** 08 9851 4028 **F** 08 9851 4021 **E** gilberts@rainbow.agn.net.au **O** 10 am–5 pm daily. Chicken, mushroom and mustard pie, frittata salads, and home-baked quiches feature on the menu here, and one or two more substantial dishes are usually available at weekends; the blackboard specials are always worth a look, too. Soups, cheese platters and ploughman's lunches are standby fare on weekdays.

Plantagenet Hotel, 9 Lowood Rd, Mount Barker **T** 08 9851 1008 **F** 08 9851 2108 **O** 12 noon–2 pm Fri, 6 pm–8 pm daily. This historic hotel has a bistro-style eatery with an à la carte menu and a wine list featuring a good selection of local wines. Meals range from steak sandwich to pastas and salads, and the Sunday night roast dinner special is very popular. The restaurant has an open fire and is nonsmoking.

Accommodation

Albany

Clarence House B&B, 110 Hare St, Albany **T/F** 08 9841 5409 **E** clarence@albanyis.com.au **W** www.albanyis.com.au/~clarence. Enjoy great views and good food at this comfortable bed and breakfast. There are just two rooms; both have ensuites, one has views over the water (allowing you to observe passing whales in season) and the other overlooks a pleasant garden.

Esplanade Hotel, cnr Adelaide Cres and Flinders Pde, Albany **T** 08 9842 1711 or 1800 678 757 (reservations) **F** 08 9841 7527 **E** reservations@albanyesplanade.com.au **W** www.albanyesplanade.com.au. A range of accommodation is available in this plush, colonial-style hotel. The excellent amenities include Genevieve's Restaurant, tennis courts and a pool. The hotel has fabulous views to the ocean and mountains.

Denmark

Cape Howe Cottages, RMB 9298 Tennessee Rd South, Lowlands Beach **T** 08 9845 1295 or 042 995 9906 **F** 08 9845 1396 **E** holiday@capehowe.com.au **W** www.capehowe.com. A choice of family-friendly cottages in a secluded location. Comfort at a reasonable price.

Mount Barker

Valley Views Motel and Chalets, Albany Hwy, Mount Barker **T** 08 9851 3899 **F** 08 9851 3800 **E** vvmotel@wn.com.au **W** members.westnet.com.au/vvmotel The motel has standard units and family rooms, as well as five self-contained chalets in a garden setting with rural views to the Porongurups. The chalets have queen-sized beds and full kitchens with cooker and microwave. The motel room tariff includes a full breakfast.

Travel Information

How to get there
By road Albany is approximately a 5-hour drive south of Perth via the Albany Hwy.
By air You can fly to Albany from Perth twice a day with Skywest. There are two or three flights per day, at 6.45 am, 11 am, or either 5 or 6 pm (**T** 1300 660 088).

Other attractions
The Great Southern region is one of Australia's great whale-watching centres, and in season (July–Aug) whales can be seen from a number of lookouts, some close to the centre of Albany, including the viewpoints at Middleton Beach Rd and at Whale World on Frenchman Bay Rd (or check recent sightings at the local tourist office). During the spring wildflower season (Sept–Nov), the area's national parks put on a brilliant display of flowers surpassing any other in Australia. The granite bulk of the Stirling Ranges, to the north of Albany via Kamballup, provides a spectacular show, with more than 1500 species of wildflowers on display, many of which are not found anywhere else in the world.

From Albany, you can drive west towards the spectacular coastal landscapes of Denmark and the old-growth forests of the hinterland. At Walpole, you can visit the Valley of the Giants, where a treetop walkway leads you through the canopies of fabulous red and yellow tingle trees (the yellow tingle is an extremely rare species).

The Gap, Blow Holes and Natural Bridge are spectacular coastal formations in Torndirrup National Park. Carved out of the granite coastline by the action of the waves, they produce spectacular waves and geyser-like water columns at high tide.

Situated 12 km south-west of the city amid some of the state's most dramatic coastal scenery, Albany Wind Farm provides about 70 per cent of the electricity needs of the town of Albany and is an impressive but slightly eerie sight.

HMAS *Perth* was scuttled during 2001 in the protected waters of King George Sound to provide a dive site for scuba divers and snorkellers. If that doesn't appeal, you can still take a trip to view the wreck from an underwater observation vessel, *Albany Reef Explorer* (**T** 08 9841 5440).

For kids

Housed in what was once a whaling station, Whale World, in Frenchman Bay Rd, Albany, is now a museum incorporating numerous fascinating displays, including film and multimedia presentations, relating to the days of whaling (**T** 08 9844 4021
F 08 9844 4621 **E** info@whaleworld.org
W www.whaleworld.org).

Events

Jan: Mount Barker Wine Festival Weekend (**T** 08 9851 2565), Vintage Blues Festival, Wignalls Wines (**T** 08 9841 2848)
Mar: Porongurup Wine Festival (**T** 08 9851 1163)
Sept: Wildflower Festival
Sept–Oct: Great Southern Wine Festival (**T** 08 9842 3265)
Nov: Franklin River Fine Wine, Food and Music Festival

Information

Albany Visitor Information Centre, The Old Railway Station, Proudlove Pde, Albany
T 1800 644 088 or 08 9841 1088
F 08 9842 1490
E avc@albanytourist.com.au
W www.albanytourist.com.au

Margaret River

Margaret River has one of the shorter histories of wine production in Australia—vines weren't planted here until the 1960s—but the range and quality of its wines has seen it become established as a leading producer with a strong national and international reputation. It is also fair to say that it has become one of the country's top wine-touring destinations, due to its winning combination of diverse wineries, well-above-average restaurants, and spectacular countryside and coastal scenery.

As they did elsewhere in Australia, members of the medical profession assisted at the birth of the local wine industry. Vasse Felix was established in 1967 by Dr Tom Cullity; Dr Bill Pannell and his wife Sandra planted vines in 1969 at Moss Wood; and Dr Kevin Cullen and his wife Di founded Cullens in 1971 after an experimental planting in 1966. Early results were so promising that Margaret River quickly began to attract significant investment and throughout the 1970s and 1980s the number of small wineries increased steadily. In the last few years it has been claimed that although Margaret River produces less than 5 per cent of Australia's wine by quantity, it accounts for more than 20 per cent of the country's premium-wine production. This statistic speaks volumes on the local industry's continuing dedication to quality.

It also reflects the region's suitability for winegrowing. Soils are generally well-drained sandy loams over clay. Surrounded on three sides by ocean, Margaret River enjoys a mild, maritime-influenced Mediterranean climate with

Key

T	Telephone
F	Fax
E	Email
W	Website
WM	Winemaker
CD	Cellar door
P	Picnic facilities
PA	Play area for children
BBQ	Barbecue facilities
GT	Guided tours
C	Cafe
R	Restaurant
O	Opening hours
B&B	Bed and breakfast
H	Hotel/Inn
M	Motel
G	Guesthouse
SCA	Self-catering accommodation

good rainfall during the winter months and low rainfall during the long ripening season, from October to April. The north of the region experiences warm, dry north-easterly winds in summer, while the south enjoys the cool, moist influence of the south-easterly trade winds. Numerous microclimates occur as a result, distinguishing a number of subregions, including Yallingup in the north-west, Carbunup in the north-east, Wilyabrup, Treeton and Wallcliffe (which includes Margaret River) in the centre and east, and Karridale in the south.

As a wine region and as a tourist destination Margaret River has shown that it can lead the way in terms of innovation, quality and style. Enjoy.

What to buy

Margaret River is famous for its Chardonnay, but, along with Coonawarra, the Yarra Valley and the Barossa Valley, is also regarded as one of the best regions in the country for producing Cabernet Sauvignon. Don't expect to find too many bargains at the older boutique wineries: the wines are very good quality and for the most part attract high prices, though recently some effort has been put into producing early-drinking wines in the lower price bracket. However, the expansion of vineyards and experimentation with a wider range of grape varieties has greatly increased the output and diversity of produce, and numerous winemakers now supply a wide range of wines at reasonable prices.

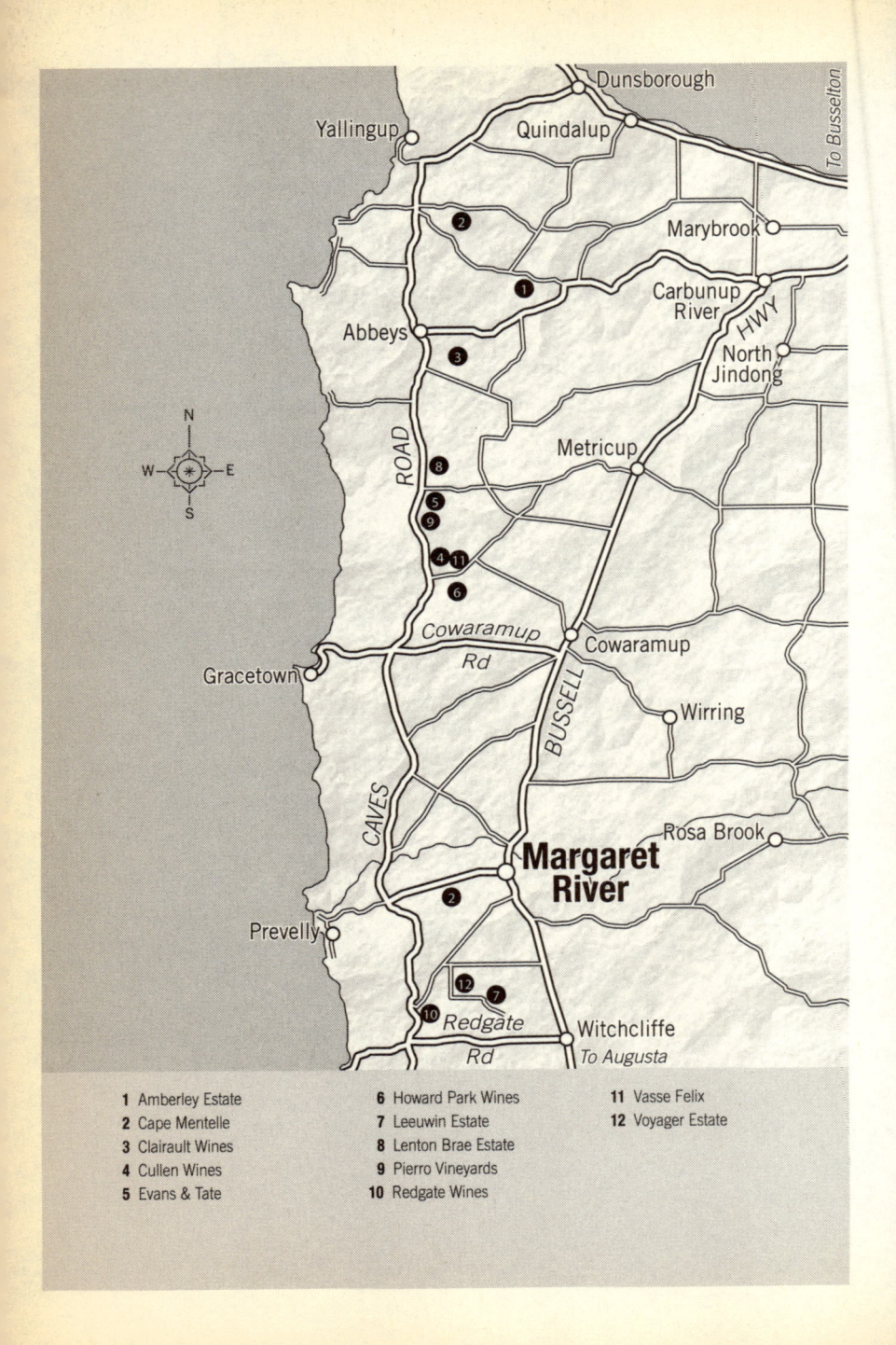

1 Amberley Estate	**6** Howard Park Wines	**11** Vasse Felix
2 Cape Mentelle	**7** Leeuwin Estate	**12** Voyager Estate
3 Clairault Wines	**8** Lenton Brae Estate	
4 Cullen Wines	**9** Pierro Vineyards	
5 Evans & Tate	**10** Redgate Wines	

Wineries

Amberley Estate

Thornton Rd, Yallingup

T 08 9755 2288 **F** 08 9755 2171

E amberley@amberley-estate.com.au

W www.amberley-estate.com.au

Paul Dunnewyk **WM**
10 am–4.30 pm **CD**
daily

A broad range of wines is produced here, with an emphasis on whites. The early Chenin Blanc was highly successful, if not everyone's cup of tea. More recently, the premium Amberley Estate label has included Semillon, Chardonnay and Sauvignon Blanc from vines that have come to maturity, as well as Shiraz, Cabernet Sauvignon, Cabernet Merlot and Cabernet Franc. The estate-grown wines are rich, mouth-filling and balanced with a bit of oak. The lower-priced Charlotte Street label includes a Chardonnay Semillon and a Shiraz Cabernet. Set amid gently sloping vineyard scenery and with an unpretentious restaurant (see Food and Dining), Amberley makes for a very pleasant cellar-door visit.

Cape Mentelle

Wallcliffe Rd, Margaret River

T 08 9757 3266 **F** 08 9757 3233 **E** info@capementelle.com.au

W capementelle.com.au

John Durham, **WM**
Simon Burnell
10 am–4.30 pm **CD**
daily
P

Cape Mentelle is very well known—almost as famous as its sister winery at Cloudy Bay in New Zealand—and the wines and location, in the heart of Margaret River, are superb. The spacious rammed-earth tasting centre is surrounded by well-kept native gardens with abundant birdlife, and the cellar looks through to the barrel room with its barriques of Cabernet. The wide range of wines gives you plenty to think about. Of the whites, the Chardonnays are often outstanding, as are the Semillon Sauvignon Blancs; the Shiraz, Zinfandel, Cabernet Sauvignon and Cabernet Merlot (Trinders Vineyard) are also consistently good.

Clairault Wines

WM Peter Stark
CD 10 am–5 pm daily
R

Henry Rd, Wilyabrup

T 08 9755 6655 **F** 08 9755 6229
E clairault@clairaultwines.com.au **W** www.clairaultwines.com.au

Clairault is located about 20 km north of the town of Margaret River. The vineyard is named after nearby Cape Clairault, a prominent local landmark. The Clairault vineyard is one of the oldest in the region; its first vines were planted in 1976. Two fine ranges are produced here, encompassing good-value Sauvignon Blanc and Riesling, as well as Cabernet Merlot and Cabernet Sauvignon. The cellar-door facilities have been upgraded and are stylishly efficient, and there are lovely gardens and a restaurant (see Food and Dining).

Cullen Wines

WM Vanya Cullen
CD 10 am–4 pm daily
P

Caves Rd, Wilyabrup

T 08 9755 5277 **F** 08 9755 5550 **E** enquiries@cullenwine.com.au
W www.cullenwines.com.au

A classic boutique winery, Cullens was one of the first to be established in the Margaret River region, by the late Dr Kevin Cullen and his wife Diana. Happily, a new generation is continuing the family tradition, and the wines are still well made and highly regarded. The range includes the all-conquering Chardonnay as well as Cabernet Sauvignon, Pinot Noir, Merlot, Sauvignon Blanc and Semillon. The winery also has a restaurant (see Food and Dining).

Evans & Tate

WM Steve Warne
CD 10.30 am–4.30 pm daily
P
PA
BBQ
C

Redbrook Vineyard Visitors' Centre, Metricup Rd, Wilyabrup

T 08 9755 6244 **F** 08 9213 1798 **E** et@evansandtate.com.au
W www.evansandtate.com.au

A public company since 1999, Evans & Tate is now the largest wine producer in the Margaret River region, but it still manages to produce fine wines at affordable prices and the visitors' centre is a classy operation. White wines predominate, with the Gnangara label offering Unwooded Chardonnay, Sauvignon Blanc and Chenin Blanc, as well as Shiraz and Cabernet. The Margaret River range includes Chardonnay and Semillon, and a Sauvignon Blanc Semillon blend, as well as Shiraz and Cabernet Merlot. The winery also has a cafe (**O** 10.30 am–4.30 pm, lunch 11.30 am–3 pm).

Howard Park Wines

Miamup Rd, Cowaramup

T 08 9756 5200   **F** 08 9756 5222   **E** margaretriver@hpw.com.au
W www.howardparkwines.com.au

A splendid addition to the range of cellar doors in Margaret River, this one has top wines from the Madfish and Howard Park ranges, as well as the Leston range of premium Margaret River wines. Good value to be found in most price brackets.

Michael Kerrigan **WM**
10 am–5 pm **CD**

Leeuwin Estate

Stevens Rd, Margaret River

T 08 9759 0000   **F** 08 9597 0001   **E** winery@leeuwinestate.com.au
W www.leeuwinestate.com.au

The Leeuwin Estate winery experience has a very special place in Australian wine tourism. Combining a winery, restaurant (see Food and Dining) and art gallery, it offers an inviting array of attractions, as well as special events throughout the year. The foundation for all of this is the enticing wines, which include outstanding Chardonnay, Semillon, Shiraz and Cabernet Sauvignon, as well as Pinot Noir, Merlot, Riesling and Sauvignon Blanc. The Art Series, which carries labels based on the winery's extensive art collection, is the premium range. Two other labels, Siblings and the fruit-driven Prelude, offer wines for early drinking. The art gallery's display of original artworks includes many of those used on the Art Series labels, and fine examples of local craftworks. The restaurant is stylish and has spacious verandahs. Leeuwin Estate also has its own airstrip, and special deals are available for lightning trips to the vineyard from Perth.

Robert Cartwright **WM**
10 am–4.30 pm **CD**
daily
11 am, 12 noon, **GT**
3 pm daily
R

Lenton Brae Estate

Caves Road, Margaret River

T 08 9755 6255   **F** 08 9755 6268   **E** info@lentonbrae.com
W www.lentonbrae.com

Lenton Brae Estate is a small winery owned and operated by the Tomlinson Family, whose wines are particularly good. It is situated in the Wilyabrup Valley of the Margaret River region, housed in a striking rammed-earth building. Try the reasonably priced Semillon Sauvignon Blanc and the award-winning Chardonnay. The Tomlinsons also make a very good Cabernet Merlot blend called Margaret River and a dessert Semillon.

Edward Tomlinson **WM**
10 am–6 pm daily **CD**

Pierro Vineyards

WM Dr Mike Peterkin
CD 10 am–5 pm daily

Caves Rd, Wilyabrup, Margaret River
T 08 9755 6220 **F** 08 9755 6308 **E** pierro@iinet.net.au
W www.margaret-river-online.com.au

Another medical man, Dr Mike Peterkin has been producing award-winning whites here since 1979. Two ranges, Pierro (made from estate-grown grapes) and Fire Gully, are available. The Chardonnays and Semillon Sauvignon Blanc blend are both very highly regarded; Pinot Noir, Merlot and Cabernet Sauvignon are also made. The Chardonnay and Pinot Noir are in great demand on release.

Redgate Wines

WM Andrew Forsell
CD 10 am–5 pm daily
P

Boodijup Rd, Margaret River
T 08 9757 6488 **F** 08 9757 6308 **E** info@redgatewines.com.au
W www.redgatewines.com.au

Redgate is a small winery with a big reputation. Whites predominate here, with Semillon, Sauvignon Blanc and Chardonnay all grown with consistently rewarding results—the Sauvignon Blanc Semillon blend is often great value. Of the reds, the Pinot Noir and Cabernet Merlot should not be overlooked.

Vasse Felix

WM Clive Otto
CD 10 am–5 pm daily
C
R

Cnr Caves Rd and Harmans Rd South, Wilyabrup, Margaret River
T 08 9756 5000 **F** 08 9755 5425 **E** info@vassefelix.com.au
W www.vassefelix.com.au

Vasse Felix was established as the first commercial winery in the region, in 1967. A new winery began operating here in 1999 and since then the range of wines has grown steadily and become more popular. Among the whites are the Classic Dry White (Semillon Chardonnay Sauvignon Blanc), Semillon and Theatre White; the reds include the Cabernet Sauvignon, Cabernet Merlot, Shiraz and Classic Dry Red (Cabernet Sauvignon, Shiraz, Merlot and Cabernet Franc). A really good restaurant (see Food and Dining) and excellent cellar-door operation make this a must-visit destination.

Voyager Estate

Stevens Rd, Margaret River
T 08 9385 3133 **F** 08 9383 4029 **E** wine@voyagerestate.com.au
W www.voyagerestate.com.au

Cliff Royle **WM**
10 am–5 pm daily **CD**
R

The oldest vines here date back to 1978, just over 10 years after vines were first planted in the area. When the current owner, Michael Wright, took over the property in 1991, he set out to expand it and develop a visitor destination that would be a showcase for the region. He also set out to ensure that, above all else, the quality of wine being made at Voyager Estate would always be the best that nature, expertise and pure hard work could provide. He achieved this goal and more. The wines are as memorable as the winery's stylish Cape Dutch architecture, immaculate gardens, and elegant restaurant (see Food and Dining). They include a range of whites at different price points, an estate Shiraz, and a Cabernet Merlot.

Wine tours and activities

Taste the South Winery Tours create personalised itineraries to suit your time frame and wine preferences; book ahead for the best service (**T** 0438 210 373 **E** tastethesouth@netserv.net.au).

Food and Dining

Margaret River produces some of the best food in Western Australia and there are several local specialities that can be matched with the fabulous wines, notably game and seafood, especially the famous marron—a kind of freshwater crayfish. You'll find them in many restaurants, or you can see them being farmed at Margaret Marron Farm, approximately 10 km south of Margaret River on Wickham Road, which also has facilities for picnics, barbecues and swimming (**T** 08 9757 6329).

The region is also well known for its cheeses. The Margaret River Dairy Co. Pty Ltd on Bussell Hwy, Cowaramup, makes a variety of delicious cheeses; you can see them being made (till around 3 pm) and taste both cheeses and yoghurts before you buy at the factory shop. Ricotta, fetta, various club cheddars and Swiss cheese are just a few of the varieties on offer, and the company also sells local ice-cream—and milkshakes—for the kids (**T** 08 9755 7588).

The Margaret River Farmers' Markets give shoppers a good opportunity to match the area's freshest produce with the latest wine releases from boutique wineries. The markets feature around 40 food and wine stalls, most operated by the producers themselves. Fresh produce includes hydroponic and organic fruit and vegetables, herbs and plants, gourmet breads, smoked fish, preserves, award-winning olive oils, chilli sauces, fudges, organic cheese, honey, ice-cream and cakes. Check the dates with the Margaret River Visitor Centre (see Travel Information). At Forest Grove Olive Farm, RMB 317 Harrison Road, Forest Grove, visitors can taste estate-bottled extra virgin olive oil (**T** 08 9757 6428).

Amberley Estate, Thornton Rd, Yallingup   **T** 08 9755 2288   **F** 08 9755 2171   **E** amberley@amberley-estate.com.au   **W** amberley-estate.com.au   **O** 11 am–3 pm daily for lunch, from 6 pm Sat for dinner. This award-winning restaurant has a good à la carte lunch menu and offers all-day coffee, snacks and cakes. It has a pleasant outlook over vineyards and valley.

Clairault Wines, Henry Rd, Wilyabrup   **T** 08 9755 6655   **F** 08 9755 6229   **E** clairault@clairaultwines.com.au   **W** www.clairaultwines.com.au   **O** 12 noon–3.30 pm. This stylish restaurant has won several awards and offers good modern Australian food. Whether you sit inside near the fires in winter or out on the terrace overlooking lawns in summer, this is a great place for lunch or coffee

Cullens Restaurant, Caves Rd, Wilyabrup   **T** 08 9755 5656   **E** enquiries@cullenwine.com.au   **W** www.cullenwines.com.au   **O** 10 am–4 pm daily. There's a strong French influence here, though the food is based squarely on fresh local produce, including vegetables grown in the restaurant's own organic garden, hand-reared local poultry and fine local cheeses. The verandah has pleasant views over the vineyards.

Leeuwin Estate, Stevens Rd, Margaret River, **T** 08 9759 0002   **F** 08 9597 0001   **E** winery@leeuwinestate.com.au   **W** www.leeuwinestate.com.au.   **O** 12pm–4.30 pm daily, from 6 pm Sat for dinner. This is one of the best winery restaurants in Australia, with the food, impeccable wines, décor and ambience all of a very high standard. The menu features local produce such as Albany oysters, crayfish, seafood, venison, fresh vegetables and cheeses. The restaurant has wide verandas and looks out over lawns and a stand of karri trees.

Vasse Felix, cnr Caves Rd and Harmans Rd South, Wilyabrup, Margaret River **T** 08 9756 5050 **F** 08 9755 5425 **E** info@vassefelix.com.au **W** www.vassefelix.com.au. **O** 10 am–3 pm daily. Built of stone and timber, with large shaded balconies, the restaurant looks out over vineyards and natural forest. The menu combines local produce with a light Asian influence—dishes include tuna carpaccio with a seaweed and sesame salad, crispy pressed duck with seared scallops, and soy beans with ginger and star anise. The excellent wines complement the food to perfection.

VAT 107, 107 Bussell Hwy, Margaret River **T** 08 9758 8877 **F** 08 9758 8899 **E** vat@vat107.com.au **W** www.vat107.com.au. **O** From 6 pm daily for dinner. A winner of the WA Tourism restaurant award in 2001, Danny Angove's restaurant has attained iconic status and gained a strong local following. Great food is served in smart surroundings, the varied menu changing to include the best regional produce, and the standard is maintained season after season. Local marron, venison and Karridale lamb are there alongside scallops, seafood and Asian-style salads. Comfortable accommodation is also available (see Accommodation).

Voyager Estate, Stevens Rd, Margaret River **T** 08 9385 3133 **F** 08 9383 4029 **E** wine@voyagerestate.com.au **W** www.voyagerestate.com.au **O** 10 am–5 pm daily. A spacious and elegant room houses one of the best restaurants in Margaret River, where you can eat a sumptuous lunch, or just enjoy a tasting plate or (generous) sandwich along with a glass of wine. Fresh local produce is everywhere on the menu: fish, chicken, lamb and beef, goat's cheese, and a range of beautifully cooked vegetables—all accompanied by Voyager's recommended wines.

Accommodation

Flag Freycinet Inn, Tunbridge St, Margaret River **T** 08 9757 2033 **F** 02 9999 4332. This convenient, modern motel in the centre of town has a restaurant, a swimming pool and pleasant gardens.

The Grove Vineyard, Metricup Rd, Wilyabrup Valley **T** 08 9755 7458 (office) or 0427 100 077 (accommodation) **E** info@thegrovevineyard.com.au **W** www.thegrovevineyard.com.au. The Grove is well located for you to make the most of Margaret River's many sights and attractions. Choose from three comfortable chalets. The facilities include tennis courts and there are lakes and lovely walks nearby. Check the website for packages and book ahead.

Heritage Trail Lodge, 31 Bussell Hwy, Margaret River **T** 08 9757 9595 **F** 08 9757 9596 **E** enquiry@heritage-trail-lodge.com.au **W** www.heritage-trail-com.au. Take your walking shoes to make the most of this luxury retreat set within a stand of majestic karri trees. It's big on creature comforts, including spa baths, airconditioning, balconies and queen-sized beds.

The Noble Grape B&B, Lot 18 Bussell Hwy, Cowaramup **T/F** 08 9755 5538 **E** noblegrape@netserve.net.au **W** www.bbbook.com.au/thenoblegrape. Six bedrooms and family rooms are available here at reasonable rates. Light breakfast is included and dinner can be arranged. The house is within walking distance of the Regional Wine Centre (see Travel Information) and only a few kilometres from some of the best wineries in Margaret River.

VAT 107, 107 Bussell Hwy, Margaret River **T** 08 9758 8877 **F** 08 9758 8899 **E** vat@vat107.com.au **W** www.vat107.com.au. Comfortable accommodation is offered in four luxurious studio apartments serviced by the restaurant of the same name. The pluses include spas, mini-bars and king-sized beds.

Travel Information

How to get there
By road Margaret River is approximately 290 km (3 hours) south of Perth.
By air Leeuwin Estate (see Wineries) has its own airstrip and special day tours operate from Perth.

Other attractions
Leeuwin–Naturaliste National Park, which stretches 120 km from Bunker Bay in the north to Flinders Bay in the south, encompasses rugged sea cliffs, windswept granite headlands, and dramatic rock formations. Cape Naturaliste offers some of the best whale watching in season and the lighthouse walk is spectacular.

In and around the park are several remarkable cave systems. Lake Cave, south of Margaret River, is probably the most beautiful small limestone cave in Australia. The lighting system has recently been enhanced to better display the delicate formations and lake. The cave is open daily and guided tours take place throughout the day; contact Caveworks to confirm tour times (**T** 08 9757 7411 **F** 08 9757 7421 **E** caveworks@margaretriver.com **W** www.margaretriverwa.com).

Ngilgi Cave lies beneath the limestone ridge that forms Cape Naturaliste at Yallingup and is one of the Cape's most visited attractions. (**T** 09 9755 2152 **W** www.showcaves.com **C PA BBQ**).

From the town of Margaret River, you can cycle along a dedicated track to the beach at Prevelly (which takes about 40 minutes). Bikes can be hired from Down South Camping (**T** 08 9758 9666) or Margaret River Cycles (**T** 08 9758 7671).

For kids
At Eagles Heritage you can see magnificent eagles at close quarters, and if you're game, so to speak, you can put on a glove and have one sit on your arm. Displays take place twice a day, weather permitting (10.30 am, 1.00 pm **T** 08 9757 2960 **W** www.eaglesheritage.com.au).

The Dolphin Discovery Centre in Bunbury is the only place in Australia that offers shore-based and boat-based interaction with wild dolphins as well as dolphin-watching tours and a fascinating and educational interpretive centre (**T** 08 9791 3088 **W** www.dolphindiscovery.com.au).

Events
Feb: Leeuwin Estate Concert
Nov: *Sunday Times* Margaret River Wine Festival

Information
Augusta Margaret River Tourism Association, Bussell Hwy
T 08 9757 2911 **F** 08 9757 3287
E welcome@margaretriver.com
W www.margaretriver.com
Margaret River Regional Wine Centre, 9 Bussell Hwy, Cowaramup
T 08 9755 5501 **F** 08 9755 5583
E ron@mrwines.com
W www.mrwines.com

Swan Valley

Key

T	Telephone
F	Fax
E	Email
W	Website
WM	Winemaker
CD	Cellar door
P	Picnic facilities
PA	Play area for children
BBQ	Barbecue facilities
GT	Guided tours
C	Cafe
R	Restaurant
O	Opening hours
B&B	Bed and breakfast
H	Hotel/Inn
M	Motel
G	Guesthouse
SCA	Self-catering accommodation

The Swan Valley was the first Western Australian region to be planted with vines, in 1830, soon after a European colony was established at the mouth of the Swan River. The site of the first vineyard is now one of the oldest wineries in Australia, Olive Farm. The region experienced two further periods of viticultural expansion, in the 1920s and again in the 1940s and 1950s. In both of these periods, migrants from a number of different countries in war-torn Europe, mainly Italians and Croatians, began to grow a range of vines and for a time the area had more land under vines than either New South Wales or Victoria. More recently, the Swan Valley has undergone a period of sustained expansion and development, the quality of the wines has been steadily improving, and the number and standard of cellar door outlets, restaurants and cafes continues to increase.

The broad, flat alluvial plain of the Swan Valley and its tributaries has deep, loamy soils that are generally well suited to grape-growing. In the northern coastal area, the well-drained sandy soils are ideal for the production of table wines. The hot dry summers and long hours of sunshine ensure that the region is able to ripen fruit sufficiently for the production of fortified wines.

The wineries of the Swan Valley are scattered along either side of the Swan Valley and lend themselves to a circuit to the north of the charming town of Guildford. Heading east of the river at the visitor centre and turning northwards at Midland along the Great Northern Highway, travellers can return via West Swan Road at Belhus. Detours left and right off the highway and Toodyay Road take in several of the best wineries. Another option is to take a cruise along the waters of the Swan River to wineries such as Olive Farm, Houghton and Sandalford (see Travel Information).

What to buy

The area produces a wide selection of premium wines as well as a number of more mundane quaffing wines. Whites predominate but reds and fortified wines are also produced in quantity and can offer good value. Chenin Blanc is one white grape variety that grows well in the Swan region, as do Chardonnay and Verdelho. Of the reds, Cabernet Sauvignon, Shiraz and Merlot are grown successfully in several areas. The Swan Valley's fortified wines, which have been produced for many years, give the likes of Rutherglen a run for their money and are well worth tasting.

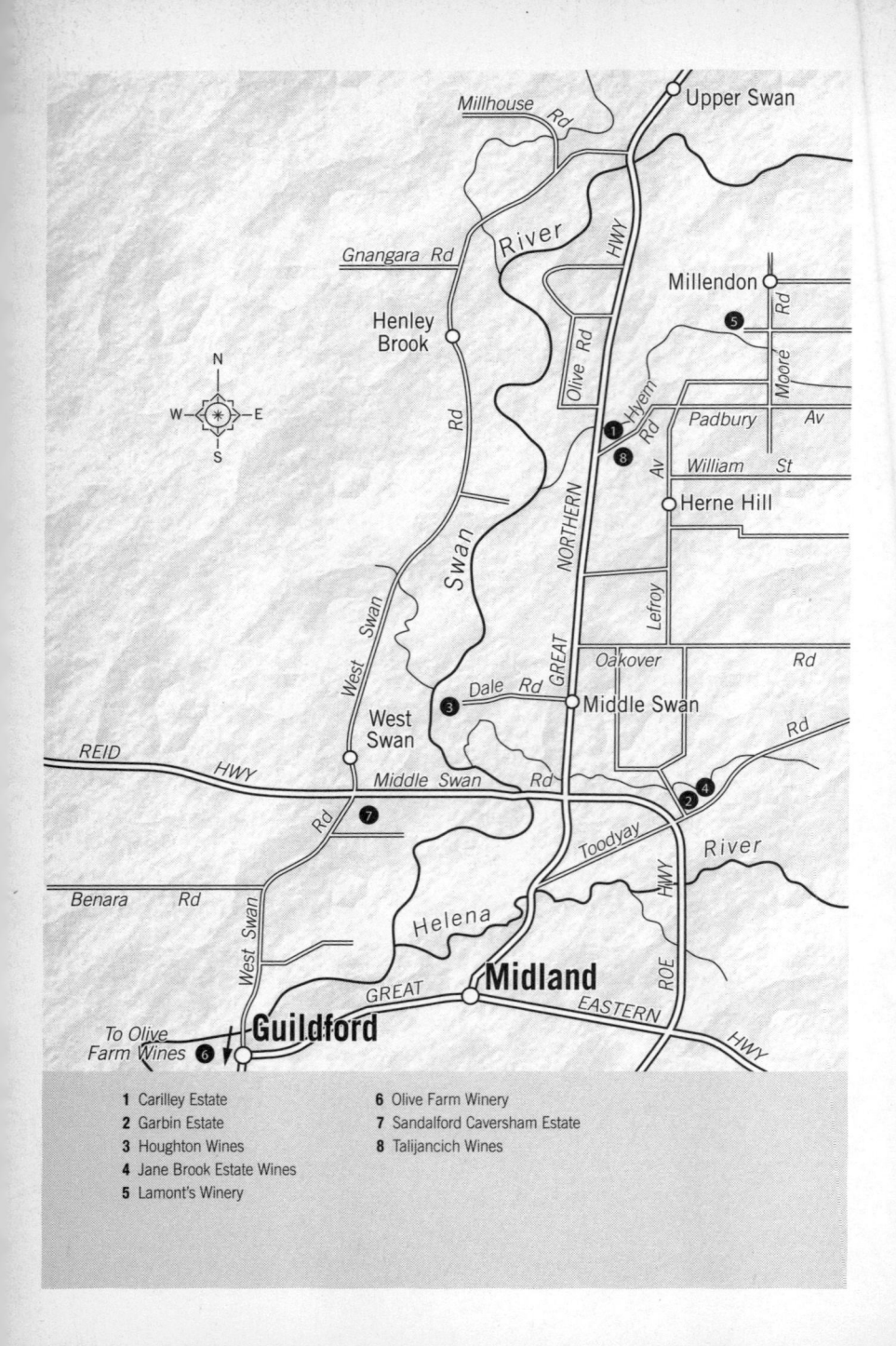

1 Carilley Estate
2 Garbin Estate
3 Houghton Wines
4 Jane Brook Estate Wines
5 Lamont's Winery
6 Olive Farm Winery
7 Sandalford Caversham Estate
8 Talijancich Wines

Wineries

Carilley Estate

Lot 23 Hyem Rd, Herne Hill

T/F 08 9296 6190 **E** cellar@carilleyestate.com.au **W** www.carilleyestate.com.au

Rob Marshall **WM**
10 am–5 pm daily **CD**
P
C

The Carija family has owned and operated vineyards in the Swan Valley since 1957, and this, their third winery, was established in 1985. Planted by the family, it spans beautiful Susannah Brook in the heart of the Swan Valley. Rich soils and intensive viticulture result in high-quality fruit, which is picked by hand. The wines are made in new French, American and Croatian oak, and in modern state-of-the-art, stainless-steel fermentation vats—the move to adopt more modern techniques has seen a significant improvement in the quality of the wines. The range includes Chenin Blanc, Chardonnay (wooded and unwooded) and Viognier, as well as Shiraz, Merlot and Malbec; the pick of the bunch are the Viognier, Chenin Blanc and 2001 Shiraz. Carilley Estate also produces limited quantities of hand-picked extra virgin olive oil from its own olive grove, and has a cafe that serves light, Mediterranean-style food and caters especially well for vegetarians.

Garbin Estate

209 Toodyay Rd, Middle Swan

T/F 08 9274 1747 **E** binwine1@bigpond.com

Peter Garbin **WM**
10 am–5.30 pm **CD**
Mon–Sat,
12 noon–5.30 pm
Sun
P

This is a welcoming, family-owned winery that makes a range of award-winning wines from old vines, including Chenin Blanc, Chardonnay, Shiraz, Cabernet Merlot, dessert wines and a Ruby Port. Of these, the Shiraz is the standout. A pleasant covered area is provided for visitors to enjoy a picnic along with wines purchased at the cellar door.

Houghton Wines

WM Rob Bowen
CD 10 am–5 pm daily
P
GT
C

Dale Road, Middle Swan

T 08 9274 5100   **F** 08 9274 5372   **E** customers@hardys.com.au
W www.brlhardy.com.au

Situated in the heart of the Swan Valley, Houghton Wines represents a good slice of the history of Western Australian winemaking. Named after Lieutenant Colonel Richmond Houghton in 1836 (though documents suggest that the first vines were planted soon after 1830), the winery produced its first commercial vintage in 1859, and has since become one of Australia's oldest continuous winemaking operations. Now part of the BRL Hardy group, Houghton has 50 ha planted with premium grape varieties, including Verdelho, Chardonnay, Semillon and Chenin Blanc. The large range encompasses the Houghton (which includes the famous White Burgundy), Crofters and Moondah Brook labels, among others. The new Houghton Regional Range is a selection of elegant, premium varietal styles from key south-west Western Australian regions, such as Frankland River Shiraz and Riesling, Margaret River Cabernet Sauvignon, and Pemberton Chardonnay, Merlot and Sparkling Chardonnay Pinot Noir.

Jane Brook Estate Wines

WM Julie White
CD 10 am–5 pm daily
R

229 Toodyay Rd, Middle Swan

T 08 9274 1432   **F** 08 9274 1211   **E** janebrook@janebrook.com.au
W www.janebrook.com.au

One of the oldest vineyards in the area, Jane Brook was first planted in the early twentieth century by the Mateljan family. Since taken over by the Atkinson family, it expanded significantly in the 1970s. The wines range from lively Verdelho and crisp Chardonnay through to rich Shiraz and plummy Cabernet Merlot. A small range of fortified wines is also available, along with a Méthode Champenoise Pinot Chardonnay. The cellar door gift shop also sells gourmet produce such as chutneys and preserves made by the Atkinson family, and the restaurant (see Food and Dining) serves soup, platters of cheese, seafood and other delicacies (bookings are recommended).

Lamont's Winery

85 Bisdee Rd (off Moore Rd), Millendon
T 08 9296 4485 **F** 08 9296 1663 **E** winery@lamonts.com.au
W www.lamonts.com.au

Digby Leddin **WM**
10 am–5 pm **CD**
Wed–Sun and
public holidays
C
R

A success story from its inception in the early 1970s, this family-owned winery has gained a reputation as one of the Swan Valley's favourite wine-touring destinations. Encouraged by Corin Lamont's late father, Jack Mann, the family established the winery in 1978 with the aim of producing full-flavoured table and fortified wines. The estate vineyard now has just over 5 ha of vines, and apart from some recently planted Shiraz, most are between 15 and 20 years old. The winery produces a wide range, from Chardonnay, Riesling and Verdelho through to sherries and fortified wines. The reds include the excellent Family Reserve Red (Cabernet Sauvignon), as well as a medium-bodied Shiraz. The whites include a Riesling, a barrel-fermented Chardonnay, and a lightly oaked Semillon Sauvignon Blanc blend. Set in a pleasant garden, the cellar door cum cafe serves a variety of tasty platters accompanied by crusty bread, among them its signature dish, grilled whole Swan River marron. It also sells the winery's own scrumptious marinated olives.

Olive Farm Winery

77 Great Eastern Hwy, South Guildford
T 08 9277 6557 **F** 08 9277 6828 **E** info@olivefarm.com.au
W www.olivefarm.com.au

Ian Yurisich **WM**
10 am–5 pm **CD**
10 am–4 pm **R**
Wed–Sun,
6 pm–8 pm Fri
for dinner

English botanist Thomas Waters came to the fledgling colony of Perth in 1829. En route to Australia, he broke his journey in South Africa, where he purchased a number of plants, including vines and olive trees. Upon his arrival at Perth, he was granted 150 acres of land in what became South Guildford. Here he planted his vines and olive trees, thus founding Western Australia's first vineyard. Today it has 30 acres under vines in the upper Swan Valley, growing 11 varieties: Chenin Blanc, Chardonnay, Semillon, Verdelho, Sauvignon Blanc, Gewurztraminer, Cabernet Sauvignon, Shiraz, Merlot, Cabernet Franc and Pinot Noir. The Classic White blend of Semillon, Verdelho and Chenin Blanc is popular, as are the white and pink sparkling wines. The winery has a cafe-restaurant with an outdoor terrace area overlooking lawns and the Swan River.

Sandalford Caversham Estate

WM Paul Boulden
CD 10 am–5 pm daily
P
GT 11 am Sat
R

3210 West Swan Rd, Caversham
T 08 9374 9343 **F** 08 9374 9389 **E** sandalford@sandalford.com
W www.sandalford.com

The cellar door area at Sandalford's beautiful Swan Valley estate is one of Western Australia's biggest, offering a comprehensive selection of wines and wine-related goods ranging from glassware to bottle openers. Visitors can taste the Premium and Element wines, as well as the Founders Reserve Liqueur Port and flagship fortified wine, Sandalera. Every Saturday at 11 am, Sandalford offers a special 3-hour package, including a tour of the historic winery and a tasting and blending session during which you blend your own wine then enjoy it over a meal in the picturesque restaurant (see Food and Dining). The tour requires a minimum of two guests and bookings are essential.

Talijancich Wines

WM James Talijancich
CD 11 am–5 pm Sun–Fri

26 Hyem Rd, Herne Hill
T 08 9296 4289 **F** 08 9296 1762 **E** james@taliwine.com.au

The Talijancich family's involvement with grape-growing and winemaking began in 1932, when they purchased a property called Peter's Wines, which was blessed with rich, fertile soil capable of producing wines of the highest quality that were unique in style and character. The family is now in its third generation of winemakers and has broadened out from award-winning fortified wines such as Muscats and Tokays to produce table wines. These encompass Verdelho, the Voices Dry White, Grenache and Shiraz, as well as a very promising Viognier. The fortifieds include the Julian James White Liqueur, Julian James Red Liqueur and a Liqueur Tokay. Talijancich hosts an annual international Verdelho tasting every August, now in its tenth year.

Wine tours and activities

Panache Tours offers flexible, small-group tours in a stretch Mercedes limo; visits can include tastings, lunch or refreshments (**T** 1300 728 279 **F** 08 9473 0527 **E** dave@panachetours.com.au **W** www.panachetours.com.au). Wine cruises are run by Oceanic Cruises from Perth (**T** 08 9325 1191) and by Captain Cook Cruises (**T** 08 9325 3341), which offers a choice of two cruises, one including lunch on board followed by a trip to Olive Farm winery, the other taking in the Houghton and Sandalford wineries and including a riverside buffet lunch.

Food and Dining

The innovative Swan Valley Food and Wine Trail map, available from the Swan Valley and Eastern Region Visitor Centre (see Travel Information), lists year-round food and wine attractions. The Midland Farmers' Markets are held every Sunday morning in the town centre opposite Centrepoint Midland shops and incorporate around 50 fresh-produce stalls (**T** 08 9576 1234).

Swan Valley Central at the corner of Great Northern Hwy and Lennard St, Herne Hill, sells a wide range of dried fruits, nuts, honey and preserves, cakes and other delectable items (**T** 08 9296 4219). In addition to being a winery, Edgecombe Brothers of Belhus is one of the area's best known providores, selling fresh produce such as table grapes and asparagus in season, as well as other fruits and vegetables and a range of preserves (**T** 08 9296 4307). Merrich Estate, 11111 West Swan Rd, Henley Brook, sells terrific olives and olive oil products (**T** 08 9296 0750 **E** merrich@bigpond.com).

Dear Friends Restaurant, 100 Benara Rd, Caversham **T** 08 9279 2815 **W** www.dearfriends.com.au **O** Wed–Sun for lunch and dinner (except Sat lunch). Dear Friends offers stylish formal dining and an award-winning wine list. The extensive modern Australian à la carte menu features a huge range of seafood including oysters, prawns and salmon, as well as meats including beef, lamb, kangaroo, and quail. Accompaniments include fresh local vegetables and imaginative salads.

Jane Brook Estate Wines, 229 Toodyay Rd, Middle Swan **T** 08 9274 1432
F 08 9274 1211 **E** janebrook@janebrook.com.au **W** www.janebrook.com.au
O 10 am–5 pm Mon–Fri, 12 noon–5 pm Sat–Sun. The restaurant serves soups, bread and a range of Mediterranean platters incorporating smoked chicken, cold meats, fetta and cheddar cheeses, marinated and sun-dried vegetables, locally grown fruit and seasonal salads. Desserts and coffee are also available.

Lamont's Winery, 85 Bisdee Rd (off Moore Rd), Millendon
T 08 9296 4485 **F** 08 9296 1663 **E** winery@lamonts.com.au **W** www.lamonts.com.au **O** 10 am–5 pm daily. This cellar door restaurant serves platters of modern Australian regional food with an emphasis on fresh produce. Daily specials are available and are good value for money.

Olive Farm Winery Restaurant, 77 Great Eastern Hwy, South Guildford
T 08 9277 6557 **F** 08 9277 6826 **E** info@olivefarm.com.au **W** www.olivefarm.com.au
O 11.30 am–2.30 pm Wed–Sun. This upmarket cafe has an interesting à la carte menu and offers fresh seasonal dishes, fish specials and great pasta. Entrees include seafood chowder, grilled scallops and duck with shiitake mushrooms. Hunter-style farmed rabbit; beef, leek and potato pie; and rosemary and garlic chicken with bocconcini and avocado salad are just a few of the mains. Local wines are available by the glass.

Padbury's Cafe Restaurant, 114 Terrace Rd, Guildford **T** 08 9378 4484
O 11 am–late Wed–Sun. This heritage building was once a gas factory and then a general store before it was restored and updated in the late 1990s. It is now a popular restaurant offering good-value family meals. The à la carte menu and specials board provide a good range of choices including seafood, vegetarian, chicken and beef main courses. Meals for children are also available, as well as morning and afternoon teas. Bookings are advisable.

Sandalford Caversham Estate, 3210 West Swan Rd, Caversham **T** 08 9374 9343
F 08 9374 9389 **E** sandalford@sandalford.com **W** www.sandalford.com
O 12 noon–3 pm daily for lunch, 6 pm–9 pm Sat for dinner. Eat in a rustic but smart limestone dining room with an open fire in winter, or outside under ancient vines in the summer months.

Accommodation

Craig Park B&B, 90 Park St, Henley Brook T 08 9296 3676 F 08 9296 3677 E jeanmal@bigpond.com. Three comfortable bedrooms are available in this country home with a swimming pool and tennis court. The rooms have queen beds, ensuite spa bathrooms and airconditioning, as well as tea- and coffee-making facilities, CD players and TVs.

Fauntleroy House B&B, Piercy St, Guildford T 08 9379 0270 E fauntleroy@bigpond.com.au W www.fauntleroyhouse.com.au. Guests at this immaculately restored property enjoy comfortable rooms and the use of a shared pool. Breakfast can be taken on the spacious verandah.

Grandis Cottages, 45 Casuarina Pl, Henley Brook T 08 9263 3400 F 08 9261 1421 E grandis@grandiscottages.com.au W www.grandiscottages.com.au. These modern cottages occupy a tranquil setting on a semi-rural property surrounded by gum trees and rose gardens. Each cottage has two double bedrooms, a well-appointed kitchen and creature comforts such as airconditioning, gas fires and spa baths.

Susannah Brook Cottages, 72 Bisdee Rd, Millendon T 08 9296 4733 E susannahb@iinet.com.au W www.susannahbrookcottages.com.au. The two self-contained cottages are set in a rural location surrounded by vineyards and orchards and close to Lamont's winery. They each have light cooking facilities (microwave and toaster) and two bedrooms (one with a queen-sized bed and the other with a double and a single). Dogs, even horses, are welcome by arrangement.

Thyme and Again Cottage, 11111 West Swan Rd, Henley Brook T 08 9296 0750 E merrich@bigpond.com. The converted early-settler's cottage nestles among trees on the Merrich Estate Olive Farm. Carefully restored, it has modern comforts such as airconditioning and a king-size bed. Breakfast is served picnic-style, in a farm-style kitchen, or on the verandah. Cosy log fires are lit on cooler evenings.

The Vines Resort and Country Club, Verdelho Dr, The Vines **T** 08 9297 3000
F 08 9297 3333 **E** reservations@novotelvines.com.au **W** www.novotelvines.com.au
This beautifully located and well-above-average resort offers golf, swimming pools and a variety of restaurants on your doorstep.

Travel Information

How to get there
By road The Swan Valley region is approximately half an hour's drive (35 km) north of Perth via the Midland Hwy.

Other attractions
There are plenty of things to see in the heritage townships of the Swan Valley. Meadow St in Guildford has some fine buildings that have been carefully restored, and James St has become a centre for antiques and collectibles. The town has several fine pubs, including the Rose and Crown, which has operated since 1841, making it the oldest continually operating pub in Western Australia. Barker and Gull's Store and the National Trust-listed Woodbridge House are well worthy of a few minutes' exploration. A few kilometres upstream from Guildford lies the tiny All Saints church at Ellenbrook, built in 1841 and now regarded as the oldest in Western Australia, as other churches that once predated it no longer survive.

For kids
At Caversham Wildlife Park and Zoo in Lord St, Whiteman, visitors can view koalas, kangaroos, wombats, Tasmanian Devils and lots more (**T** 08 9248 1984 **W** www.cavershamwildlife.com.au).
Whiteman Park in Whiteman has plenty to keep kids entertained, ranging from picnic sites and walks in the bushland to a vintage electric tramway and motor, bus and tractor museums (**T** 08 9249 2446). At Supa Golf, at 10250 West Swan Rd, Henley Brook, kids get to use oversize clubs and balls while they learn the game (**T** 08 9296 5566).

Tours of the Gumnut Factory, at 231 Toodyay Rd, Middle Swan, allow visitors to see a range of objects being handmade from Western Australian nuts and seedpods (**T** 08 9409 6699).

Events
Jan: Symphony at Sandalford (**T** 08 9374 9302)
Feb: Houghton annual outdoor folk and blues concert, Houghton's Winery (**T** 08 9274 9525)
Mar–Apr: A Taste of the Valley (**T** 08 9379 9400)
Apr: Swan Valley Olive Oil Celebration, Merrich Estate (**T** 08 9692 0752)
Oct, second week: Spring in the Valley (**T** 08 9379 9400)

Information
Swan Valley and Eastern Region Visitor Centre, cnr Meadow and Swan Sts, Guildford **T** 08 9379 9400
E visitorcentre@swan.wa.gov.au
W www.swanvalley.info

Index

Wineries, cafes, restaurants & accommodation

Abercorn Wines, 59, 61
Acacia Grove, 78
Accommodation Creek Cottages, 90
Affleck Vineyard, 2, 3, 7
Ainsworth Estate, 225, 231
Alkoomi, 237
All Saints, 215
All Seasons Quality Resort, 183
Allandale Winery, 31, 41
Amberley Estate, 249, 254
Amethyst Lodge Bed & Breakfast, 231
Andrew Harris Wines, 59, 61
Andrew Harris Wines cafe, 66
Annie's Lane, 116, 118
Arrowfield Wines, 14, 50, 52
Ashton Hills Vineyard, 95, 97
Audrey Wilkinson Vineyard, 31, 34
Austin's Barrabool Wines, 186, 188
Australian Regional Food Store, 44, 45

Bago Vineyards, 24, 25
Balcony, The, 101
Bald Mountain Vineyards, 83, 85
Balgownie Estate, 176, 177, 180
Balgownie Estate Restaurant, 182
Ballandean Estate, 83, 85
Balnaves of Coonawarra, 128, 130
Barilla Bay Oysters, 170
Barossa Small Winemakers Centre, 105
Barossa Weintal Resort, 113
Barrel Room Cafe, 88
Barrique Cafe Restaurant, 10
Batcheler's Terrace Vale Wines, 31, 34
Bay of Fires, 151, 155
Bazzani Restaurant, 182
Beaumonts, 219
Beetle Nutt Cafe, 10
Best's Great Western, 196
Bethany Wines, 105, 107
Beverley Vineyard Restaurant, 88
Bimbadgen Estate, 31, 34
Bird in Hand Winery and Olive Grove, 100
Black Rabbit B&B, The, 209
Blackjack Vineyards, 177, 179
Blaxlands, 45
Bloodwood Wines, 71, 73
Blue Gum Japanese Restaurant and Guesthouse, 20
Blue Wren Winery Restaurant, 67
Blue Wren Wines, 59, 61
Bowen Estate, 128, 130
Brand's of Coonawarra, 128, 130

Briar Ridge, 31, 35
Brindabella Hills Winery, 3, 5
Broke Estate/Ryan Family Wines, 33, 42
Broke Village Store, 44
Brokenwood Wines, 35
Brook Eden, 151, 155
Brown Brothers Milawa Vineyard, 215
Bullers, 216
Bushman's Cottage, 68
Byronsvale B&B, 183

Ca Marche, 25, 27
Cafe at Cargo Road Wines, 76
Cafe Beltree, 45
Cafe Shamrock, 219
Campbells Winery, 216
Canobolas Cabins, 78
Canobolas-Smith Wines, 71, 73
Canowindra Riverview Motel, 20
Cape Howe Cottages, 244
Cape Mentelle, 249
Capercaillie Gallery, 41
Capercaillie Wine Company, 31, 41
Cargo Road Wines, 71, 73
Carilley Estate, 261
Carrington Restaurant and Motel, The, 12
Cassegrain Wines, 24, 25
Castaway Bar and Restaurant, 28
Cathcart Ridge Estate, 196
Catherine Vale Wines, 33, 42
Cellar Restaurant, 45
Chain of Ponds Vineyard Cottage, 102
Chain of Ponds Wines, 95, 97, 101
Chapel Hill Winery, 138, 140
Chapel Hill Winery Guest House, 147
Chardonnay Lodge, 134
Chateau Leamon, 177, 179
Chateau Tanunda, 105, 107
Chatsfield, 238
Chiverton Wines, 15, 17
Cipriani's Flinders Country Inn, 209
Civic Motor Inn, 21
Clairault Wines, 250, 254
Clare Valley Motel, 124
Clarence House, 243
Clonakilla, 2, 3, 6, 9
Clover Hill, 151, 156
Coal Valley Vineyard, 163, 165
Cobb & Co Cottages, 134
Cockfighters Ghost Vineyard Cottage, 47
Cockington Green, 13

Coldstream Hills, 222, 225
Coleman's Restaurant at Kilikanoon, 123
Collits' Inn, 68
Conmel Cottage, 159
Coombend Estate, 163, 168, 171
Coriole Winery, 138, 140
Cork St Cafe, 10
Coterie, The, 145
Country Comfort Inn, 28
Country Comfort Mudgee, 68
Country Guesthouse Schonegg, 11
Cow Cafe, The, 46
Cowra Breakout Motor Inn, 21
Cowra Estate, 14, 15
Cowra Smokehouse, 19
Craig Park B&B, 267
Craigmoor Restaurant, 67
Craigow Vineyard, 163, 165
Crays Waterfront Restaurant, 28
Crittenden at Dromana Estate, 204
Critters Cafe and Wine Bar, 208
Crocodile Cafe, The, 45
Crosswinds Vineyards, 163, 165
Cruikshank Callatoota Estate, 50, 52
Cullen Wines, 246, 250
Cullens Restaurant, 254
Cunningham's Inn, 230
Customs House Cafe, 89

d'Arenberg Winery 138, 140
d'Arrys Verandah Restaurant, 145
Dairy, The, 47
Dalrymple Vineyards, 151, 156
Dalwood vineyard, 30
De Bortoli, 225
De Bortoli Winery restaurant, 230
Deeb's Kitchen and B&B, 67
Delamere Vineyard, 151, 156
Denman Motor Inn, 55
Denman Royal Hotel, 55
di Lusso Estate, 59, 62
Dingo's Retreat, 46
Dolwendee Farm Stay Cottages, 56
Domaine A, 163, 166
Domaine Chandon, 226
Dominique Portet, 226
Doonkuna Estate, 3, 6, 9
Drayton's Family Wines, 31, 35

Earl of Spencer, 242
Elderton Wines, 105, 108
Eldredge Vineyards, 116, 118
Eldredge Vineyards cafe, 123
Elliot Rocke Estate, 59, 62
Elmslea Homestead, The, 12

INDEX 269

Elsemore's Caprera Grove, 33, 42
Eltons Cafe, 67
Elysium Vineyard, 33, 43
Esca, 34, 45
Esplanade Hotel, 243
Evans & Tate, 250

Falls Vineyard Retreat, The, 17, 21
Falls Wines and Vineyard Retreat, 15, 17, 21
Farmer's Daughter Wines, 59, 63
Farmer's Market, 19
Fauntleroy House B&B, 267
Fee & Me, 158
Felsberg Winery, 83, 85
Fergies Hill Spa Cottage, 90
Fergusson's of Yarra Glen, 230
First Creek Wines, 31, 36
Fisherman's Co-op, 27
Flag Freycinet Inn, 256
Flynn's Beach Resort, 28
Food on Wood, 219
Fortunes Restaurant, 182
Four Points by Sheraton, 191
Fox Creek Wines, 138, 141
Frankland Estate, 238
Freycinet Vineyard, 163, 168

Gap Vineyard, The, 196
Garbin Estate, 261
Gartelmann Hunter Estate, 31, 41
Geebin Vineyard, 163, 167
Geebin Vineyard and B&B, 171
Giardino Cafe and Farm Tours, 89
Gib Street Cafe, 10
Gidgee Estate, 3, 8, 9
Gilberts, 238
Gilberts Wines Restaurant, 243
Globe Inn, The, 12
Golden Grove Estate, 83, 86
Goulburn River Stone Cottages, 68
Goundrey Wines, 239
Grandis Cottages, 267
Granite Ridge Wines, 83, 86, 90
Grant Burge Wines, 105, 108
grapefoodwine, 10
Grapevine Restaurant, 67
Grazing, 11
Grosset Wines, 116, 118
Grove Vineyard, The, 256
Gundaroo Wine Bar, 11

Hahndorf Hill Winery, 95, 97
Halls Gap Colonial Motor Inn, 199
Hamilton's Bluff Wines, 15, 18
Hardy's Tintara Vineyards, 138, 141
Hartzview Vineyard, 163, 167, 171
Healesville Hotel, 231
Heart of Mudgee, 66
Helm Wines, 2, 3, 6, 9
Heritage Trail Lodge, 256
Heron's Rise Vineyard, 171
Hickinbotham, 204
Hidden Creek Wines, 83, 86
Highland Heritage Estate, 71, 74

Highland Heritage Estate Restaurant, 76
Hollick Wines, 128, 131
Holm Oak Vineyard, 151, 153, 153
Holroyd B&B, 220
Home Hill Winery and Restaurant, 163, 167, 170
Hope Estate, 33, 43
Horseshoe Vineyard, 50, 52
Houghton Wines, 260, 262, 265
Howard Park Wines, 240, 251
Huntington Estate, 58, 59, 63, 67

Ibis Wines, 71, 74
Ilkley Cottages, 68
Innes Lake Vineyard, 24, 26
Iron Pot Bay Wines, 151, 153

Jacob's Restaurant, 112
James Estate Wines, 50, 53
Jane Brook Estate Wines, 262
Jeanneret Wines, 116, 119
Jeir Creek Wines, 3, 7
Jill's, 208
Jim Barry Wines, 116, 117, 119
Jindalee Estate, 186, 188
Jingalla Wines, 240
Jojoes cafe, 182

Kalari Wines, 15, 18
Kamberra Wine Centre, 3, 5
Kangarilla Road, 138, 142
Katnook Estate, 128, 131
Kilgour Estate Winery, 186, 188
Kiltynane Estate B&B, 231
Kimbarra Wines, 197
King River Cafe, 219
Kookaburra Restaurant, The, 199
Krinklewood Vineyard, 33, 43
Kurrajong Vineyard Cottages, 47

La Baracca, 208
La Colline Cafe, 76
La Colline Wines, 71, 74
Lake George Winery, 2
Lake's Folly, 30, 31, 36
Lakeside Cafe and Cellar, 76
Lambert Vineyard, 3, 8
Lamont Winery, 263
Langanook Wines, 177, 179
Langmeil Cottages, 113
Lark Hill Winery, 3, 8
Le Cafe, 219
Le Parisien, 190
Lebrina restaurant, 170
Leeuwin Estate, 251, 254
Lenton Brae Estate, 251
Lillydale Estate, 226
Lillydale Vineyards Restaurant, 230
Lilydale House B&B, 191
Limeburner's, 145, 146
Lindenderry Country House Hotel and Vineyard, 209
Lindenwarrah Country House Hotel, 220
Lolli Redini, 76

Long Point Vineyard, 24, 26
Lots of Goodies Country Kitchen, 89
Lunch on the Pond, 101
Lynne Vale Estate, 183
Lynwood Cafe, The, 11

McGuigan Wines, 31, 36
McLaren Ridge Log Cabins, 147
McLarens on the Lake Motel and Restaurant, 147
Macquarie Seafoods, 28
McWilliams Mount Pleasant Wines, 31, 37
Madew Wines, 3, 8
Maggie Beer Farm Shop, 112
Main Ridge Estate, 205
Majella Wines, 128, 131
Mandurang Valley Winery, 177, 180
Margan Family Wines, 31, 37
Marion Park Gardens B&B, 231
Marions Vineyard, 151, 153
Market 190, 145
Marsh Estate, 31, 37
Marwood Retreat, 199
Maximillian's, 101
Meadowbank Estate, 163, 166
Meadowbank Estate restaurant, 170
Mercure Grand Mount Lofty House, 102
Merlot Restaurant, 220
Milawa Lodge Motel, 220
Milimani Estate Vineyard, 3, 9
Mill, The, 19
Millinup Estate, 241
Miramar, 58, 59, 63
Mitchell Winery, 116, 119
Mojo's on Wilderness, 46
Montara Winery, 197
Montgomery's Hill, 236
Moorilla Estate, 163, 166
Moorooduc Estate, 205
Morning Star Estate, 205, 208
Morris Wines, 216
Mount Broke Wines, 33, 43
Mount Compass Venison, 144
Mount Horrocks Wines, 116, 120
Mount Horrocks Wines cafe, 123
Mount Langi Ghiran, 197
Mountain Grand Guest House/Boutique Hotel, 200
Mountain Tea House, 78
Mudgee Homestead Guesthouse, 68
Muranna Herb Farm and Cottages, 210
Murrumbateman Winery, 3, 7

Naked Bean Cafe, The, 242
Neagles Rock, 116, 120
Neila, 20
Nepenthe, 95, 98
Noah's Bar and Grill, 55
Noble Grape B&B, The, 256
Novotel Barossa Valley, 113

Oakridge, 227
Old Convent, The, 77
Old Mill Cafe, 77
Old Stone House, The, 12
Oldfields B&B, 124
Olive Farm Winery, 258, 260, 263, 265
Orange Mountain Wines, 71, 74
Orlando, 109
Orlando Jacob's Creek Visitor Centre, 105

Padthaway Estate, 128, 133
Padthaway Estate Historic Homestead, 135
Panorama Vineyard, 163, 168
Paringa Estate, 206
Paringa Estate Winery Restaurant, 208
Parkville Hotel, 78
Passing Clouds, 176, 177, 180
Peak Restaurant, The, 209
Penna Lane Wines, 116, 120
Penny's Hill Wines, 138, 142, 146
Petaluma, 95, 98
Petaluma's Bridgewater Mill, 101
Peter Lehmann Wines, 105, 109, 114
Pettavel Winery, 186, 189
Pettavel Winery Restaurant, 190
Pfeiffer Wines, 217
Philippe Brasserie, 55
Piccadilly Restaurant, 101
Pierro Vineyards, 252
Pieter van Gent, 59, 64
Pipers Brook cottages, 160
Pipers Brook Vineyard, 150, 151, 156, 157
Pipers Brook Winery Restaurant, 159
Pipers of Penola, 133
Plantagenet Hotel, 243
Plantagenet Wines, 239
Plovers Ridge Country Retreat, 160
Poacher's Pantry Smokehouse and Cafe, 10
Poet's Corner Winery, 59, 64, 67
Poole's Rock Wines, 31, 38
Portabellos Cafe, 28
Prospect House, 171
Providence Vineyard, 151, 157
Punt Road, 227
Punters Corner Vineyard Retreat, 135

Quarry Cellar Door and Restaurant, 17, 20

Red Dot Cafe, 146
Red Hill Retreat, 210
Redfingers Cafe Bar & Grill, 134
Redgate Wines, 252
Reilly's Country Retreat, 125
Reilly's Wines, 116, 121, 125

Rendezvous Restaurant, 219
Richmond Grove, 14, 105, 110, 114
Rising Sun Hotel, The, 125, 126
Ristorante Leonardos, 242
Robert Channon Wines, 83, 87
Robert Stein Vineyard, 59, 65
Rochford's Eyton Restaurant, 230
Rosemount Estate, 49, 50, 53
Rosevears Estate, 151, 154
Rosevears Waterfront Tavern, 158
Rothbury Escape, 47
Rothbury Estate, 14, 31, 38
Royal Mail Hotel, 199
Rutherglen Wine Experience, 219

Sailor's Rest, 191
Salix Restaurant, 209
Salopian Inn, 146
Salt 'n' Vines Bar and Bistro, 124
Salters restaurant, 113
Saltram Wines, 105, 110
Sandalford Caversham Estate, 260, 264, 265
Sarah's Cottage, 136
Scarborough Wine Company, 31, 39
Scotchmans Hill, 186, 189
Selkirks, 77
Seppelt Great Western, 193, 198
Seppelts Wines, 105, 110
Sevenhill Cellars, 116, 121
Seville Estate, 227
Shaw and Smith, 95, 99
Sherwood Estate, 24, 26
Silk Hill Wines, 151, 154
Skillogalee House and Windamere Cottages, 125
Skillogallee Wines, 116, 121
Splash Restaurant, 45
St Matthias Vineyard, 151, 154
St Peter's Vineyard, 193
Stanthorpe Wine Centre, 83, 87
Stanton & Killeen, 217
Starline Alpaca Farm Stay, 47
Staughton Vale Vineyard B&B, 191
Stillwater River Cafe, 158, 159
Stonier Wines, 206
Strathlynn Wine Centre and restaurant, 151, 154, 159
Summit Restaurant, 101
Surveyor's Hill Winery, 3, 5
Susannah Brook Cottages, 267

Talijancich Wines, 264
Talunga Wines, 95, 99
Tamar House, 159
Tamar Ridge, 151, 155
Tamar River Retreat, 160
TarraWarra Estate, 228
Tatachilla Winery, 138, 142, 142
Tatehams at Auburn, 124, 125
Taylors Wines, 116, 117, 122
Tempus Two Wines, 31, 39

T'Gallant, 206
Thyme and Again Cottage, 267
Tim Adams Wines, 116, 122
Tom's Creek Retreat, 28
Tonic, 77
Tower Estate, 31, 39
Trinity Cottage, 47
Tuck's Ridge, 206
Tuileries, 220
Turkey Flat winery, 105, 111
Turner's Bar & Grill, 77
Turner's Vineyard, 74
Turner's Vineyard Lodge, 71, 78
2 Faces, 191
Tyrrell's Vineyard, 31, 40

Upstairs at Hollick, 134

Valley Farm Vineyard, 231
Valley Views Motel and Chalets, 244
Vasse Felix, 246, 252, 255
VAT 107, 255, 256
Verona Cellars Cafe, 55
Verona/Small Winemakers Centre, 31
Views' End Bed & Breakfast, 192
Vines Cafe and Bar, The, 199
Vines Resort and Country Club, The, 268
Vineyard Cafe, 89
Vineyard Cottages, 90
Vinifera Wines, 59, 65
Voyager Estate, 253, 255

Wallington Straw Bale, 14, 15, 18
Wandin Valley Estate, 31, 42
Wandin Valley Estate villas, 47
Wantirna Estate, 222
Warrawang Earth Sanctuary, 102
Water Wheel Vineyards, 177, 181
Watervale and Rosebrae Cottage B&B, 125
West Cape Howe Wines, 240
Whirlwind Farm, 113
Wignalls Wines, 237
Willow Creek, 207
Windowrie Estate, 15, 19
Wineglass Bar & Grill, The, 67
Wirra Wirra Vineyards, 138, 143
Wirrakee Restaurant, 182
Woodstock Winery, 138, 143
Woongarra Motel, 220
Wyndham Estate, 31, 40
Wynns Coonawarra Estate, 128, 132

Yarraman Estate, 49, 50, 54
Yarraman Estate Cottages, 56
Yass Valley Wines, 3, 7
Yering Station, 228

Zema Estate, 128, 132

Activities

A Taste of the Valley (Swan Valley), 268
Ace Hi Ranch (Cape Schanck), 211
ACT Wine Industry Network (Canberra), 19
Adelaide Hills Visitor Information Centre, 103
Adelaide Hills Wine Region Inc., 103
adventure playground (Orange), 79
Age of Fishes Museum (Canowindra), 22
Albany Escape Tours, 241
Albany Limousines, 241
Albany Reef Explorer, 245
Albany Scenic Tours, 241
Albany Visitor Information Centre, 245
Albany Wind Farm, 245
All Saints church (Ellenbrook), 268
animal sanctuary (Lake Liddell Recreation Area), 56
animal sanctuary (Mylor), 102, 103
Apex Park, 221
Ararat Visitor Information Centre, 200
Arthurs Seat Maze, 211
Arthurs Seat Reserve, 210
Ashcombe Maze, 211
Augusta Margaret River Tourism Association, 257
Aussie Wine Tours (Cessnock), 44
Australia's World Peace Bell (Cowra), 21
Australiana Corner (Cowra), 22
Australiana Tours (Cowra), 19

Baker's Fresh Vegies, 207
Bald Rock Information Centre, 90
Balloon Aloft (Hunter Valley), 48
Banjo Paterson memorial, 79
Barker and Gull's Store, 268
Barossa Farmers Market (Angaston), 112
Barossa Kiddypark, 114
Barossa Valley Tours, 111
Barossa Wine and Visitor Information Centre (Tanunda), 114
Barrington Tops National Park tours, 54
Beerenberg Jams' Strawberry Farm (Adelaide Hills), 100
Bench Mark Tasmania Wine Gallery (Launceston), 157
Bendigo Farmers' Markets, 181
Bendigo Pottery, 184
Bendigo Produce Barn, 181
Bendigo Visitor Information Centre, 184
Bendigo Winegrowers Association, 184

Bendigo Winery Tours, 181
Billabong Koala and Wildlife Park (Port Macquarie), 29
Blessed Cheese (McLaren Vale), 100, 144
Blessed Cheese cafe (McLaren Vale), 145
blowhole (Cape Nepean National Park), 211
blowhole (Torndirrup National Park), 245
Bonorong Wildlife Park (via Hobart), 173
Boonoo Falls National Park, 90
Borganna Nature Reserve (Hastings River area), 29
Bridestowe Estate Lavender Farm (near Scottsdale), 161
Bullers Calliope Winery Bird Park, 221
bushwalking (Lake Canobolas), 79
Butcher, Baker and Winemaker Trail, 112

Cadbury Chocolate Factory (Claremont), 173
Canal Rocks, 257
Canberra region, 4, 9, 13
Canberra region events, 13
Canberra Visitors Centre, 13
canoeing (Lake Glenbawn State Park), 56, 57
Canowindra Motel Winery Tours, 19
Cape Naturaliste, 257
Cape Nepean National Park, 211
Cape Schanck Lightstation and Museum, 210
Capercaillie Gallery (Lovedale), 41
Captain Cook Cruises, 265
Carlyle Winery Tours, 218
Cascade Brewery, 172
Cataract Gorge and Reserve, 161
Caversham Wildlife Park and Zoo, 268
Caveworks, 257
Central Deborah Gold Mine (Bendigo), 183
Chairlift Ride, 210
Cheviot Beach, 211
CJ Dennis drinking fountain (Auburn), 126
Clare Valley Cycle Hire, 122
Clare Valley Experiences, 122
Clare Valley Visitor Information Centre, 126
Cockington Green (Canberra region), 13
Colley's Seafood, 242
Coonawarra Vignerons, 136
Corriedale Clip farm spinning mill (Canberra region), 13
Country Lane Antiques (Mudgee), 66

Cowra Breakout, 21, 22
Cowra-Canowindra region, 14, 19, 21, 22
Cowra Visitor Information Centre, 21, 22
Cunliffe & Waters, 229
cycling (Clare Valley), 126
cycling (Margaret River), 257
cycling (Rutherglen), 221
cycling (Wangaratta), 221

d'Anvers Chocolates (Devonport), 158
Darbys Falls Observatory, 22
Dare's Hill Circuit drive (Clare Valley), 126
Discovery Air tours (Mudgee or Canowindra), 65
Discovery Science and Technology Centre (Bendigo), 183, 184
Dolphin Discovery Centre, 257
Donnelly's Castle (near Stanthorpe), 91
Down South Camping, 257
Dromana Strawberry Festival, 211

Eagles Heritage, 257
Eden Gate Blueberry Farm, 242
Edgecombe Brothers of Belhus, 265
Endeavour Museum (Wollombi), 56

Fairy Penguin Twilight Tours, 161
farm tours (Clare Valley), 126
farm tours (Qld), 88, 89
Farmer's Market (Cowra), 19
Farmer's Market (Great Southern), 242
Farmer's Market (Margaret River), 254
Farmer's Market (Midland), 265
Farmer's Market (Yarra Glen), 229
Filipo's Tours (Granite Belt), 87
Fisherman's Co-op (Port Macquarie), 27
fishing (Lake Glenbawn State Park), 56, 57
fishing (Storm King Dam, Stanthorpe), 91
Flynn's Beach (Port Macquarie), 29
Ford Discovery Centre (Geelong), 190
Fordwich Grove Olive Farm Shop, 44
Forest Grove Olive Farm, 254
fossil museum (Canowindra), 22
fossil tours, 133
Franklin River Fine Wine, Food and Music Festival, 245

Gallivantours, 190
Geelong Visitors Information Centre, 192

Geralka Rural Farm (Clare/Spalding Rd, 126
German Model Train Land (Hahndorf), 103
Giardino Cafe and Farm Tours (Amiens), 89
Girraween National Park, 90
Glengarry Bush Maze, 161
Global Ballooning, 232
Go Wild Ballooning, 232
Gold and Heritage Museum (Beaconsfield), 161
Gold Creek Village (Hall), 13
gold fossicking (Ophir Reserve), 79
gold mine tours (Bendigo), 183
Golden Memories Museum (Millthorpe), 70
goldrush towns (Gulgong and Hill End), 69
golf (Duntryleague golf course), 79
Gooramadda Olives, 218
Gourmet Trail (Mudgee), 66
Grampians and Halls Gap Visitor Information Centre, 200
Grampians and Mount Zero Olives, 198
Grampians Grape Escape, 200
Grampians National Park, 200
Grampians/Pyrenees tours, 198
Grape Expectations (Cessnock), 44
Grape Grazing Festival (Yarra Valley), 232
Grapevine Getaway Winery Tours, 218
Great Gnome Hunt, 211
Great Ocean Road, 192
Great Southern Farmer's Market, 242
Great Southern Food and Wine Touring Guide, 242
Great Southern Wine Festival, 245
Great Western Picnic Races, 200
Green Eggs in Great Western, 198
Greenhills Adventure Playground (Victor Harbor), 148
Grubb Shaft Gold and Heritage Museum (Beaconsfield), 161
Guildford (Swan Valley), 268
Gulgong Pioneer museum, 69
Gumnut Factory, 268
Gunadoo Gold Mine, 79

Hahndorf activities, 100, 103
Halls Gap Wildlife Park and Zoo, 200
Hans Heysen's former home, 103
Harley Davidson motorcycle tours (Mudgee), 65
Healesville Sanctuary, 232
Henry Lawson Centre (Gulgong), 69
Henry Parkes Museum (Tenterfield), 90
HMAS *Perth*, 245
HMS *Investigator*, 211

horse studs (Upper Hunter), 54, 55
hot-air ballooning (Canowindra), 22
hot-air ballooning (lower Hunter Valley), 48
hot-air ballooning (Yarra Valley), 232
Hotson's Cherries, 218
Houghton annual outdoor folk and blues concert, 268
Hume Weir Trout Farm, 218
Hunter Bell Cheeses (Muswellbrook), 54
Hunter Valley Cheese Factory (Pokolbin), 44
Hunter Valley Gardens (Pokolbin), 48
Hunter Valley Harvest Festival, 48
Hunter Valley Wine Country Visitor Information Centre, 48, 57
Huntley's Berry Farm (Blayney Road), 75, 76
Huon Pine walk, 173

Integrity Tours (Adelaide-based), 144

Japanese Gardens (Cowra), 21, 22
Jazz in the Vines, 232
John Riddock Interpretive Centre, 135

Krazy Putt (Gravelly Beach), 161

Lake Cave, 257
Lake Glenbawn State Park, 56, 57
Lake King, 221
Lake Liddell Recreation Area (Muswellbrook/Singleton), 56
Lake Moodemere, 221
Lark Distillery (Hobart), 173
Lavender House (Rowella), 161
Leeuwin-Naturaliste National Park, 257
limestone caves (Margaret River), 257
Limestone Coast Discovery Tours (Naracoorte), 133
Living Wings and Things Butterfly House (Bendigo Pottery), 184
Longest Lunch, 232
Lowanville Farm, 207
Lyndock Lavender Farm, 114
Lyndock Recreation Park, 114

McLaren Vale and Fleurieu Visitor Centre, 148
McLaren Vale Tours, 144
Macquarie Mountain Tours, 27
Margaret Marron Farm, 253
Margaret River Cycles, 257
Margaret River Dairy Company Pty Ltd, 253
Margaret River Farmer's Markets, 254
Margaret River Regional Wine Centre, 257

Margaret River Visitor Centre, 254
Mary McKillop Interpretive Centre, 135
Mary McKillop school, 136
Maynard Pioneer Park (Clare), 126
Melbourne Food and Wine Festival, 232
Melrose Park Deer Farm (Mudgee), 66
Merrich Estate, 265
Midland Farmer's Markets, 265
Milawa Cheese Company, 218
Mill Providore and Gallery (Launceston), 158
model trains, 103
Montgolfier ballooning, 232
Montrose Meats, 229
Moorooduc Station, 211
Mornington Park, 211
Mornington Peninsula Vignerons Association, 211
Mornington Railway Preservation Society, 211
Mount Arapiles, 200
Mount Barker Wine Festival Weekend, 245
Mount Buffalo, 221
Mount Lofty Botanic Gardens (Crafters), 103
Mount Ochtertyre, 221
Mount Wellington (Hobart), 173
Mudgee Honey Haven, 66
Mudgee Taste Trail, 66
Mudgee Visitor Information Centre, 69
Mudgee Wine Tours, 65
Muscat Trail, 221
Muswellbrook Visitor Information Centre, 57

National Dinosaur Museum (Canberra region), 13
National Museum of Australia (Canberra), 13
National Wool Museum (Geelong), 192
Ngilgi Cave, 257
Norm's Coolies Performing Sheepdogs (Tanunda), 114
North Brother Mountain (Dooragan National Park), 29

Oceanic Cruises, 265
Onkaparinga River National Park, 148
Onkaparinga Woollen Mills (Lobethal), 100
Orange Botanic Gardens, 79
Orange Region Vignerons Association, 79
Orange Visitor Information Centre, 79

Panache Tours, 265
Peninsula Visitor Information Centre, 211

INDEX 273

Penny Royal World (Launceston), 161
Penola-Coonawarra Visitor Information Centre, 136
Penola Memorial Park, 136
Peppermint Bay resort, 169
Peregrine Ballooning, 232
picnic spots, barbecues and swimming (Clare Valley), 126
picnics (Storm King Dam (Stanthorpe), 91
Pindari Cellars (Launceston), 157
Pinot Noir Celebration, 211
Pomonal Berry Farm, 199
Porongurup Wine Festival, 245
Port Macquarie Visitor Information Centre, 29
Port Macquarie/Kempsey region, 27, 29
Portarlington Pier, 190
Puffing Billy, 232
Pulpit Rock, 211

Questacon (Canberra), 13

RailTrail, 221
Railway Museum (Yass), 13
Rawson Falls (Hastings River area), 29
Red Hill Annual Show, 211
Red Hill Cheese factory, 207
Red Hill Long Lunch, 211
Red Hill Markets, 208
Red Rock Olives, 198
Reds & Whites (Orange region), 75
Reptile Centre (Canberra region), 13
Riesling Trail (Clare), 126
Rokewood Orchards, 218
Rose and Crown (The), 268
Rutherglen stagecoach tour, 218
Rutherglen Wine Experience and Visitor Information Centre, 221
Rutherglen Wine Show, 221

Salamanca Markets, 169
Salamanca Place, 172
scuba diving (King George Sound), 245
Seahorse World (Beauty Point), 161
Seal and Sea Seal Adventure Tours (Beauty Point), 161
Sharam Cottage (Penola), 136
Sherwood Wine Embassy (outside Port Macquarie), 27
skateboarding/roller skating (Orange), 79
snorkelling (King George Sound), 245

Sorrento Long Lunch, 211
South Australian Whale Centre (Victor Harbor), 148
Southern Spirit Tours (McLaren Vale), 144
Spirit of Tasmania 1 and 11 (Devonport/Melbourne), 160, 172
Spirit of Tasmania 111 (Devonport/Sydney), 160, 172
Spring in the Valley, 268
Stanthorpe Visitor Information Centre, 91
Stawell Gift, 200
Stawell Gift Hall of Fame, 200
steam train (Timbertown), 29
Story Book Cottage (Tanunda), 114
Strawberry farms (Adelaide Hills), 100
Sugarloaf Rock, 257
Summer Wine Weekend, 211
Summerhill Farm, 208
Sunday Times Margaret River Wine Festival, 257
Sundown National Park, 90
Sunny Ridge Strawberry Farm, 207
Supa Golf, 268
Swan Valley and Eastern Region Visitor Centre, 265, 268
Swan Valley Central, 265
Swan Valley Food and Wine Trail map, 265
Swan Valley Olive Oil Celebration, 268
Symphony at Sandalford, 268

Tahune Forest Airwalk, 173
Talune Wildlife Park (Gardners Bay), 173
Tasmanian Art Gallery and Museum, 172
Tasmanian Chairlift, 161
Tasmanian Maritime Museum, 172
Tasmanian tiger (thylacine) exhibit, 172
Tasmanian Travel and Information Centre, 173
Tasmanian Wine Centre (Hobart), 169
Tastes of Rutherglen, 221
tenpin bowling (Orange), 79
The Great Escape tours (Stanthorpe), 87
The National Science and Technology Centre (Canberra), 13
Timbertown pioneer village (Wauchope), 29
Toffee and Treats (Penola), 136
Torbay Asparagus, 242

Torndirrup National Park, 245
Town Beach (Port Macquarie), 29

Udder Delights cheese factory (Lobethal), 100
Upper Hunter Tours, 54
Urimbirra Wildlife Experience (Victor Harbor), 148

Valley of the Giants, 244
Valleybrook Wine Tours (Launceston), 157
Victorian Olive Groves, 208
Victorian Wine Week, 232
Vineyard Shuttle Service (Cessnock), 44
Vintage Blues Festival, 245

Wacky Wood (Tanunda), 114
Wallace's Mornington Peninsula Winery Tours, 210
War, Rail and Rural Museums (Cowra), 22
Warrawang Earth Sanctuary (Mylor), 102, 103
Waterbird Haven Trust (Tamar River), 160
waterskiing (Lake Liddell Recreation Area), 56
Western Plains Zoo (Dubbo), 69
whale-watching, 244
Whale World, 244, 245
Whiteman Park, 268
Wildflower Festival, 245
wildflowers (Stirling Ranges), 244
Willabran Figs (Houghton), 100
Winery Walkabout (Rutherglen), 221
Winter Wine Weekend, 211
Wollemi National Park, 56
Wonambi Fossil Centre, 133
Wood Works Gallery (Bungendore), 13
Woodbridge House, 268
Wyangala Waters State Park (outside Cowra), 22

Yallum Park (Coonawarra), 135
Yarra Valley Dairy Company, 229
Yarra Valley Game Meats, 229
Yarra Valley Pasta Shop, 229
Yarra Valley Platters, 229
Yarra Valley Regional Food Group, 229
Yarra Valley Regional Food Trail, 229
Yarra Valley Salmon Caviar, 229
Yarra Valley Visitor Information Centre, 232
Yarra Valley Winery Tours, 228